Shared Services and Municipal Consolidation

A Critical Analysis

**BY MARC HOLZER
AND JOHN FRY**

Published by:
Public Technology Institute
1426 Prince Street
Alexandria, Virginia 22314
www.pti.org

Printed in the United States of America
ISBN-13: 978-1460997857
ISBN-10: 1460997859

Table of Contents

PREFACE

The authors wrote this manuscript to take advantage of the work product from a project conducted by the National Center for Public Performance. The original intent of the project was to provide a literature review that would inform elected and appointed officials in the State of New Jersey about municipal efficiency, specifically relating the impact on municipal efficiency of various forms of collaboration and restructuring in the delivery of public services.

The initial research was performed under the direction of the authors, but it benefitted from the significant contributions of the faculty, staff, and doctoral students at the Rutgers School of Public Affairs and Administration. The faculty, who helped with editing, insight, and research direction, include Gregg Van Ryzin, Norma Riccucci, Bob Shick, and Alan Shark. Staff who assisted include Eileen Burnash and Ginger Swiston. The doctoral candidates, several of whom had earned the doctorate in public administration by the completion of this project, include:

Atta Ceesay	Weerasak Krueathep	Alicia Schatteman
Etienne Charbonneau	Sunjoo Kwak	Tiankai Wang
Alex Henderson	Weiwei Lin	Xiang Yao
Tae Hee Kim	Gautam Nayer	

We have added to the initial work product by reflecting on what were the next steps in order for elected and appointed officials in local government to move forward with new initiatives to promote efficiency in the delivery of public services. This effort, which goes beyond the initial literature review, is encompassed in Section II. Jonathan Wooley assisted in the final preparation of the manuscript.

Finally, the authors, as they progressed through the many versions of this manuscript, felt they had continued to learn as they went through this editing process, much of the learning coming from practitioner colleagues and organizations committed to improving the performance of local government. Rather than keep these insights to ourselves, we took the liberty of adding text bars throughout the text, which are formatted so they can be distinguished from the original work. Although we cannot begin to acknowledge the multitude of these individuals and organizations that furthered our knowledge base, we would like to express our appreciation for their contributions.

— *Marc Holzer*

John Fry

Introduction

Increasing municipal government efficiency is an important, but certainly not a new, emphasis. In fact, it has been a topic in the public administration literature for at least a century, if not longer. The present economic crisis has sharpened concerns about the rising costs of government. Elected officials are attempting to respond to the public outcry and to their own feelings that something is amiss with government. However, there is no one recipe for government efficiency, and the literature on municipal government has not provided clear answers.

> **After completing the research that is the basis of this book and writing an initial draft of the manuscript, the authors formed the Shared Services Institute within the National Center for Public Performance, which has enjoyed a thirty-year history of observing and enhancing government performance. The Institute created outreach programs in New Jersey, both to get a street view of the changing map of local government services and to try to transfer best practices from other states and countries to its home state, a state that seldom looks beyond its borders. Much of our recent learning is anecdotal, rather than empirical. Because of its currency, it deserves a place in this book. This recent learning is highlighted throughout the text in this manner.**

The main responsibility of local government is to deliver services to the public. Government provides services that otherwise would not be provided by individual citizens or by the private sector, because there is not sufficient financial incentive. Toward that end, local government provides services such as parks and recreation, road maintenance, and sewer services. Government also provides some services that are regulatory in nature. That is, they are provided for the good of all, because individual interests or inclinations might not be in the best interests of the public, as a whole. These regulatory services include, for example, police protection, criminal justice and dispute resolution, building code enforcement, planning and zoning, and animal control.

A group of services provided to individuals or properties may be provided either publicly or privately. These include solid waste collection and disposal, water and other utility services, and senior citizen transportation.

Services such as solid waste collection and disposal, water and other utility services, and senior citizen transportation are the most likely to be considered as services that do not need to be provided by government. An alternative being looked at more seriously in the face of fiscal stress is an extension to privatization. That is, that government not only does not need to be involved in producing the service, but also it does not need to be involved in providing the service. Referred to as service abandonment, this action leaves the relationship for the service between the vendor and the consumer. Service abandonment reduces tax costs to zero, but the costs to the consumer may rise without government negotiating a larger contract. Franchised service delivery may mitigate these cost increases by having government involved only in negotiating the contract for its taxpayers, but incurring almost no costs for administration of the service.

Finally, there are services that are required by the government in order to have the capacity to provide publicly visible services. These internal administrative services include purchasing, general management, and information technology. But no matter what the reason, if government provides the service, it will be funded by local taxes, user-based fees or fines, or grants and aid from higher levels of government (ultimately from other taxes).

If we are to reduce the costs of government, local governments must deliver public services more efficiently. Working smarter or harder are ways to become more efficient. Management can provide increased incentive to workers or utilize better supervision to achieve greater worker productivity. Investments in technology, tools and equipment can reduce the operating costs of providing services. More effective resource allocation can achieve the service delivery goals of government at lower costs. These operational improvements are important, but organizational arrangements are also opportunities for efficiency.

This book examines how best to align services with the right level and configuration of government to optimize efficiency of service delivery. The examination includes alternatives using other entities to deliver the service, whether they are other governments on the same level, other levels of government, additional levels of government, or private entities. We have not comprehensively investigated abandonment of a service, although we have commented on ways to protect the public in doing so. We recognize this is a viable option; some services are not provided by government in some states and regions (garbage collection, for example). Our examination considers whether governments, themselves, should be reconfigured in order to maximize the efficiency of service delivery. Consolidation and, to a lesser extent centralization and regionalization, would change the organization of government. Contracting and joint agreements would not change the structure of government, but would alter the methods of delivering service. All of these alternatives represent changes in the structure of service delivery, not just in the operations required to deliver the service.

The research that is the basis of the chapters in the first section of this book was conducted in late 2008 and early 2009. Each chapter concludes with a summary of the major conclusions. The focus of the research is to examine the measurement and improvement of municipal efficiency as it relates to optimal municipal size, municipal consolidation, service delivery consolidation, and optimal service delivery arrangements. The goal is to provide information on what is known about these subjects and on what could be used in any jurisdiction, assuming existing laws allow the options that are discussed.

One of the hurdles for any centralized government, in looking at the organization of service delivery by its constituent municipalities, is gleaning information from the results in other states or countries that may have a different tradition of governmental organization. Most of the efforts of centralized governments have relied on the premise that the problem of municipal government inefficiency was due to too many governments, particularly targeting small municipalities as the bastions of inefficiency. These centralized governments are simply following conventional wisdom about economies of scale in their pursuit of municipal consolidation. It is hard to fault them for that. The argument is compelling on its face and even gets almost universal support, not for the action of consolidating municipalities, but for the less disruptive reforms of consolidating services, such as through shared service agreements. The assumption of economies of scale suggests that larger municipalities will be able to produce services more efficiently, because, as the population served increases, the resources needed to provide the additional services required will not grow proportionately as fast as the quantity of services that are provided. Put another way, the increased cost of each additional unit of service is supposedly less for municipalities of large size than for municipalities of small size.

Not only does this sound right, but governments continually act on this assumption. They form regional districts to provide a service more efficiently over a larger area. They join with other municipalities to create a larger service need, which the merged department can address more efficiently. And, of course, they repeatedly look at consolidating adjoining municipalities to reduce tax dollars. Consolidationists claim it is only "illogical" notions like home rule and vested political interests that get in the way of reducing the cost of government through such mechanisms.

In the chapter on municipal consolidation, we do not find any clear evidence that consolidation generally reduces the costs of government. Yet, typically, centralized governments looking for ways to reconfigure local governments to reduce tax burdens ignore this lack of evidence in the public administration literature on consolidation. Sancton (1996) observes that the Royal Commission on Local Government chaired by Lord Redcliffe-Maud ignored the **lack of evidence** in its own statistical analyses that existing large local governments delivered services more efficiently than smaller ones and recommended the formation of large single-tier governments in England in 1969.

Although our research looks independently at the relationship of municipal efficiency to municipal size, municipal consolidation, consolidation of municipal services, and alternate mechanisms for municipal service delivery, the links between these are evident and compelling. When describing the results, a logic chain became apparent. First, evaluate the impact of size on efficiency so that where economies of scale come into play, they can be used to create effective reforms. Then, if size is a factor, evaluate the effectiveness of municipal consolidation and the consolidation of services as two alternative reforms. Continue to evaluate other service delivery arrangements and develop an optimal array of such arrangements to improve local government efficiency. At every step, the measurement of efficiency is an important issue.

The chapters in the first section of this book use the logic described above. The findings suggest the sequence in which we have presented the chapters because of the lack of conclusive and overriding information about economies of scale. The research reveals ambiguities and inconsistencies that do not support universal action, such as a state mandate for consolidation of municipalities possessing certain characteristics. Instead, the research leads to the conclusion that the specifics of each situation need to be evaluated in a comprehensive manner, being realistic about what could be achieved in a proposed reform. While this is an adequate way to proceed, it does not provide simple directions or comprehensive solutions. Hints in the literature that suggest there might be answers are tempting, however. They prompt a series of questions that could pursue the development of a fuller understanding of service delivery and, ultimately, a plan to harness that understanding to improve efficiency.

The research leads to the recognition that different service types show increased efficiency in relationship to some municipal characteristics. The most actionable finding is that labor-intensive service types are more efficiently delivered in smaller municipalities, but capital-intensive service types are more efficiently delivered in larger municipalities or other larger government organizations. Are there other features of service types that fit better to some reforms, but not others? Perhaps, although it does not appear there have been any significant attempts to understand the relationships to characteristics of service types.

Service delivery arrangements often produce benefits in some ways, but detriments in others. Are there ways to configure service delivery reforms to take advantage of the benefits observed for a specific service delivery arrangement but at the same time mitigate the disadvantages of that arrangement? While the literature discusses varied service delivery mechanisms, there is no comprehensive comparison of them and no resulting guidebook on how to match the mechanism to the need.

A most perplexing question emerges when the literature is analyzed as a whole. Why does the literature recognize the beneficial impact of economies of scale on consolidation of services (such as shared service arrangements) but not on consolidation of the municipality? The logical implication of the findings in the literature is to expect municipal consolidation to produce benefits in some service types and not in others, perhaps even producing detrimental changes in some types. The logical extension of this is that service consolidation would be effective, and, therefore, should be implemented for some service types, but not for others. However, it is not the case that interest in consolidation of services is limited only to service types such as those that are capital-intensive, for which one would expect benefits from increased size of the organization delivering the service. Consolidation of services is a popular reform even for labor-intensive services like public safety. The literature does not demonstrate that such reforms have led to inefficiencies, despite the findings about relative inefficiencies that are associated with the increased scale resulting from such reforms.

> **The inconsistency in the perception of economies of scale for labor-intensive services in total municipal consolidation as opposed to functional consolidation (of specific services) spills over into the initiatives of centralized governments. It is not uncommon for a centralized government to choose an answer based on "common-sense" and implement it, rather than analyzing the relative efficiency of structures that are already in place. Further, government officials have ignored their own data and made decisions to undertake initiatives based only on conventional wisdom. It seems officials are convinced they know the best answer without demonstrating its effectiveness empirically. Further, they are often "hell-bent" on implementing their answer whenever they can get traction. This is the political process determining how the search for efficiency proceeds, without the assistance of rational information.**

These "loose ends" demonstrate there is a long way to go to develop a comprehensive understanding of municipal service delivery. The research on size, consolidation, service consolidation, and alternate service delivery mechanisms helps our understanding of many of the ingredients of municipal efficiency and even yields modest information about how some of the factors react when combined. However, we remain far short of a recipe for achieving municipal efficiency. To that end, we began to look for more insights into the characteristics of service types that municipalities deliver to the public; into the features of service delivery arrangements; and into how these service characteristics align with differing service delivery arrangements. This increased understanding of the ingredients of municipal efficiency has positioned us to make recommendations about what arrangements are most likely to produce positive improvements in efficiency for particular service types.

Each of the first five chapters contains a list of conclusions. The final chapter in the first section of the book is an overview of these findings in each of the subject areas and an attempt to pull the findings together. The integration of the findings on each of the subjects researched about municipal efficiency confirms our sense that we are on the verge of understanding how to promote municipal efficiency but have not yet gotten there. The second section of this book is an attempt to take that next step and get closer to an answer, or a range of answers, which municipal or other government officials can evaluate in specific circumstances and put into practice.

First, we present a comprehensive inventory of municipal services. The inventory fully accounts for all aspects of municipal service delivery. It contains a table of the delivery characteristics of each service, which essentially are the operational requirements of that service. Any service delivery arrangement must fit these needs, if the municipality considers it for implementation.

In the following chapter, we delineate the service delivery arrangements, indicating the comparative strengths and weaknesses of the characteristics of each. This chapter builds on the initial research in which we found what is known about structures to promote municipal efficiency.

The final chapter links each service type, as defined by its requirement characteristics, to the service delivery arrangements best suited to it in order to meet those requirements. Of course, this analysis is conceptual, but we expect specific municipalities can apply these results to the actual circumstances of their service, yielding significant insight into how best to arrange the delivery structure to maximize efficiency while producing the quality of service that is appropriate.

We look to both practitioners and academics to critique and extend our effort. We have assembled some of the characteristics of service types found in the literature, and we have added to them. We have started to examine service delivery arrangements to see how they affect efficiency of the delivery of different service types. We have pursued two goals – in the long run, to move toward the ultimate recipe for service delivery reform; and, in the interim, to provide increased understanding for putting together variations that work until we have a universal solution. Having an increased understanding that we can use immediately is critical. The public and their elected representatives are not willing to wait. We must provide them with the best, most useful information to determine actions that they should implement now.

Section I:

The Background

CHAPTER 1

Municipal Size and Efficiency

Policymakers generally believe that larger municipalities exhibit greater efficiency. They have managed to do so despite a lack of consistent evidence supporting this belief. On more than one occasion, a government commission has authorized and accepted research on this topic showing no basis for the belief, but has continued to use the assumptions of the conventional wisdom that "bigger is better."

There is an extensive literature on municipal size and the efficiency of the delivery of municipal services. The belief that larger governments would be more efficient has motivated much of this work and, further, has motivated the call for consolidation to cure the supposed inefficiencies. The literature provides little support for the size and efficiency relationship, and, therefore, little support for the action of consolidation, except as warranted on a detailed, case-by-case basis.

Analyzing the Literature on Optimal Municipal Size

The literature reveals that the size of local government and the closely related issue of fragmentation are not concerns specific to only one state or to only this period in time. New Jersey, New York and Indiana have recently formed commissions to study the same concerns. As an example of the enduring nature of the concern with fragmentation, the 1970 *New Jersey County and Municipal Government Commission Report on Joint Services—A Local Response to Area Wide Problems* advanced these same issues almost forty years ago. Despite the continuing interest, New Jersey is not unique in letting conventional wisdom make its way into the laws it has enacted even recently (New Jersey Public Laws, 2007):

> Consolidating local units, structurally and administratively streamlining county and municipal government, and transferring services to the most appropriate level of government for delivery would help to alleviate the property tax crisis by reducing the administrative costs of local government and making the delivery of local services more efficient due to economies of scale.

Most legislators in every state have in mind that there must be an optimal size or range of sizes for a municipal government entity—one that maximizes cost efficiency and that minimizes duplication of efforts. In this conceptualization, which has commonly been the basis of the actions of jurisdictions that exercise control over local governments, size relates to the need for consolidation.

The literature has a different perspective. It is not surprising to find that there are no easy answers, no optimal size, and no ideal government structure in the literature. Aside from substantive issues, there are a number of factors that influence the ability to measure the relationship between government size and expenditures reliably. Among these are the array of services under the responsibility of a local government, the quality of services provided, the willingness of citizens to fund local government services and the wealth of the citizenry. The long-running North Carolina Benchmarking Project reflects on these sources of inconsistency in comparisons of municipal efficiency:

> Because of the inadequacies of efficiency measurement and lack of uniformity in cost accounting rules, most cities and counties wishing to compare their services with other jurisdictions are well advised to focus primarily on measures of effectiveness and quality, where cost accounting and the differentiation of multiple duties are not at issue, and only secondarily on measures of efficiency. (Ammons and Rivenbark, 2008, p. 310)

Although there are predominant themes relating size to the efficient delivery of municipal services, there are discrepancies. Our discussion starts with the predominant themes, but it then delves into specific service areas and the underlying factors involved in these specific service areas. It will also discuss types of efficiency and suggest that there are a number of different ways to obtain increases in efficiency.

Overall Relationship between Municipal Size and Efficiency

The preponderance of the literature discusses the U-shaped curve between municipal size (as measured by population) and cost per capita to deliver municipal services (see Figure 1). Cost measures, often taking the form of cost per capita, are commonly used in this kind of analysis as general indicators of efficiency. In other words, the U-shape suggests that in the smallest governments, one finds the greatest costs or inefficiencies, that there are some gains in efficiency (costs savings) as size increases, but these level off in the middle ranges of size, and for the largest municipalities some inefficiency returns.

However, even the general discussion of the (inverted) U-shaped nature of the relationship between size and efficiency has variations. This clear statement is a starting point: "The consensus among researchers who have studied consolidation efforts is that nearly 80 percent of municipal services and activities do not possess economies of scale beyond a population of approximately 20,000 residents." (Katsuyama, 2003) Gabler uses a threshold of 25,000 (in 1960 population numbers) and is more emphatic about the diseconomies at the large end of the scale: "The results of this present study suggest that large cities tend to employ and spend more per capita than the smaller jurisdictions and that this tendency is attributable—in part— to the effects of city size." (Gabler, 1971, p. 138) The 1987 report of the Advisory Commission on Intergovernmental Relations, "The Organization of Local Public Economies," provides further support for these numbers. The report reviewed the studies of several researchers and concluded that per capita costs generally fall with increasing size for municipalities with populations up to 25,000, remain fairly constant for those up to 250,000, but then rise significantly.

The U-shaped curve seems relatively consistent and generalizable across social and cultural contexts. A study of water supply in rural India (World Bank, 2008, p. 3) provides more evidence of the U-shape, but in this case, it is applied to households and in a very different context. "The size classes 500 to 1,000 households and 1,000 to 1,500 households have relatively lower cost, compared to smaller or larger piped water supply schemes." Post-war amalgamation in Japan also showed the U-shaped function, but with somewhat different levels of population, indicating 115,109 persons was the threshold at which efficiency gains would reverse (Mabuchi, 2001).

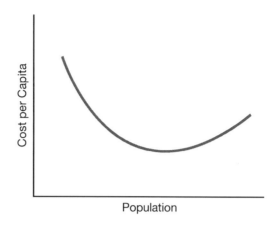

FIGURE 1A. *Hypothesized shape of the relationship between size of jurisdiction and cost of public services.*

Several studies show little or no relationship between size and efficiency. In a study of counties providing local services in Iowa, the authors see no evidence for the 'bigger is better' mantra.

> The big county is not superior in most respects. Per capita expenditures of the large county exceed those of four of the five smaller counties. Per capita taxes, similarly, are higher in the big county functions but were generally no higher than the per capita expenditures in smaller counties, except for hospitals, highways, and capital outlays. The evidence from the double-sized county indicates that economies of scale leading to lower taxes and spending have not transpired. Factors such as quality of services, organizational slack, and willingness of residents to pay for services must be considered in order to draw more definitive inferences concerning the advantages of plans for structural reorganization. The Iowa data, however, do not support the view that bigger is necessarily more efficient. (Koven and Hadwiger, 1992, p. 324)

The message of the author clearly focused on opposing consolidation. The heading for the article makes that completely clear: "Consolidation may not produce savings or be politically feasible." (p. 315) Note that capital outlays are an exception, which is a point that is evident in other references.

Australia enacted many consolidations based on the widespread acceptance among policy makers that larger municipalities would exhibit greater economic efficiencies. Byrnes and Dollery (2002, p. 405) reviewed the literature to determine if an empirical basis existed for this view. They concluded "The lack of rigorous evidence of significant economies of scale in municipal service provision casts considerable doubt on using this as the basis for amalgamations."

An early study from Ontario, Canada finds little support for the relationship between size and efficiency, including even among the smallest municipalities (Bodkin and Conklin, 1971, p. 478). The study investigated the proposition of consolidation promoting efficiency and stated

"...our calculations suggest that quite small municipalities, even those with populations in the range of 5,000 to 10,000 persons, can provide fire and police protection, sanitation and waste removal, conservation of health, recreation, and general government services as cheaply, or even more cheaply, than can the larger municipalities."

Boyne (2003) presents a review of empirical studies of public service performance, concluding that little support is found as to the proposed relationship between organizational size and service performance. Many factors assumed to be important had little or no impact on performance. There is only moderate support for the proposition that additional resources, including both financial and real resources, will lead to better services. The author makes two important points. Resources are differentiated from organizational size, which has no significant effect on performance. Resources may have a more significant impact than was shown in the studies he reviewed, if financial resources were separated from real resources. Further, he posits that financial resources, such as budget appropriations, may be acting through real resources, such as staff quality and quantity, but the relationship is masked in the studies by including both in a traditional multivariate analysis. On one factor, the author gives a positive thumbs-up: managerial variables have a significant impact on performance. We discuss management further under types of efficiency.

Although the focus of Mera's article is economic development, in his review of several studies that investigated government expenditures per capita, he finds little evidence of a relationship between population size and efficiency: "This conclusion is not unique; it confirms earlier studies which tend to show that the expenditure per capita is not very much related to the population size when the expenditure is one way or another adjusted for quality differences." (Mera, 1973, p. 312) A study of the relationship between fragmentation and sprawl also notes the effect on public expenditures. "Fragmentation is associated with lower densities and higher property values but has no direct effect on public service expenditures." (Carruthers and Ulfarrson, 2002, p. 336)

Impact on Specific Service Types

The literature shows not all service types react to municipal size in the same manner. In fact, some effects are opposite to the general finding of the U-shaped curve, depending on the service rendered to the public. Bish (2001) reviews over fifty years of literature on amalgamation in coming to the conclusion that policymakers need to change their thinking about governance, abandoning the belief in large hierarchical organizations and moving to a research based understanding of the conditions under which local governments can function successfully.

One general distinction in the overall relationship between size and efficiency stands out: capital-intensive versus labor-intensive services. Generally, capital-intensive services, such as water delivery, sewer services, and road maintenance become more efficient or less costly with increasing size. This is fairly intuitive. Not as intuitive is that labor-intensive services not only fail to benefit from increasing size of a municipality, but also may actually show diseconomies of scale. Jake Haulk, President of the Allegheny Institute for Public Policy in Pittsburgh, says research shows that towns are most efficient in delivering services such as police, fire protection and roads at a population of about 15,000 (Cauchon, 2006). The small towns often fill needs specific to the tiny areas they serve. Police services are the most studied example of such labor-intensive services.

An enduring article from half a century ago summarizes these effects succinctly. Hirsch states that growth and consolidation will have little impact on the 80–85 percent of all expenditures resulting from public education, fire protection, police protection, refuse collection, and other horizontally integrated services. Growth and consolidation will affect water and sewerage services, which represent 8–10 per cent of total expenditures, resulting in a decline in per capita expenditures in all but a handful of the very largest metropolitan areas. Administrative services, which account for 3–6 percent of total expenditures, demonstrate the most complex relationship to size. In smaller communities, the expenditures per capita will decline with increasing size. In medium-size communities, growth and consolidation will lead to increases in per capita expenditures. (Hirsch, 1959) Administrative services appear similar to other labor-intensive services, but show efficiency gains at the low end of municipal size, reversing that trend at the higher end, much like other labor-intensive services.

A different conceptualization produces the same conclusion. Services that require capital investments generally have the following characteristics—they are easy to measure; are needed infrequently; possess economies of scale in relation to the population served; and may be produced most efficiently for large populations. Conversely, services that are labor-intensive are difficult to measure, are performed frequently and regularly, and are likely to possess diseconomies of scale (Bish, 2001). The author also observes that most researchers conclude that approximately 80 percent of local government activities do not show economies of scale beyond populations of 10,000 to 20,000. The remaining 20 percent are for specialized services needed infrequently by small municipalities.

Other studies mirror the results for water services (Fox and Gurley, 2006; Tynan and Kingdom, 2005; World Bank, 2008; Bodkin and Conklin, 1971). It is not surprising that water services are often delivered as a contractual service with either a private or public provider or are provided through a regional authority. These mechanisms are better at amassing the required capital for infrastructure development and enhancement. Tynan and Kingdom note, however, that a desire for increased customer responsiveness has been pushing the transfer of services to the municipality, which will result in cost increases.

Public works services can incur high capital costs for equipment, but unlike water and sewer systems, these are not at the level of infrastructure development. Some authors have investigated road maintenance in rural New England and found it behaves like water and sewer services rather than like police services (Deller, et al, 1992). Deller and Halstead (1994, p. 247) conclude: "small town governments may best match local demand with services, but at high cost." The first, but not the only factor, is the scale efficiency obtained with increasing size. "The data strongly support the notion of economies of size in the production of rural road services." (p. 258) One option would be to consolidate this service, but efficiencies are also possible through joint or cooperative purchasing.

The second factor the authors point to is not scale efficiency, but allocative efficiency (management use of resources). Small towns do not use resources efficiently. Deller and Halstead (p. 258) seem to link the bulk of the 40 percent higher-than-necessary costs with the inefficient use of inputs. In sum, the authors boldly state: "... the current institutional arrangement of placing rural road maintenance responsibilities in the hands of town officials is highly inefficient in terms of both size economies and managerial efficiency," and then back off with: "These results, however, should not necessarily be used to promote reforming smaller units of government into larger, more economically efficient units."

When we turn our attention to police services, the initial research is strongly in favor of small departments. These results are in part because of perceptions of safety and responsiveness, but they are also directly related to efficiency and cost containment. A government commission report reviews the work of Ostrom and her colleagues, as well as others, examining police services:

> Their work consistently demonstrates that smaller units tend to be more responsive providers of police services. ...No study has found a large police department (over 350 officers) able to perform more effectively in delivering direct services to citizens in similar neighborhoods than smaller departments. Frequently small departments deliver better service at lower cost. (Advisory Commission on Intergovernmental Relations, 1987, p. 27)

This report showed similar results for small town efficiencies in other service areas, such as education.

Allocative efficiency (management of resources) is more effective in small departments, but it is slightly offset by the U-shaped curve of scale efficiency (size economies) in the middle range of department size (Drake and Simper, 2000, p. 67). Drake and Simper assert the reasons for the better management efficiencies are that "effective resource usage and cost control are easier to accomplish in smaller police forces than in larger ones." Scale efficiency leads to the results that predominate in the literature. First, there is a diseconomy of scale in the largest departments—efficiency declines with increasing size. But at moderate levels of size, larger size units show greater efficiency. These gains in efficiency within the moderate size departments are relatively small.

Ostrom and Whitaker's work refutes the theory that size will beget efficiency in policing. Although there is some evidence that there are gains at the lower end of the size spectrum, because of less responsive performance at medium sizes and above, the evidence supports the provision of services by smaller departments. The initial study compared three independent communities adjacent to Indianapolis with three matched neighborhoods within the city. The citizens in the independent communities were victimized less, received assistance more, the assistance came more rapidly, and the residents rated the police-citizen relationships as good in a higher percentage (94% versus 82% of residents). The police departments in the independent communities achieved a higher level of performance. The authors' conclusion was, "Our findings strongly suggest that in the area studied, small police forces under local community control are more effective than a large, city-wide-controlled police department in meeting citizen demands for police protection." (Ostrom and Whitaker, 1973, p. 76)

Three years later Ostrom reviewed a series of empirical studies:

> In general, examining the full set of respondents, we found consistent but weak relationships between size of jurisdiction and general evaluations of police services. All significant relationships run counter to those predicted in the simplified consolidation model. Feelings of safety decrease with size; fear of break-in and attack increase with size; and the rating of police honesty decreases with size. In regard to the cost of police services, we found a positive relationship between city size and per capita costs. (Ostrom, 1976, p. 48)

The author concludes that small departments are better performing than are large ones:

> ...with regard to regular patrol, immediate response to reported crimes, criminal investigation, the provision of emergency services, and other neighborhood-level police services, very small- to medium-sized police departments consistently perform more effectively and frequently at less cost than do large police departments. (Ostrom, 1976, p. 72)

Pachon and Lovrich disagree and re-analyzed the data on public perceptions of police in 15 cities. They assert that the effects Ostrom saw were due to the socioeconomic characteristics of the respondents:

> ...[T]here appears to be very little evidence of a negative relationship between jurisdictional size and citizen satisfaction when controlling for socioeconomic characteristics. Quite to the contrary, the overwhelming trend is in the opposite direction: in five of the six partial correlations calculated there is weakly positive relationship between city size and citizen satisfaction! The strength of this positive relationship is particularly evident in the small suburbs category. (Pachon and Lovrich, 1977, p. 42)

The authors also refute Ostrom's statement that large police departments are not more efficient or economical. However, they produce no additional data or analysis, simply stating that the evidence is still inconclusive.

A study of English libraries is one of the few instances in which the population served was considered in assessing the relationship between municipal size and efficiency (Stevens, 2005). Although no direct effect of population density on expenditures was in evidence, an indirect one exists. Costs are lower either where a large young population (under 16) or a large senior population (over 65) exists. Costs are higher in areas serving a large economically deprived population. Although not as detailed in evaluating other factors, another study of libraries in New South Wales, Australia found that efficiency can be achieved for population levels between twenty and thirty thousand persons (Worthington, 1999).

Considering the different relationships between size and efficiency for different service types, it is difficult to conclude that one size of government is optimal in all circumstances. Bish (2001) takes this statement further by observing that even in a service category, there can be both functions that small governments deliver more efficiently and functions that large governments deliver more efficiently. For example, police services include both routine patrol (favoring small) and specialized homicide investigations (favoring large). The conclusion is that no single size of organization is suitable for all services, even within a service type.

> It is precisely Bish's point about the varying efficiency of small and large governments, depending on the service delivered, that seems to elude officials charged with the responsibility to find ways to cut the cost of government. Most states continue to pursue the one-size-fits-all philosophy, providing incentives to governments who merge and disincentives to municipalities for remaining small, as though economy of scale operates under all conditions. We have seen it does not.

Some Additional Detailed Findings

The details in the work of Gabler; Revelli and Tovmo; Katsuyama; and Boyne provide evidence of how difficult it can be to identify effects that are consistent. We present them here, in part for completeness, but also to demonstrate the inconsistencies in the results in the literature.

Gabler studied efficiency in three states: Texas, Ohio, and New Jersey (Gabler, 1969). Many results are not consistent in all three states. When he looked at the medium size municipalities (25,000 to 250,000 population), the only systematic relationship between size and per capita expenditures was for fire protection in Texas, in which size led to higher per capita cost. Size and public employment rose together for parks and recreation in Texas and Ohio, and for administration, police, and fire in Texas. No other relationships are significant in the three states and service areas studied. Given these mixed results for medium-sized populations, Gabler concludes that no major economies or diseconomies of scale exist.

Among the larger cities (over 250,00 population), Ohio shows greater police expenditures with increasing size, but this is not related to greater manpower needs. Texas shows no relationship between size and costs or employment other than a slight tendency for expenditures for administration to increase with size. In New Jersey, diseconomies of scale exist in total expenditures per capita, total employment, administrative employment, expenditures for sanitation, employment for sanitation, expenditures for police, and expenditures for fire. No other relationships are evident other than an economy of scale for highway expenditures and employment. (Table 1A compares expenditure data in New Jersey's two largest cities with 34 smaller cities.)

Table 1A. *Per Capita expenditures per 100 Population for Selected Functions by City Size in New Jersey.*

City Size 1960 Population	Total	Highways	Police	Fire	Sanitation and Sewerage	Parks and Rec.	General Control
34 Cities (25,000–250,000)	139.93	6.11	15.87	13.38	11.43	5.46	3.21
Jersey City (276,101)	192.39	4.29	24.47	18.34	9.68	6.21	4.15
Newark (405,220)	211.50	4.06	30.02	20.52	14.02	3.90	2.96

Reformatted from "Economies and Diseconomies of Scale in Urban Public Service" (Gabler, 1969, p. 432). Expenditure data are from 1962 and are divided by the 1960 census figures of population.

Gabler's study also looked at the effect of population density on expenditures per capita and employment per capita. The findings are less significant and uniform than those for population size. There are not clear-cut findings for service areas that apply across all three states, although his general finding that larger cities experience diseconomies of scale is supported more often than it is not. His later study (Gabler, 1971) confirms these mixed results, but also shows that the largest cities do experience diseconomies of scale.

A study from Norway that looked at both population size and population density adds to the lack of consistency, associating these factors with efficiency (Revelli and Tovmo, 2007). These authors found a negative relationship between size and efficiency (larger governments were less efficient) and a positive relationship between the sparseness of the population and efficiency. Rural areas attained higher levels of efficiency.

A study from Norway that looked at both population size and population density adds to the lack of consistency, associating these factors with efficiency (Revelli and Tovmo, 2007). These authors found a negative relationship between size and efficiency (larger governments were less efficient) and a positive relationship between the sparseness of the population and efficiency. Rural areas attained higher levels of efficiency.

The general finding of Katsuyama's review of studies of consolidation was that there was a population threshold of 20,000, beyond which economies of scale do not persist (Katsuyama, 2003). However, for the 20 percent of municipal services that are highly specialized, used infrequently, or require large capital investments, the results are different. Spreading large capital costs over a larger population will reduce the cost per capita. Katsuyama agrees with others that, on the other hand, labor-intensive services show diseconomies of scale with increasing size for populations in excess of the population threshold at 20,000. Under that threshold, some studies indicate there may be economies of scale from consolidation, either with a larger municipality or between two smaller municipalities.

New Public Management (NPM) theory contends that disaggregating large municipalities into smaller units enhances performance. The NPM perspective is not focused entirely on cost efficiency. The belief is that large organizations are bureaucratic, inefficient and lack the managerial flexibility to meet their goals. Boyne analyzed data on six service areas to evaluate this anti-consolidation position. The study uses five dimensions of performance (service coverage, quality, speed, efficiency, and administrative effectiveness) with measures of scale based on workload and output, not population. Since there is no direct relationship to municipal size in the tested hypothesis, the application of the findings is difficult. Boyne states that only in half of the cases, the smallest units were the best performers and, when performance declined with scale, the very largest units showed a reversal of the trend. The author states further that the negative relationship between scale and performance reverses at a very large scale. This result is present in social services, waste recycling, planning, and housing. (Boyne, 1996)

> **Smaller governments do some things that allow them to provide services more cost-effectively. Salary scales are known to be lower in smaller units of government, which is accepted. The downside is that smaller units may face more personnel transitions because individuals use them as stepping-stones. Hiring individuals with a connection to the community offsets this issue. We have observed that smaller units reduce costs through the use of part-time personnel, broad banding using staff who wear many hats, and volunteerism. The trade-offs are in convenience to the public due to lack of staff availability and lesser levels of expertise in specific services. For the most part, citizens in smaller communities seem to accept these limitations.**

Comments and Conclusions

The main dependent variable in this analysis, expenditure per capita, is a difficult one to measure. David Ammons, who serves on the National Performance Management Advisory Board, a joint effort of eleven leading public interest associations to develop a comprehensive, conceptual framework for public sector performance management, expresses serious concerns about the complexity of measuring efficiency across jurisdictions. He is also one of the highly regarded faculty at University of North Carolina's Institute of Government, where they have conducted the practice of comparative performance measurement and benchmarking for at least a decade. He and his colleagues have grappled with cross-jurisdictional comparisons in North Carolina.

> Expenditure data is inconsistent. In the face of these complexities, too many local governments resort to reporting "FTEs per 1,000 population" or "cost per capita" for services overall or for the services of a particular department. These are

extremely crude measures of efficiency, if they can be called efficiency measures at all. (Ammons and Rivenbark, 2008, p. 310)

Reagan Burkholder, who, as the principal of Summit Collaboratives, LLC, has been gathering and reporting data in a small consortium of municipalities in New Jersey, provided testimony before New Jersey's Local Unit Alignment, Reorganization, and Consolidation Commission, a body formed to make recommendations to improve municipal efficiency, about many causes of comparative inconsistency, such as:

▶ Additional services that were provided under identical department names

▶ Similar services that are categorized under different department names in different towns

▶ Loaning of personnel during peak needs in other departments, with no concomitant budgetary accounting

▶ Personnel that routinely provide services in multiple departments without appropriate division of labor expenses

Factors such as these affect both the overall expenditures of a municipality and its division into department budget lines. This is even more problematic in a line item than in a program-based budget. Perhaps a greater impact than accounting inconsistencies is afforded by varied levels of services offered by municipalities. This can be the result of policy decisions about service levels, provision of the service by another level of government, or varied expectations of service levels by the public in different municipalities.

There is no evidence in the academic literature of a detailed analysis of the array or depth of services included in accounting or departmental categories. And there is no evidence that the studies examined in this review controlled for these difficult inconsistencies. This affects the precision and use of the results, rather than the overall findings.

If the relationship between size and efficiency is confounded by varying levels of service provided by different governments, one might expect to see differences in public satisfaction with the services delivered. Academics do study citizen satisfaction, but they often find there is little or no evidence that service productivity actually enhances such satisfaction (Moore et al, 2005). Anyone who has lived or worked in a small town knows the expectations for some services are diminished. Although this does not mean that a citizen is willing to wait 23 minutes rather than six for an EMS response, it does mean he/she may be accustomed to the tax assessor not being available or the construction code official having part-time hours. The literature indeed suggests that citizen expectations do play a role in citizen satisfaction ratings (Van Ryzin 2004, 2006). But it is not clear how different expectations, if they exist, should be dealt with systematically across the diversity of a large state.

Although a few of the references presented earlier did address demographic factors in looking at the relationship between size and efficiency, most studies do not take demographic or other external factors into account. The distinctions studied are for internal variables, such as service type or forms of efficiency. This is a limitation in the literature.

Although the literature does not reveal strong and consistent relationships between size and efficiency in the delivery of local government services, some relationships are evident. The first relationship describes the overall effect of size of government on efficiency. However, the general relationship does not hold when specific services are considered. The last point, about the difficulties of measuring efficiency, is very important in the determination of what promotes municipal efficiency:

▶ The Inverted U-shaped Curve

There is an inverted U-shaped relationship between size and efficiency on a general level. Efficiency increases with population size up to about 25,000 people, at which point it is stable until size is about 250,000 people. Efficiency declines with increasing population size after that. The inverted U-shaped curve that describes the relationship between municipal size and efficiency offers two opportunities for improvement: the very smallest and the very largest governments. The literature defines the smallest as populations less than 20,000 to 25,000. The largest are municipalities with populations in excess of 250,000. The literature suggests states should examine their largest governments as well as their smallest governments for ways to increase efficiencies.

▶ Service-Specific Relationships

The literature finds that the specifics of the service are very important in the relationship between size and efficiency. The (inverted) U-shaped relationship is not consistent when evaluating specific service types. Much of the literature argues that small municipalities are not less efficient, generally. Small municipalities, those under 25,000, are less efficient only when services are specialized or capital-intensive. The most important finding, which changes how one should interpret the inverted U-shaped curve, was the difference in the relationship between size and efficiency in capital based services as opposed to labor-intensive services. Larger municipalities will deliver specialized and capital-intensive services more efficiently. Smaller municipalities (as low as 5,000 population is cited by the literature) deliver labor-intensive services more efficiently. The literature even suggests that the details of tasks within a service type are critical. For example, small communities deliver police services more efficiently for routine patrol tasks, but large municipalities perform better in traffic light maintenance and special investigations. Over 80 percent of municipal services are of a routine and labor-intensive nature. Allocative efficiencies (management of resources) are more important than scale efficiencies in these routine service situations.

▶ Capital-Intensive Services

Efficiency gains are related to size for capital- or infrastructure-intensive services such as sewer and water. The literature supports the finding that this same concept is operative for seldom used and specialized services, such as a high technology crime lab. This suggests that contracting, sharing, or receiving specialized services from a larger entity can make selected services more efficient.

▶ Labor-Intensive Services

Labor-intensive services are more efficient in smaller governments. This finding of increased efficiency in smaller units is an important conclusion. Police, fire, and education are all predominately labor-intensive services.

The literature only offers burdens of management control and excess administration in larger governments as an explanation for the observed inefficiencies. Reduced levels of services and expectations in smaller towns may also be operating to reduce costs.

▶ Complexity of Measuring Efficiency

An additional finding from the literature is the difficulty in determining one measure of efficiency that works well at the level of a municipality, or even for a service area. There are many distorting influences on cost per capita as a measure of efficiency, leading to a serious lack of comparability between jurisdictions. Varying definitions of expenditure measures across jurisdictions and policy decisions leading to different services levels make comparisons of efficiency of services imprecise and perhaps unreliable.

There are many inconsistencies in the literature. Even the most consistent findings of the inverted U-shaped curve and the relationship for capital-intensive versus labor-intensive services have variations supported by some authors. For example, we could not reconcile the debate over police responsiveness and inefficiency in small versus large units. Different authors observed greater managerial efficiencies in small units, but others saw relative efficiencies in large units.

The evidence does not support the common wisdom, which purports that scale efficiencies are key to reducing the cost of municipal government. Ignoring the evidence and the details of the relationships between size and efficiency has led to the continuing and misleading assumption that merged governments will reduce the tax burden on the public.

CHAPTER 2

Municipal Consolidation and Efficiency

The unquestioned assumption that contends that larger municipalities exhibit greater efficiency is the source of most of the interest in consolidation. The argument flows from the assumed inefficiencies of small size to the corollary that there are too many municipalities, leading to the belief that consolidation is the logical solution. Much as the casual assumptions differ from the findings in the literature reported in the prior chapter on size, so, too, does this chapter report a lack of supporting evidence that consolidation provides an answer to municipal inefficiency. In part, this is because of a complex, rather than simple, relationship between size and efficiency. In addition, consolidation, itself, can be problematic, both in the implementation and in the documented achievement of improved efficiency.

Consolidation of municipal government has been studied broadly and is a major area of interest for states in their attempts to control the costs of local government. Overall, the literature indicates that there is no compelling evidence for consolidation across the board. Without more positive and consistent evidence, it is wisest to pursue consolidation, when it is warranted in a specific situation, based on a careful analysis of the projected costs of service delivery under the proposed consolidated government.

> **Recent proof of the difficulties in achieving municipal consolidations is provided by New Jersey, where there have been only three consolidation attempts since the enactment of a more flexible (and incentivized) consolidation statute in 2007. The first attempt, in which the consolidation study commission recommended merging Wantage Township and Sussex Borough, was defeated three to one by the Wantage voters, who did not trust the state government and their role in the consolidation. Chester Borough and Chester Township, who had looked at consolidation several times in the past, have delayed further action for a year due to the state rescinding funding for the implementation of consolidation. Princeton Borough and Township, with a prior history similar to the Chesters, are beginning their study with a commission formed in July 2010. The commission was formed, with explicit recognition that the study may recommend more shared services, rather than full municipal consolidation. In sum, there have been no implementations yet under the 2007 law.**

The most significant lesson from the literature is that consolidation is beneficial in some situations, but not in others; there are no rules of thumb this determination. Rather, a case-by-case analysis is necessary, evaluating the goals of the consolidation against the realistic possibility of how those goals would be achieved by a merger. One author warns, "do not base recommendations on a comparison of an actual situation with an ideal." (Bish, 2001, p.27) The literature does indicate that consolidation is more successful if implemented voluntarily, rather than mandated. In many cases, the interest in consolidation has triggered a review of other mechanisms to provide government services efficiently and effectively.

> **Achieving municipal consolidation voluntarily is possible. New York State has more recent success than New Jersey, but its new law was enacted earlier in 2005, with continuing refinements to it to promote consolidation and remove legislative obstacles. One advantage New York has is that one party, the village, can choose to dissolve without need for agreement from the next highest level of government, the town, which must continue to provide services to residents in the former village, since they are within the boundaries of the town, both before and after dissolution. The Village of Pike is the only one to dissolve since 2005, but there are five others which recently approved dissolution by referendum and three more that have scheduled referendums to approve a dissolution.[47] Dissolution is a one-sided consolidation within the town in which the village is located. In New Jersey, one of the two consolidating entities always ends up with a tax increase, before the supposed efficiencies of consolidation are implemented. Even after those efficiencies, the smaller town usually will see much greater tax reductions, due to a higher prior tax rate, than the surrounding larger town. This makes a two-town positive referendum hard to achieve.**

Analyzing the Literature on Municipal Consolidation

One of the primary questions for those concerned with municipal efficiency is whether the formation of larger political jurisdictions through municipal consolidation results in greater cost-efficiency of service delivery. Going beyond the relationship between municipal size and efficiency, and aside from purely cost considerations, we inquired whether there were other benefits to consolidation examined in the literature and under what circumstances any of these benefits may or may not be appropriate.

---

[47]Recent information on dissolutions in New York State was provided by Steven Fountain of the New York State Comptroller's Office on July 14, 2010.

There is a commonly held belief that efficiency will be improved by reducing the number of units of government and combining them into larger units. Karcher's book *New Jersey's Multiple Municipal Madness,* (1998) is his treatise on the concept that there are too many municipalities in New Jersey. Karcher reviews reasons new governments were created, finding that some were for the benefit of a small group of people or for other reasons, which would not be perceived now as benefitting the state as a whole. He concludes that the current fragmentation is not appropriate and discusses both voluntary and mandatory consolidation as approaches to resolving the current inefficient situation.

> **Many states feel they are unique in the fragmentation of their local governments. Despite Karcher's focus on New Jersey, it is ranked 24th in the 2007 Census of Governments with 1,383 local governments (U.S. Census Bureau, 2007).[48] If he looked northward, he would have counted over 4,000 governments in New York State. This total mushrooms to over 11,000 when special districts are included (New York State Office of the State Comptroller, 2010). It is not a problem restricted to the congested northeast. Indiana also outpaces New Jersey. Indiana has in excess of 3,000 governments, of which cities, townships and towns comprise about half.**

A study of Post-War Japan accepts the premise of consolidation. The author states that it is widely accepted that "amalgamation will increase the efficiency of local government ..." (Mabuchi, 2001, p. 12). However, the author maintains that responsiveness to local residents is also an offsetting issue in consolidation. "... it is also generally believed that there is a negative effect on democracy." Throughout the literature, there is tension between the basic belief in efficiency of larger governments and concerns about the unforeseen consequences of consolidation.

Governing Magazine recounts the experience in the state of Iowa, and that is reinforced throughout the text below. Iowa faces a similar situation to several states, with well over 3,000 local governments in a state that is not densely populated. Iowa has 36 local governments for every 100,000 people. With a stagnant tax base and few options, Iowa's governor proposed replacing all the local governments with 15 regional governments. Although the proposed consolidation was not well received in a state that is proud of its local police forces and fire districts, the article states that the municipalities of Iowa are working together now to a much greater extent. So far, there have not been tremendous cost savings from this increased cooperation. "For local officials, saving a lot of money right away isn't as great a concern as doing things more

---

[48] The Census is kinder about the number of local governments than most states are. For example, they believe New York has a mere 3,403, including special districts, which is less than New York's self-reported number of 4,172, without special districts. Whatever the right number, the point remains that what is "madness" to some, is only half-bad in the context of all the states.

efficiently when they can, whether that means streamlining internally or reaching out to new partners." (Greenblatt, 2006)

A Case for Consolidation?

Although there is some support for reducing the number of governments and, consequently, increasing the size of the remaining governments, there is a considerable body of literature that does not support consolidation. Most of the interest in consolidation has been focused on reducing the number of small municipalities. A 1987 report by The Advisory Commission on Intergovernmental Relations (ACIR), entitled *The Organization of Local Public Econo-mies,* reviewed several studies. The report concluded that per capita costs generally fall with increasing size for municipalities with populations up to 25,000, remain fairly constant for those up to 250,000, but then rise significantly. This pattern is represented by an inverted U-shaped curve relating municipal size and efficiency. Katsuyama's review (2003) of the work of those studying consolidation efforts concludes that the vast majority of services show no economies of scale beyond a population of approximately 20,000.

Norway has been reducing the number of municipalities substantially since 1952, when the ini-tial thrust was to form municipalities of at least 2,000 inhabitants. The evidence from an empiri-cal analysis of these consolidations showed that consolidation did reduce per capita expenditures (Hanes, 2001). However, there were two important caveats. The first was that the results were not significant when the researcher controlled for selection bias. The second is that the cost sav-ings from consolidation declined with municipal size of the consolidated municipality.

As a body, these findings do suggest success in merging the smallest municipalities. However, a tense debate rages between states and localities over just what local government should look like (Fox and Gurley, 2006). Municipalities across the country have pushed back regarding proposals for consolidation, and the debate ensues in New Jersey, New York, and Ohio. There is significant debate about whether consolidation is the best way to help citizens. Much of the debate is about cost savings. Many studies have found that larger municipalities are not gener-ally the most efficient for specific service types.

A comprehensive review of fifty years of evidence about the relationship between the structure and performance of local governments in metropolitan areas leads Bish (2001) to conclude that consolidation eliminates the very characteristics of local government that are critical to the most successful and least costly government systems. The author introduces his study with the major recommendation: "policymakers need to change their way of thinking about urban gov-ernance, from the obsolete and discredited idealization of large hierarchical organizations to a research-based understanding of the conditions under which cities can function successfully...." (Bish, 2001)

Byrnes and Dollery (2002) find that the research on economies of scale in local government does not support the proposition that substantial efficiency gains would flow from the forma-tion of larger local governments. Efficiency and economy may not be the strongest arguments for consolidation (Ho, 2004). It is difficult to prove or to promise future tax savings. Voters are not easily swayed by promised savings, perhaps because they fear cuts in service as a logical extension of tax savings. There are other alternatives to achieving cost efficiency in services.

Sancton (1996, p. 268), who has studied municipal consolidation in Canada, proclaimed that "The days of large-scale centrally imposed municipal reorganization are clearly over." He was stunned that the policy-makers were unaware of the academic literature about the impact of scale on local government costs that showed precious little evidence to support a consolidationist position. His study cited statistical work in Great Britain, which was largely ignored by the Royal Commission on Local Government when they recommended large, single-tier units of local government for England. He also observed that the United States had come around, noting that the Advisory Commission on Intergovernmental Affairs, although it was previously a staunch advocate of metropolitan consolidation (as indicated at the beginning of this review), had reversed its position by 1987 and was supporting "fragmentation."

> **Despite Sancton's belief that centrally imposed municipal reorganization is behind us and the turnaround, now over twenty years ago, by the Advisory Commission on Intergovernmental Affairs, both New Jersey and New York formed a special commission in 2007 to look at local government consolidation. New York's Commission on Local Government Efficiency and Competitiveness was established by executive order to "make recommendations on ways to consolidate and eliminate taxing jurisdictions, special districts, and other local government entities where doing so would improve the effectiveness and efficiency of local government." New Jersey's legislature established the Local Unit Alignment, Reorganization and Consolidation Commission "to develop criteria to serve as the basis for recommending the consolidation of specific municipalities, the merger of specific existing autonomous agencies into the parent municipal or county government, or the sharing of services between municipalities or between municipalities and other public entities." Although consolidation was not the only objective of either commission, both states recognized fragmentation that resulted in too many governments. As Sancton observed in Canada, there has been a softening of the call for consolidation in New York and New Jersey, as well as a reduction of funding to encourage it.**

Fox and Gurley (2006, p. 2) provide a comprehensive review of whether consolidation works, but conclude: "...no single policy advice can be given on whether consolidation is a good idea, with the facts and circumstances of each case determining whether consolidation or not (sic) is beneficial." Governments should not assume consolidation will solve problems, because benefits and costs are specific to each situation. Consolidations may, but do not inevitably, save money.

Other studies support this notion of the importance of the specific circumstances, if only because of their absolute disagreement with one another. Jordan sees consolidation as the solution to the problem of governance following the successful consolidation of smaller units into the Greater Amman Municipality (Malkawi, 2003). However, Malkawi feels the practice of consolidation preceded the perception of the problem of the multiplicity of administrative units, and, therefore, was not implemented as a solution to the problem. Ostrom has a similar concern: "We find in the described studies a consistent pattern of evidence that contradicts the assumptions made by proponents of consolidation; we cannot support their belief that consolidation affords "the" solution to "the" urban problem." (Ostrom, 1976, p. 70)

Both Fox and Gurley (2006) and Ostrom (1976) see size economies as being service-specific. As was detailed in the previous chapter, *Municipal Size and Efficiency,* infrastructure-intensive services show benefits of size, which makes an indirect case for consolidation of smaller units or some other measures that would reap the same benefits. Fox and Gurley (2006) observe that bureaucrats have been noted for being efficient at the things they want to do, and inefficient at those they do not. In these instances, alternative delivery mechanisms could be identified in hopes of obtaining the same benefits that are expected from consolidation, but without the efficiency losses, which occur because of the unwanted implementation of consolidation. Economies of scale are not the only criteria on which to determine the benefits of consolidation. The authors mention that land area, population density and geographical attributes may affect the benefits of consolidation.

In Western Germany, mergers that occurred in the 1960's and 1970's show significant economic impacts, such as a 20 percent lower level of debt. The authors find that the financial situation of city regions where the core and the hinterland are separate administrative districts is worse (in terms of public debt as a ratio to tax income) than in single district regions. Further, in evaluating economic impacts on the governments, mergers are superior to a "strategy that relies solely on soft or hard functional cooperation." (Blume and Blume, 2007, p. 707)

On the negative side of the ledger, there are several concerns that must be considered to understand the impact of consolidation. Consolidation, by its nature, reduces government competition without necessarily reducing overall government size (Fox and Gurley, 2006). To be cost effective, consolidation must be accompanied by the elimination of redundant workers, at least in the long term. The authors also note transition costs can be quite high in specific instances, particularly if infrastructure modifications or enhancements are required or capital-funded facilities are added. This emphasizes the point that consolidation only reduces costs if expenditures of the combined governments are lowered.

> Even though towns embark on consolidation to cut costs, the commitment to reduce resources may not follow. The political will to reduce staff is difficult to attain, particularly in small towns where the Mayor is close to the employees, with whom he or she has developed a relationship and may even be a neighbor. In addition to the personnel problem of imposing layoffs, some of the public may perceive the reduction of combined resources as reducing services. It is easier for the governing bodies to use an attrition-based reduction, but this solution may exacerbate the problem caused by transition costs.

The transitional costs for a Canadian consolidation creating the City of Abbotsford were about $1.5 million in 1995 Canadian dollars. Annual projected savings were $1 million (Vojnovic, 1998). Campbell and Selden (2000) analyzed the transitional costs for a consolidation between the City of Athens and Clarke County, Georgia that was completed in 1991. The estimates of the 1991 costs were:

▸ $470,353 for one-time operating and capital costs necessary only because of the unification

▸ Nearly $5 million to implement the recommendations of consultants who conducted classification and compensation studies

▸ More than $2 million for annual personnel costs due to the harmonization of the pay and fringe benefit packages

A World Bank report that analyzes different models of government structure confirms the concern with a loss of competitiveness that results from consolidation. The report elaborates that there is less incentive to be responsive to local needs (Slack, 2007). The author references Boyne's 1992 empirical review of consolidated versus fragmented governments in the United States. One source of the cost difference is that compensation levels rise to the highest levels in the pre-consolidated governments. An additional factor mentioned by Slack is that service levels also rise to the highest expectation of the most serviced community. Gregory C. Fehrenbach, a consultant for the New Jersey League of Municipalities, noted that when towns merge, residents are often unwilling to give up services. He used an example of two towns, one with twice-a-week trash collection and the other with weekly collection. Because the residents of the town that had trash picked up twice a week did not want to give that up, both towns ended up having twice-weekly service. "You can't just make the assumption that larger is better," Fehrenbach said. (Peters, 2007)

Transitions to achieve a consolidated government can take two to three years to work out and require a melding of different service cultures of the organizations (Rosenfield and Reese, 2004). This is not a trivial matter, nor should it be assumed that the most effective service culture will emerge. The bottom line is also affected by compensation packages, which will rise to the highest level among the pre-consolidation governments, and by an increase in equipment and technology necessitated by a larger workforce.

Consolidations are often weighed without being realistic about how the merged government will operate. It is logical to assume that scale efficiencies, for the services in which they are operative, will increase after consolidation, because they are based on economies derived from increased size. On the other hand, allocative efficiencies, which are derived from managing the use of resources, cannot be assumed to increase with size. In fact, Fox and Gurley (2006, p. 35) reflect on the practical realities of such a drastic change as consolidation: "The involved people, local and national bureaucrats, local and national politicians, and service deliverers, may thwart or enable the consolidation, depending on the design. They will to a very real degree determine whether it works or fails."

Some of the literature has looked at other benefits of consolidation. Although these are often financial in nature, they are not of the same ilk as direct cost savings for increasingly efficient operations of government. The Toronto consolidation, establishing a single-tier government from what had previously evolved into a two-tier government, is a well-known and completed consolidation which has been the source for several of the articles found in the literature search. Although the literature does not make the case that the Toronto consolidation created cost savings, one of the changes that occurred because of the consolidation was the ability to make citywide planning decisions that would never have made it through six units of government (Grant, 2007). In essence, the benefits of regional planning have accrued without the difficulties of implementing and achieving a regional outlook among distinct governments.

In a similar manner, long-term economic growth and vitality is easier to achieve in a single government structure, rather than across several individual governments in a region (Ho, 2004). The approved consolidation of the City of Louisville with Jefferson County is a good example to support the author's point that consolidation will be encouraged only if there are perceived concerns about an area's economic future. As the Brookings Institution (2002, p. 2) concludes:

> ... an agenda of transformation to a changing community—one with a resilient economy and high quality of life that are increasingly imperiled by economic change, persistent racial divides, decentralization, and the relatively low education levels of its people. This agenda charts how a renewed Louisville can build on its assets, strengthen families, fix the basics, influence metropolitan growth, and sustain its neighborhoods in order to make itself a top-rank "competitive city." In doing so, it takes a deliberately broad view of "competitiveness."

An analysis of a fire district merger in Ada County, Idaho found the potential to increase service levels with no increase in costs (Curry, 1999). This proposed merger of four fire districts would allow an increase in staffing and the ability to make the chief officer responsibilities more specialized. Standardized training for paid and volunteer members and an enlarged prevention department would also be possible without increased costs.

Obstacles to Consolidation

Sancton (2001a) examines the arguments of public-choice theorists against consolidation. The main argument is that maintaining many municipalities in the same area increases the level of competition between the municipalities and allows each municipality to determine its own service and tax package to attract particular residents and businesses. Public-choice theorists have addressed the issue of whether competition between municipalities is detrimental to planning and development in a regional area. They argue that regional planning is unnecessary, noting the development of infrastructure in the U.S. succeeded without a plan. They counter the argument promoting redistribution of wealth in a merged urban area by stating that such redistribution is the province of central, not municipal, governments, so it should not be a reason for consolidation.

Different needs for services do present one of the difficulties in consolidating communities, particularly if they are greatly different, such as urban and rural areas. These areas often have different service requirements and, consequently, different service costs and tax bases (Sancton, 1996, 2001a). If the merged community resolves the issue by providing service equity throughout the entire area, costs may rise, because it is not usually acceptable to reduce service to the lowest pre-consolidation levels. There is a related issue in terms of the higher amounts of regulation that typically have evolved in urban areas. A merged rural area may not welcome the increased government intervention which could conflict with notions of self-sufficiency.

Two consolidation studies in New Jersey, which have occurred since the 2007 enactment of the new consolidation law, were similar in that there was a small Main Street community surrounded by a larger township. In both cases, the prior tax rates in the downtown boroughs were higher, leading to a greater savings for the boroughs from consolidation. The benefits to the surrounding townships were harder to see and came about only 1) through state subsidization of the increased costs due to consolidation, or 2) through a negotiation of shared cost reductions. Mechanisms can be created through negotiation that do not base the tax bills solely on equalized property values, the most common way to determine the tax bill in a state where property taxes are the primary means to support local services. Although this may appear counter-intuitive to one who believes the economy of scale argument, the off-the-shelf apportionment of taxes in a consolidated municipality in New Jersey will create a higher tax bill in the town that had fewer tax problems prior to the merger. The larger townships often do not want the Main Street problems and their accompanying costs, even when the Main Streets are rural or suburban.

Service delivery subtleties affect how much area to include in a consolidated metropolitan area. The type of service is important. Functions such as regional planning are best in a broad area that might include heavily developed and sparsely developed areas that need to be considered in relationship to each other for planning purposes. However, that same combination of heavily and sparsely developed areas has a very different impact on functions such as garbage collection. The policies and procedures that make sense in a densely populated area may produce inefficiencies in a sparsely populated area.

One study looked specifically at legislative impediments to consolidation in its review of fourteen detailed case studies about city-county consolidations in the United States from 1967-1999 (Leland and Thurmaier, 2004). Most of these attempts were unsuccessful or took several tries before they were completed. Most of the successful ones reduced the total number of elected officials in order to show cost savings. The successful cases needed a vote of the state legislature to pass special legislation supporting a consolidation process. Some cases required a constitutional amendment. But legislation can be too restricting and create further obstacles. In North Carolina, for example, the law that authorized consolidations stated that the larger government entity must be abolished.

An important distinction arises in assessing the feasibility of consolidation. Although there is some connection between the two, the financial efficiency of a consolidation is indeed different from the political feasibility of accomplishing it. *Optimal Consolidation of Municipalities: An Analysis of Alternative Designs* presents an econometric model for estimating the cost savings of a potential consolidation. The model is applied to municipalities in Allegheny County, Pennsylvania. The authors conclude: "... citizens are much less likely to accept a consolidation plan that greatly disturbs the existing tax and service levels." (Carey et al, 1996. p. 103)

The tension between financial and political considerations is demonstrated in a study of voluntary consolidation potentials being encouraged by the centralized government of Norway. The author first remarks on considerations of cost: "Cost efficiency can be improved by unifications, and central government has therefore designed a framework to stimulate voluntary mergers. Efficiency gains are larger among authorities with a small population base." (Sorensen, 2006, p. 92) However, in the same article, Sorensen also recognizes the difficulty of achieving consolidations in some of the same governments which may have the most to gain financially:

> Local politicians and top administrators in small municipalities remain more reluctant to merge than leaders in more populous municipalities. Elimination of revenue disparities would certainly further consolidations, but local leaders (and probably citizens) are prepared to pay a price (in terms of diseconomies of scale) to persist as independent polities. (Sorensen, 2006, p. 92)

The study in Norway describes political transaction costs as obstacles to consolidation. The central government has promised to maintain grant levels in local governments, which are generous, to compensate for diseconomies of scale. However, the promises may not be credible. Property rights have been nullified after consolidation, prompting municipalities with high revenues to oppose merger with poorer neighbors. Expected changes in party representation in a consolidated government lead to opposition to consolidation. More senior politicians, particularly those from small governments, oppose consolidation.

> **Rutgers Shared Services Institute conducted a mailed survey of all voters in the Township of Wantage, New Jersey after over 75 percent of the voters rejected consolidation with the Borough of Sussex. Although the results have not been published yet, one of the factors behind the vote was the lack of trust that the state would deliver the promised funding incentives for consolidation. In the subsequent year, the Joint Consolidation Study Commission of Chester Borough and Chester Township, New Jersey extended the study for another year, when the funding was taken out of the state budget. The Commission is waiting to see if the state will re-instate incentives for consolidation.**

The popular press is more direct in discussing whether consolidations are based purely on financial considerations. "Consolidation has very little to do with saving money," Carl A. Bergmanson, mayor of Glen Ridge, New Jersey, said at a group discussion on consolidation. Bergmanson elaborated that large city governments were often far more inefficient than the governments of small municipalities like his (Peters, 2007).

Political representation in the consolidated government is an obstacle and may become a problem after consolidation. The issues vary depending on the types of communities that will be combined, their respective populations, and the electoral process in place, or that will be put in place. In Vermont, the population in the Town of Essex outnumbers that of the Village of Essex Junction. In a 2006 article in the *National Civic Review,* Santucci argues for a proportional representation scheme to achieve equity between these two communities. This unusual approach attempts to ameliorate the problems with more conventional voting systems, which the author reviews in coming to his voting system recommendation for the merged towns. Each potential consolidation situation may present different problems that require a solution specific to the needs of the communities involved.

> **Representation is one of the main obstacles to address in a consolidation plan. Conventional electoral systems, even those with wards, do not provide an answer to the problem of unequal population. The smaller town, often with the downtown center, fears its differing service needs and culture will be abandoned by the representatives of the larger government. This concern exists despite the presence of existing towns that successfully meld downtown cores with surrounding less**

> densely populated areas that have differing needs. These existing solutions suggest at-large representatives will appropriately represent the needs of all the areas in their towns, but it does not qualm the fears of those who will be absorbed. In the end, rising costs in the small town may make representation a secondary, but still important, issue.

In Ottawa, Canada, the representation of rural areas is an issue. Much like the Vermont consolidation, representation by population would result in no effective representation for the rural areas, but a different mechanism would be in conflict with democratic principles (Sancton, 2003). Eventually, Headingley, the most rural community, was allowed to secede from the Ottawa consolidation.

Sancton (2000) also mentions different or non-existent unions as an obstacle to consolidation. In the province of Ontario, legislative amendments were needed to allow the formerly non-unionized Pittsburgh Township employees to enter the Kingston union with accumulated seniority rights. Although the changes were legally enacted, the unions were not pleased with the solution.

The Monroe County Council of Governments (COG) was formed in 2000 as a voluntary association of municipalities in Monroe County, New York. In 2003, COG and the RUMP Group, an organization of local business leaders, combined their efforts to look at further opportunities for cooperation or consolidation to counter the fiscal stress affecting local government (Center for Government Research, 2003). The conclusion in Monroe County was that the timeline on achieving cost savings through consolidation was far too long, because of the structural and legal changes that would be required by a physical merger. Since the GRIP-NAPA report of over thirty years ago, recommending a two-tier government and establishing an initial central agency to encourage collaboration in Monroe County, cooperation and innovation have occurred incrementally throughout the county.

For Monroe, the success of functional cooperation in the past represents an obstacle to consolidation. COG is a regional association that maintains a focus on promoting efficiency for municipalities throughout the county. This same phenomenon occurred in British Columbia (Sancton, 2005). A successful implementation of a two-tiered government utilizing regional districts has staved off the consolidation movement so popular in Canada in the latter part of the 20th century.

Lessons Learned

The lessons from consolidations that were completed add insights as to obstacles that derailed or stalled consolidations. McKay (2004) found that efforts to achieve efficiency in a newly consolidated government could take a back seat to concerns of achieving equity and uniformity throughout the consolidated area. The other concerns McKay raises from this case study are general questions about change management, such as clarity of goals, roles, and deadlines and good communication.

In a study of five Canadian consolidations, greater needs for service delivery and governance in rural areas echo the concern with increased costs generated by the equity issue (Vojnovic, 2001). This study also detected the harmonization of salaries as a cost containment issue resulting from consolidation. The overall results in salary costs were mixed for the five mergers because some mergers resulted in a reduction of employees and one, Abbotsford, set reasonable expectations for salaries before the consolidation occurred. Abbotsford also established a political forum of residents of the former districts that approved all initiatives. This mechanism might have provided the courage to keep costs in check.

> **The attempt to bolster the political feasibility of achieving a consolidation may have the opposite effect on the financial feasibility of the consolidation. Prior to forming a consolidation study commission, two mayors in New Jersey told their staffs there would be no reductions in staff. As they worked through the fiscal impact of consolidation, it became clear that reductions were needed to offset the costs of the transition, including harmonization of wages. Although it is hard to establish concretely, it appeared the staff recognized the need to reduce resources in a merged municipality, even though they wanted to keep their jobs.**

However, in an earlier study, Vojnovic (1998) noted that Abbotsford had also reduced staff in the consolidation, which helped it to reduce administrative costs. The staff members were affected by relocation, new work standards, and an increased level of required teamwork within the larger municipality. The employees also faced a significant increase in workload, which resulted in delays in processing inquiries, complaints and applications.

In four of the five mergers in the Vojnovic 2001 study, increased specialization occurred after the merger in two distinct areas. Employee specialization resulted from a greater volume of work that was repetitive. Equipment specialization, such as that resulting from the need for better accounting and information systems, followed from increasing the complexity of managing a larger organization. Vojnovic found that there has been little evidence of cost savings in the consolidation of larger municipalities. He attributes this lack of success to diseconomies of scale, higher wages resulting from specialization, and greater transition costs, such as those required to restructure a larger bundle of services.

Over a ten-year period, Sancton has written frequently on consolidation, with a focus on the Canadian attempts to find a better method to govern and deliver services to its citizens. Different structures have been implemented throughout the last fifty years. Some of the variety in the nature of the attempts is due to the fact that Canada has vested more powers in its provinces to mandate restructuring, without approval of the municipalities, than the United States has permitted in its states.

Sancton (2001b) blames this central power for some of the difficulties that have resulted, comparing provinces that mandated consolidation with one province that allowed it to occur as the municipalities desired. The Greater Vancouver Regional District (GVRD) was formed with the consent of its member municipalities. The consolidations that occurred in Toronto and Montreal, which have been beset with more severe problems, were mandated and did not achieve agreement of the consolidated municipalities. Vojnovic (1998) agrees that voluntary consolidations are more successful and that centrally imposed timeframes act as an impediment to success.

Sancton (2001b) states that the GVRD model is more similar to what is practical in the U.S., where states cannot mandate consolidation (without legislative or constitutional changes). The mobilization of forces in Vancouver to promote a regional solution created support for the solution that was eventually implemented. The provincial mandates in Ontario and Quebec did not need this support. Therefore, they did not obtain it, nor did they have it when it was needed.

Although this chapter focuses on consolidation, the Canadian experience is not just a crucible for consolidation. It offers lessons about consolidation as a remedy to other structures of governance, even though the subsequent consolidations largely have not succeeded for other reasons. Sancton (2005) provides a history of the actions and reactions in Canadian governance. The main thrust of the 1950's and 1960's was to form two-tier governments. A metropolitan layer of government is established for functions that benefit from a metropolitan level solution, such as land use planning and infrastructure maintenance and development. Local municipalities continue to provide services such as zoning and recreational programs. (Note that two-tier governments are discussed further in the chapter *Alternative Service Delivery Arrangements and Efficiency.*)

The formation of two-tier governments occurred in four provinces. Ontario, Quebec, and Manitoba have subsequently abolished these two-tier governments to resolve unforeseen problems. On the other hand, British Columbia established a network of regional governments in the 1960's, which still exists, and that provided metropolitan level solutions, although British Columbia never recognized them as a separate layer of government. They replaced many special purpose bodies (special districts) that had been formed previously by multiple municipalities.

> **The two phenomena we have observed to be getting increasing attention in the last couple of years are exactly what British Columbia accomplished almost fifty years ago. Special districts continue to be brought back under the municipalities that created them. Regional collaborations are being studied and promoted with great passion from a number of different organizations, more often with the initiation from local officials than from state or county leaders.**

The new regional districts encouraged inter-municipal cooperation and allowed municipalities to opt out of regional services (or cooperate with other municipalities, even outside the region). The board of directors of each regional district consists of members of municipal councils. The directors have numbers of votes proportional to the population they represent in the region. Sancton likes the solution:

> Although it is impossible to determine objectively an ideal institutional model for metropolitan governance, it is hard to imagine a mechanism that could better combine local self-government through established municipalities with the existence of an institution at the metropolitan level that can both provide a degree of consensual metropolitan leadership (the strategic plan) and a framework within which municipalities can voluntarily cooperate with each other. (Sancton, 2005, p. 325)

In 2006, British Columbia produced a primer on its regional districts (British Columbia Ministry of Community Services, 2006), which emphasized the reasons for their success. It states that the regional district serves the interests of the municipalities, rather than sitting over the municipal governments. They rely on borrowed power rather than statutory authority. They are consensual organizations that provide only the services to which their constituent municipalities agree. Unlike the municipalities, regional districts must match the benefits and costs of the services to the citizens that benefit from the services.

A two-tier government has inherent conflicts between the two governing tiers. In addition to Canada, London, Rotterdam, Copenhagen, and Barcelona have shown this form to be unstable (Sancton, 2001a). In Toronto, Ontario by the 1970's, the two-tier government showed sources of conflict in that the suburbs did not want to support rebuilding deteriorating central city infrastructure and in that the upper-tier was spending an increasing share of total municipal revenues. A move to have the upper-tier council directly elected was successful in 1988, but it led to increasing conflict between the two levels of government. In 1996 Toronto decided to merge into one government as the City of Toronto for the stated purpose of saving money. Sancton (2005) sees this move as removing all ability of the rural and peripheral areas to self-govern. Other parts of this chapter show there is considerable doubt about whether the goal of saving money was realized by the Toronto consolidation.

Manitoba's effort to create the Corporation of Greater Winnipeg resulted in the abolition of the Corporation within ten years, despite the attempt of the initial effort to avoid the political conflicts of a two-tier government. The directly elected members of the Corporation sat on 13 community committees that advised the main council on local matters. These committees were advised by residents' advisory groups that were chosen at open community meetings. The interest in these advice and consulting functions waned, increasing suburban political strength led to conflicts over funding central city infrastructure, and, generally, tensions between the two levels led to the demise of the Corporation.

Quebec reacted to its two-tiered problems in 2000 by merging the communities in Montreal and Quebec City. In Montreal, the Mayor wanted to promote social equity by using the stronger suburban tax base. The opposition Liberal Party won the election in 2003 by pledging to provide a legislative mechanism for de-mergers, which they did. Despite a confusing set of rules that required public approval, fifteen de-mergers were approved in Montreal and one in Quebec City, reversing the consolidations that had occurred only years earlier.

An analysis of the 2004 Quebec referenda on the de-mergers of municipalities determined citizen preferences regarding consolidation and fragmentation (Tanguay and Wihry, 2008). The authors observe that the referenda on consolidations, which had been imposed from above, approved many consolidations which had not taken place but were justified on economic grounds. Thus, voters may well be expected to favor a merger if they expect a reduction in the tax-price of local services.

The Quebec legislature also created the concept of metropolitan communities (Sancton, 2005), which are similar to the regional districts that have been successful in British Columbia. They have responsibility for functions such as regional planning, waste disposal, regional infrastructure, and regional parks. The alleged success of British Columbia's regional districts is attributed to a number of factors, in addition to the steadfast refusal to treat them as another level of government. The regional districts have demonstrated flexibility in providing a hybrid of services, both upper- and lower-tier, based on the requirements of the municipalities. When required, the districts have also acted as administrative agencies for projects or services undertaken jointly by their member municipalities, further demonstrating their ability to accommodate specific local needs (Vojnovic, 1998). The results of creating the metropolitan communities in Quebec are not yet known. Over the last fifty years, Quebec City has been a two-tier government, a consolidated government, and now a government with a regional district.

Specific Attempts

The literature describes both successes and failures. The term "success" is often used to mean completed and "failure" to indicate abandoned. Both the economic and political feasibility need to be considered when evaluating a proposed consolidation, but not all attempts consider all aspects of the proposed merger. Of those attempts at consolidation that were completed, there are opposing camps about whether the consolidation was actually a success in achieving the goals it intended or in delivering other benefits that were not anticipated. Some of the reports below were prepared by or quote those with an interest in the consolidation. The varied results reported include estimates of savings that might not be realized in the merged community, if the merger is completed.

Overall, Benton and Gamble (1984, p. 190) underscore mixed results in the literature:

> An article a few years ago declared that "metropolitan reorganization via consolidation is not a dead issue, but it is certainly not very healthy" (Marando, 1979, p. 426). The author of that article builds a strong case for his conclusion by citing numerous instances of rejection by voters, court cases that require concurrent majorities for affected areas, and more significantly, a lack of evidence that con-

solidation produces economies in government (Marando, 1979, p. 419-21). However, the more general literature pertinent to governmental reorganization and the issue of "economies of scale" in government is divided to the point that there is no definite answer to the question of scale. On the one hand, part of the literature reports diseconomies of scale (Bish and Ostrom, 1973; Gabler, 1969; Hirsch, 1959; Schmandt and Stephens, 1960). On the other hand, some studies have shown mixed results, with economies of scale for some categories of expenditures, diseconomies for other categories, and no relationship for the rest (Alesc and Dougharty, 1971; Hirsch, 1968; Morgan and Pelissero, 1980).

> **The voters in Wantage Township, New Jersey, 75 percent of whom voted against consolidation, ironically answered a mailed survey in the majority (52 percent) that they agreed that, in general, consolidation is a good idea. Although this could be a NIMBY (Not In My BackYard) reaction, conversations we had with some vocal opponents suggest the voters do not perceive or do not believe the benefits.**

A 2004 study showed that, since 1990, only five city-county consolidations have succeeded: Athens/Clarke County, Georgia in 1990; Lafayette Parish/City of Lafayette, Louisiana in 1992; Augusta/Richmond County, GA in 1995; Wyandotte County/Kansas City, Kansas in 1997; Louisville/Jefferson County, Kentucky in 1999. (Ho, 2004) As mentioned above, Leland and Thurmaier (2004) cite fourteen case studies of city-county attempts beginning in 1967, most of which were not completed.

The consolidation of Athens with Clarke County, Georgia provides some lessons for the would-be consolidator (Campbell and Selden, 2000). The authors detail additional costs of $7.5 million, which were presented earlier in this chapter. Despite these high costs, the authors conclude that consolidation can be efficient and result in cost savings in some departments. They emphasize that the amount of money saved in a merger will depend on the design of the new government, as reflected both in its charter and the policy and management decisions of its elected and appointed officials. A comment in this study, which bears consideration because of its political ramifications, is that the unification charter determined that water rates would be equalized by increasing the rate paid by city users and decreasing the rate paid by county users.

Table 2A (see next page) examines total expenditures between 1990 and 1997, which included the two years preceding and six years following unification. The comparison of the general fund total operating expenditures for Athens-Clarke County(in real dollars) with the expenditures of three unconsolidated city-county governments in Georgia over the same eight-year period shows that in Athens–Clarke County they increased at a rate noticeably lower than in the three comparison groups in both the short and long term.

Table 2A.

Comparison of Total General Fund Operating Expenditures*
*Percentage Change Since 1990 in Real Dollars***

City/County	Short-Term (1990-92)	Long-Term (1990-97)
Albany–Dougherty Co.	43.08	58.34
Gainesville–Hall County	15.52	40.43
Warner Robins–Houston Co.	8.87	33.41
Athens–Clarke County	6.74	20.97

* General fund expenditures related to education, library, hospital, garbage collection, and garbage disposal were excluded from the analysis since they do not appear in Athens-Clarke County's General Fund expenditures.

** Expenditures were adjusted for inflation using 1989 as the base year.

Although the table shows only the percentage change (of increase) for total expenditures, the article also examined the sub-categories, which are not shown in the table. In the sub-categories, there were some declines in costs in the five years after unification in Clarke County. General government expenditures (including internal support units) declined by nearly 10 percent, the only major function to experience a decrease in expenditures. Finance expenditures decreased both in the short and long term, although one of the non-consolidated comparison groups also decreased.

A consolidation of Jacksonville with Duval County led to a long-term impact of a 1.6 percent tax increase from 1969 to 1981 (Benton and Gamble, 1984). Over the same period of time, the comparison area (Tampa-Hillsborough County) reported a 1.8 percent increase. (Prior to consolidation the tax rate was declining in both Jacksonville/Duval County and the control area, but the long term impact over six years eventually showed an increase in costs in both areas resulting in the 1.6 and 1.8 percent increases in the tax rate over the total period.) Consolidation certainly did not prove to be an instrument that reduced the amount of revenue derived from the citizenry in the long run. In fact, these findings are opposite to the main hypothesis that consolidation will reduce costs and, therefore, taxes. Consolidation had an insignificant impact on property tax revenue in both the short and long run. Public safety expenditures increased as a result of this consolidation, as was suggested by Ostrom's work in the 1970's. Prior to consolidation the rate of change for public safety expenditures had been a decline of 0.1 percent, similar to the decline in the Tampa/Hillsborough County area. After consolidation, the merged Jacksonville entity showed an annual increase of 3.3 percent.

Prior to consolidation, the estimate of savings in another Florida community considering consolidation were reported in a local newspaper article (Sharockman, 2004). A study estimated that West Oldsmar homeowners would save $100 or more a year, and Oldsmar would see more than $100,000 in additional revenues annually if the city incorporated the 142-acre enclave into its boundaries. The savings to homeowners would come in the form of lower property taxes, as well as reductions in taxes, fees or surcharges that residents now pay for garbage collection, water, and sewer service.

In the county of Westchester, Pelham Manor and the Village of Pelham decided not to merge. Pelham Manor was smaller, but had a more valuable property base. Therefore, even if there were some savings in consolidation, Pelham Manor's taxes might have gone up. Residents of Pelham Manor would, in effect, have picked up more of the costs for the newly merged community than their neighbors. They would have contributed more with less say in how taxes were spent. (Fessenden, 2006)

The Toronto forced consolidation into a megacity has engendered considerable controversy. The merger occurred in 1998 and all the savings or costs reported below are in Canadian dollars from that period. An article from the *Toronto Gazette* has considerable detail about the problems that followed the Toronto consolidation (Sewell, 2000):

> The provincial government first estimated that the Toronto amalgamation would save up to $250 million. What the province seemed to forget was that 73 per cent of the $5 billion spent annually by municipal governments in Toronto was spent at metro level on services that had been centralized or amalgamated years ago: police, transit and social services. The only savings possible would come from the $1.5 billion spent by the local governments on things such as libraries, parks and recreation, planning, public health, garbage collection, water and sewage and fire services.

Attempts to cut salary costs were reportedly foiled by lean staffing prior to consolidation and an increase in fire salaries to the highest of the pre-consolidation levels. Although some cuts were realized ($134 million), they were offset by increases in the first two years ($154 million), by the high costs of necessary studies, buying new technology, and equipping centralized facilities.

Sewell sees the reduction in executive staff that occurred after the consolidation as stripping the government's ability to provide powerful executive level advice for changing times. The reduction of departments from 52 to 6 and of divisions from 206 to 37 was accompanied by the reduction of area managers by a third, from 1,837 to 1,204, and of executive management positions by two-thirds, from 381 to 154.

With 850 of the most senior staff removed from the workforce, local government suffered a loss in corporate memory and expertise. This loss of senior talent reduced the productivity of the workforce and the ability of the city to plan for its future.

Sewell continues by reporting that cuts made to litter services have had an impact on the public in this traditionally clean city. Recreation programs, once free as a matter of social policy, now have user fees attached, leading to a decline in participation and fewer programs being offered in the downtown area. Public transit fees were increased. Response has slowed for tree maintenance, building permits, and variance hearings. Finally, the author contends the creation of one large council has led to inaccessibility to local decision-makers and the shift of power into the backrooms of the mayor's office.

A more recent article on Toronto (Grant, 2007) sees the same problems as were evident at the time of consolidation. However, it also sees the benefits of a central government for regional planning. It summarizes the changes in the size of the municipal government as showing decreases in the administrative staff within the context of an overall increase of over 4,000 positions for the entire staff.

Although the Brookings Institution study of the approved Louisville/Jefferson County merger did not evaluate the impact because the merger was not completed at the time of the study, the details of the agreement are interesting because they allowed for considerable flexibility and power to be exercised by the merged Metro Mayor and Council:

> Small incorporated cities will not be affected by the merger either. All of their existing powers are preserved. All fire departments and other service districts will also continue to operate as separate entities with all their current powers. The merger referendum does not specifically require the merger of the police or any other government departments. Decisions on consolidating these departments will be made by the Metro Mayor and the Metro Council after the new year. (Brookings Institution, 2002, p. 4)

The consolidation of the Halifax Regional Municipality was implemented to save money and reduce the competition between municipalities for economic development (Sancton, 2005). The new municipality implemented three different tax rates—urban, suburban, and rural—corresponding to different levels of service. The author states that there is no evidence that savings occurred. The effect of the consolidation specifically on police services in Halifax was studied (McDavid, 2002). The study concluded that consolidation led to overall cost increases, lower service levels, and no effect on the crime rate.

The 1999 Halifax Regional Municipality Citizen Survey asked citizens about the consolidation (Poel, 2000). Citizens did not have a favorable assessment of the HRM amalgamation decision or the performance of their Council, did not see the geographical, social and economic diversity of the HRM region as a strength, and did not think municipal services had improved.

Comments and Conclusions

It is natural and practical to seek the development of criteria to determine where consolidations would be most effective. Such criteria would focus scarce resources or maximize the probability of early successes for a state trying to lead its municipalities to greater efficiency. Because the literature does not agree on a "one size fits all" solution and because the estimation of potential cost savings or changes is complex, specific criteria are not effective in identifying consolidation candidates.

The literature makes a clear distinction between the rational financial basis for consolidation and the political or cultural environment that will allow consolidation to occur, much less make it pay off. There are not enough credible examples from which to draw consistent lessons. What we do know is that there has been significant resistance to consolidation.

> **The resistance to consolidation, even in the face of intensive media messages about too many governments, has weakened the initial resolve of centralized governments. In both New York and New Jersey, the 2007 actions that pushed for consolidation have been reinterpreted to weaken the focus on consolidation as the primary thrust. The centralized governments in both states have recognized other effective alternatives and their municipalities have increased their vigor in pursuing them, particularly shared services, but accompanied by significant growth in the interest in regional solutions. Some of this interest comes from the belief that regional solutions can get beyond the small reductions in costs resulting from sharing or consolidating only two towns, in favor of creating regional service centers where appropriate expertise is possible without creating excess capacity.**

There are no clear answers about whether consolidation works. Among those consolidations which were realized (i.e., completed), the impact is very mixed. Even the evidence as to whether small municipalities should consolidate is not uniformly consistent in the literature. Some of the explanation for the mixed results may lie in controlling the diseconomies associated with consolidation, but some diseconomies may be inherent in an increasing scale of operations. Sources of diseconomy include harmonization of salaries and services, the need to provide better information and management systems in a larger entity, the need to create a new or enhanced management structure to preserve allocative efficiency, and the increased specialization of employees and equipment.

It is important to be realistic about the transitional costs, both financial and organizational, in evaluating a potential consolidation. Uniformity, in the guise of equity of services or of salaries and benefits, can counter any potential cost savings. It is prudent to reduce annual operating costs, through a reduction in the workforce or the facilities and equipment, in order to offset the transitional costs of consolidation. Reductions in employees, however, can increase workloads and cause poor response to citizens' requests. Political representation is an issue that must be resolved in a merged government. Considerations of the use of the broadened tax base are a political decision.

Although transitional costs, including the need for additional facilities and equipment, are significant, the literature usually indicates reasons other than financial for a failure to consolidate. The literature noted that the need for structural changes to accomplish consolidation is a disincentive. If these changes, which are usually legal and organizational, are undertaken, the desired gains in efficiency will require a relatively long timeframe to achieve. Political concerns of elected officials and parties in power have scuttled consolidations. The loss of local control of the level of services and their delivery is a concern of the public, as well as elected and appointed officials. This includes the differences in perceived needs for services and desirability of regulation in different types of areas, such as urban and rural. Differing tax bases and tax rates present obstacles or opportunities, depending on the policy goals of the consolidation. Fear of job loss and increased workload are issues for unions and employees. Combining different unions, or union and non-union municipalities, presents an obstacle. Ironically, successful regionalization and prior inter-governmental cooperation provide alternative paths to achieving greater efficiency and, therefore, reduce the perceived need to take on the more drastic changes required by consolidation.

The literature addressed legislative impediments, but they are specific to individual states and countries. The Canadian literature indicated that the lack of relevant laws in the United States prevents mandatory consolidation from being imposed by states, but considered this a good thing. There were other specific references to laws allowing consolidation, which added restrictions that made consolidation less attractive. Some labor laws required amendment for specific consolidations to occur.

The mixed results for the consolidations that have been completed indicate that some have been successful in reducing costs or providing other benefits. The literature about the recent restructurings in the United States, however, seems to favor consolidation of functions to a regional or county level, as opposed to a complete merger of municipalities. For example, the consolidation of fire districts in many states has led to reduced costs, but service improvements, including reduced response times, sometimes are the most important result to the public. The municipalities that contain fire districts have remained separate.

Consolidation of other specific functions has provided benefits other than cost savings, but these are sometimes perceived as disadvantages by part of the affected population. Regional or centralized land use planning or economic development has been a popular restructuring because of the benefits of equity of service delivery and broadening a tax base to provide funding to restore deteriorating infrastructure. However, what are seen as benefits by some can have grave political consequences. These supposed benefits have been the source of dissatisfaction with the consequences of a merger. Whether equity and the redistribution of wealth or resources are beneficial is a political policy determination. There are other results of consolidation that also will be perceived as benefits or disadvantages, depending on the interests of the individual or group.

The largest portion of the data that is available on consolidation is from the initiatives of other countries. They have undertaken more consolidations than have been attempted in the United States. However, the fact that the political situation and the cultural conditions are often so different is a major concern for attempting to arrive at recommendations that apply to any of the states in the U.S.

In the final analysis, if the question is "Do we consolidate and where?," the literature review shows there is not adequate information to say "yes" or "no," and there are certainly not concrete criteria to follow through on a "yes" answer. The literature indicates that governments have achieved only a small portion of the attempted consolidations, and the results of those achieved are mixed. These are the major findings, which we have discussed in detail above:

▶ Cost Savings Are Not Assured

The literature does not consistently support the general belief that increasing the size of municipalities will lead to cost savings. The overall inverted U-Shaped curve relationship between population size and costs per capita masks the details of size relationships that vary with the nature of the service being delivered.

▶ Implementation of Consolidation Is Costly and Time Consuming

The financial costs of consolidation include costs of the transition, of salary and service harmonization, and of additional facilities, equipment, and infrastructure (both physical and administrative) resulting from the merger. Transitional costs can be substantial if the consolidated government requires new facilities or infrastructure. There is a tendency to create a wage and benefit structure that rises to the highest wage levels of the pre-merged governments. It will normally take years to complete a consolidation. It is a complex task to achieve, as opposed to simply assuming a better organizational culture and better procedures in the merged government.

▶ Savings Only Result from Reductions in Resources

Like any potential restructuring, the costs and benefits of consolidation will be specific to the conditions and issues of the governments that are involved. The costs and benefits should be assessed with recognition of the results that can be achieved realistically. The proposed merger must be evaluated as to how positions, equipment, or facilities can be reduced, if not immediately, then in the long run, so that these savings will balance the costs of the transition and increased on-going costs resulting from higher uniform service levels and wage and benefit structures among merged municipalities. Even staff reductions can be costly if it is necessary to offer incentives to get them to occur.

▶ Most Consolidation Attempts Fail

Governments have not achieved the majority of recent voluntary attempts at consolidation. Of those that have been achieved, the results, measured in terms of costs savings or improved quality or responsiveness of service delivery, are mixed. Further, the results of consolidations are not consistently beneficial in terms of long-term financial and political considerations.

▶ Politics Is an Obstacle

The literature most often cites political considerations, running the gamut from multiple concerns of the public to concerns of political parties about shifts in the balance of power, as the most significant obstacles to consolidation. Local leaders and their publics are willing to pay the price of inefficiency in order to retain local control. To be effective in consolidating, politics should be contemplated and resolved in the broadest terms, including the interests of elected officials, employees, and the public, which values local control.

Evaluations of potential mergers must be specific to the needs and situations of the communities involved. The mere attempt to consolidate often focuses an evaluation on ways other than consolidation to achieve increased efficiencies, even when the merger of governments does not result. This consideration of alternatives has led to better arrangements for service delivery in many situations.

CHAPTER 3

Consolidation of Service Delivery and Efficiency

At this point, we have examined size as a determinant of municipal efficiency, and, despite a lack of consistent evidence that bigger is better, we have looked at the implications of municipal consolidation. Results were mixed, with the most consistent finding that consolidations should be examined on a case-by-case basis. Another major finding from reviewing municipal consolidations is that the evaluation often does not continue the interest in municipal consolidation, but instead redirects attention to functional consolidation, that is, consolidation of services, as the method of restructuring.

This has a great deal of appeal based on the findings in the literature on municipal size, which suggest the efficiency-generating capabilities of size vary with the type of service being delivered. The classic split is between labor-intensive services that are most efficient in small municipalities and capital-intensive services that are most efficient in large municipalities. The appeal would be validated, if the literature showed service consolidation being fostered in capital-intensive or specialized services, but being avoided or showing negative results in labor-intensive services. This is not the case. In fact, municipalities often pursue police services as shared (as well as centralized) services, even though police services, particularly patrol services, are labor based. The literature offers no explanation for this logical inconsistency.

> **The misdirected focus solely on economy of scale is put on a more productive path by considering excess capacity. Although the literature does not provide much information on the notion of excess capacity, it seems to be a factor in whether a collaborative agreement will yield efficiency gains or quality improvements. Excess capacity exists because of the need to be able to respond even though the service is not needed at all times or is not always needed with a high level of expertise. Excess capacity is common in services that include needs that are unscheduled or need expertise, but only on occasion. Section II of this book discusses excess capacity and its sources, noting which service delivery arrangements can reduce under-utilized capacities. Evaluating the excess capacity in services may be more productive than focusing on scale, although scale is one mechanism to reduce excess capacity.**

The literature on overall municipal consolidation warned that consolidation is only cost-effective if the merged municipality can reduce resources, that is, if it requires fewer employees or less equipment/facilities to deliver equivalent service. The concept of achieving reduced resources is also appropriate for service consolidations, as are concerns about the resulting service quality. It appears that municipalities must address both of these areas of concern as they evaluate specific arrangements, rather than as a universal mechanism to identify potentials for service consolidation.

Analyzing the Literature on Consolidation of services

Consolidation of services has been a popular starting point to identify optimal arrangements for delivering municipal services that maximize cost efficiency or achieve other benefits. The consolidation of services with other governments can take several forms, and has multiple terms to describe the arrangements: inter-local agreements, shared services, service transfers, government partnerships, contracts with government, and many other variants. The most common term is "shared services," and that is the term used throughout this book. Typically, one entity delivers the services to another. For example, a small township may contract with a larger neighboring town for police services.

The literature reflects the fact that service consolidations, primarily through the mechanism of shared services, are the most common form of service delivery other than the direct delivery of service by municipalities. Shared services is a successful tool to increase efficiency of local government service delivery. In this chapter, the focus is on a transfer or consolidation of the service delivery to another existing government entity, which is the most common form of restructured service delivery. The next chapter, *Alternative Service Delivery Arrangements and Efficiency*, examines other options for service delivery, including those that involve non-government entities, create a new government entity, or shift the full responsibility to a more central government for all the local governments within that central government (essentially, a mandated transfer of responsibility). Both practitioners and academics understand and accept shared services. Some of the other options are more esoteric, may require definition specific to state laws or require modified legislation, and may be described with different terms or definitions in different regions and countries.

Government Use of Consolidated Service Options

In 2005, the consulting firm Accenture conducted a survey of 143 senior-level government managers in 13 countries, including the U.S. The research indicated that shared services are a common practice in many states in the U.S., and internationally:

> Many governments have started to implement some components of a true shared services operating model, but few have implemented them all; thus, few governments have achieved the full potential of their shared services. While many government organizations have started the journey toward a true shared services

model, most still have a ways to go. Beyond lower costs, the focus must be on improved service to customers. (Accenture, 2005)

Another survey conducted in Broome County, New York, among elected officials, provides more details about the status of utilizing shared services in local governments. The final report from the Broome County shared services summit identifies services and candidates for optimal sharing of services, noting courts, health insurance, parks and recreation, and highways as the best services to target for implementation (Sinclair, 2005). In New Jersey, a review of a series of case studies (Holzer et al, 2007) includes some important services the Broome County study ignored, perhaps because the delivery of these services is located at a higher level of government in New York State. Fire, police services, solid waste, public works, parks and recreation, and library services are the focal points for inter-local service agreements in these case studies. The Accenture report adds human resources, property management, legal services, finance, and information technology to the list. A different position is that the most obvious functions for sharing are highly regulated transaction-based processes such as revenue collection and benefit payments (Price Waterhouse Coopers, 2005).

The Broome County report echoes the international survey conducted by Accenture on the extent of service sharing. It finds that while a lot of sharing occurs, particularly in the use of highway equipment, snow removal, parks and recreation, dog control, and fire services, governments produce many services directly. The survey results show that half of the services inquired about were only shared by one or two governments, indicating that there is an opportunity for many more governments to share these 21 service types.

The mechanisms by which sharing occurs are mostly informal. The Broome County study surveyed only elected officials, and not staff. One might expect that elected officials would depend on their staff to review and utilize more formal mechanisms. However, based on interviews with municipal staff, Holzer et al (2003) came to the same strong conclusion that informal mechanisms lead to cooperation between governments.

Informal networks are particularly effective with capital-intensive services, such as road maintenance, which requires expensive equipment that may be underutilized unless municipalities share the equipment. Although there are seasonal peaks in road maintenance, it is a scheduled activity, unlike a fire response, so managers of the entities can accomplish the planning between themselves. This happens informally even without agreements on many occasions, because Public Works Directors typically have fostered good working relations with their peers. Thurmaier and Wood's work in Kansas on inter-local agreements finds that a majority of cities and counties have at least one such agreement. The research concludes that a "norm of reciprocity" culture exists, creating networks of service sharing (Thurmaier and Wood, 2002, p. 590).

An additional important fact surfaced in the Broome County study. Broome County's local government officials expressed interest in exploring additional service sharing. They targeted sixty-six services for further investigation. Officials seem to believe that service sharing is a worthwhile strategy for improving the cost effectiveness of their governments or improving the services that they provide to residents.

Motivations for Consolidating Service Delivery

There is no question as to whether there are good reasons for sharing services. It is a regular topic discussed on state websites, and there are many programs to encourage these forms of inter-governmental collaboration.

Economies of scale are a key reason for service sharing in communities all over the world and at varied levels of political jurisdictions. Most African countries have already recognized the benefits of regional integration and participate in at least one regional arrangement. (Foroutan, 1992) In the United States, regional integration often helps by consolidating sub-regional markets in order to benefit from economies of scale. For example:

> With shrinking revenues and growing service demands, Michigan communities are joining forces to provide services to their constituents. Joint, or shared, services are agreements between local governments to combine resources to provide a service to their communities. This combination is a cost saving method for municipalities that want to maintain service levels but find that tax laws inhibit their ability to fund them individually. The result is a classic example of economies of scale .... (Davis, 2005)

In the City of Buffalo, it was estimated that a different proposed model of delivering services would have reduced the local tax levy by 9 to 13 % (Center for Government Research, 2006). The city would continue to provide core governance, administrative, and other key services, but contract out for services other governments or the private sector could provide.

Some municipalities have begun to see promise in selling their services and are soliciting partners to contract with them. The Mayor of Pittsburgh made an offer to provide services such as trash-hauling, animal control, building inspection, computer, ambulance, firefighting, personnel, police and public works, and bulk purchasing to the suburbs. The reaction of the suburban municipalities has been mixed, although Pittsburgh feels the rate they are charging for the services is break-even. The inner ring suburbs have been more interested in contracting for services than the more distant municipalities. A newspaper article on the announcement by the Mayor cites desire for autonomy, fear of loss of control, and concerns about the quality of the service as the reasons many of the municipalities are not interested. (Allen, 2008)

However, there is consensus in the literature that shared services should go beyond cost savings and focus on improved service to customers. "The primary motivation for the introduction of shared services should not be cost savings but rather improvements in service delivery and quality." (Spoehr et al, 2007, p. 5) To extend this further, there are opportunities to not just improve service, but also entirely change the nature of the service delivered. To develop breakthrough enhancements in service delivery, it is sometimes necessary to justify the cost of acquisition of the tools or infrastructure required for development, such as software or hardware. Shared services, or some other arrangement which spreads the initial costs, can make this investment practical.

> **Despite the literature's call for a focus on quality of public services, most of the documentation of evaluations of service delivery alternatives concentrates on financial improvement, not quality improvement, when there is any attempt to quantify success. However, we have observed that quality improvements share the stage with cost reductions in most cases, and, in some, may take the lead. Quality is an equally important factor because few collaborations go forward if there is a potential reduction in service quality. Some collaborations, particularly involving very small governments, occur principally to correct management problems or to provide better coverage that cannot be provided by a small government. Police shared services usually start from one of these perspectives, even though they may save money, too.**

The area of Information Technology and E-governance is an example of how shared services could change the nature of the service by centralizing operations. Most towns have a website. They vary in their quality and effectiveness in serving the public, but they fall far short of the potential suggested by E-governance models. The development of capacities such as E-commerce is expensive and requires technical skills not typically available in small municipalities. The area of records retention, records storage, and disaster recovery is another technologically-based service, the development of which is constrained by the limited resources of small municipalities. The necessary communication and network infrastructure, advanced indexing and retrieval software, and storage and back-up facilities require extensive capital investment. A larger entity can make these costly investments in technology because it spreads the costs of the basic tools over a larger population, reducing the initial cost per capita to develop the technology infrastructure for all the municipalities that will benefit from the technology.

To improve business processes in the implementation of shared services, such as with information technology services, the Accenture report (2005) recommends outside expertise should be used in the planning and implementation of new technologies. This additional cost is practical because the Accenture report focused on larger governments. Smaller local governments could obtain some of the benefits of outside expertise with the support of County Shared Service Offices or government industry associations such as state chapters of Government Management Information Sciences.

Expertise is important in what might be considered non-technical arenas, such as road maintenance. "Due to small size and relative isolation, rural governments are inherently limited in developing either effective policy or efficient delivery systems. These structural barriers have prevented many rural public officials from developing the capacity, resources, and expertise needed for managing increasingly complex problems." (Deller et al, 1992, p. 355) The authors write about production consolidation as a viable option where physical consolidation is not. Specifics include cooperative arrangements, state or regional circuit rider programs, jointly hired engineers or cooperative purchasing of equipment.

A study of social care managers showed they did not believe the cost savings were the significant benefit (Stephenson, 2008). The study found, "Shared services could help deliver quicker response time and flexibility, standardized services and delivery of new services." Interestingly, the managers, who did not view the cost savings as substantial, felt that the savings from sharing services would not exceed 11%—still an attractive number to many.

The problems of inefficiency in local governments can have several solutions. The International City/County Management Association (ICMA) routinely surveys what solutions municipalities implement, including restructuring:

> Inter-municipal cooperation was the most common form of restructuring (55 percent of all reported restructuring cases since 1990). Privatization was next most common at 28 percent, followed by reverse privatization at 7 percent and governmental entrepreneurship at 6 percent. Cessation of service (4 percent) was the least common restructuring alternative....
>
> Mutual aid agreements represent the simplest and most common form of cooperation. Joint production of a service was the next most common, followed by contracting with another government. Formation of special districts was rare." (Warner and Hebdon, 2001, p. 323)

As opposed to using private contracting, "contracting governments turn to other governments as vendors for services that risk contract failure." (Brown, 2008, p. 372) Monitoring and oversight can also be provided at a lower cost than what is required to monitor an outside (non-governmental) contractor, but the cost saving benefits of contracting still accrue because of economies of scale.

Indianapolis accomplished broad service transfers with the implementation of UniGov (Rosentraub, 2000). UniGov includes a consolidated city-county government, four independent cities, and more than fifty other units of local government. This city-county consolidation program concentrated a limited or select group of urban services at the regional (defined as county) level while permitting most other critical urban services to be delivered by administrations and agencies serving different, often much smaller, areas within the county. Structurally, UniGov is a multilayered local government system under which authority for economic development, public works, parks, transportation, and some elements of public safety is transferred to the county (or regional) level—the first layer in a multi-tiered structure. The consolidated government is the final authority for land use and economic development programs for the entire county.

The ICMA also provides insight into what conditions lead to adopting shared services (and private contracting) as a solution to the problems of efficient service delivery (Warner and Hefetz, 2002b):

▶ Governments using higher levels of cooperation and privatization show lower average per capita expenditures. Moreover, the efficiency effect is greatest for suburbs.

▶ Both cooperation and privatization are higher among higher-income municipalities. Whereas cooperation is favored by higher-poverty municipalities as well, privatization is not.

▶ Municipalities with council-manager forms of government were more likely to pursue higher levels of privatization in 1992, but less likely to pursue privatization in 1997 and more likely to pursue cooperation. Professional management is not significantly related to cooperation.

▶ Larger metropolitan places are less likely to engage in cooperation. They have the least to gain from economies of scale.

A 1997 survey of local governments in New York state indicated population size has a significant impact on local government restructuring, including inter-municipal cooperation and privatization—"larger townships and counties were more likely to restructure." (Warner and Hebdon, 2001, p. 327) Jeong used the ICMA data and concluded that population size does not explain the choice of joint production (although the focus was on contracting out); joint production was also encouraged by a reformed county political structure (specifically elected county executives, who may not be termed "reform" in all local governments) and robust financial resources (Jeong, 2006).

Leroux and Carr studied the determinants of cooperation among municipalities in Michigan for various public works services. The analysis documented the role economic factors play. Cooperation in road improvements and construction is more likely when there are high per capita property taxes, or when there is a greater reliance on inter-governmental revenues. However, cooperation in lower cost activities like traffic signs, signals, and street light maintenance was not related to per capita property taxes. The wealthiest communities cooperate more, except on roads. Populous and high growth governments cooperate more on roads. Cooperation is more likely in a service area to which a large portion of the budget is devoted. (Leroux and Carr, 2007, p. 352)

Municipalities have taken advantage of unusual events by forging collaborative efforts that allow the municipalities to share the benefits and responsibilities of a facility. In two situations, the development of a regional asset by an outside organization led to sharing. The Nature Conservancy developed the Greater Hanover Recreation Park, but three boroughs own and maintain it (Luzerne County, 2005). In addition, the *Boston Globe* reported that two cities in

Massachusetts benefited from a fire station built by a developer as part of an agreement between the parties (Conti, 2008).

Barriers to the Consolidation of Services

When there are financial incentives to sharing services, municipalities do not necessarily enter into a collaborative agreement. Many factors can stand in the way. Researching possible sharing situations requires time and resources to evaluate the benefits and the methods of sharing.

An open-ended approach to sharing services was recommended by the New York State Commission on Rural Resources (2005) in its report to promote increased collaboration in highway services. This report recommended authorizing the municipal highway official to enter into inter-municipal agreements without the prior approval of the governing body. A sample resolution was included in the report to delegate this authority from the chief executive officer of the municipality, resulting in a standing agreement to collaborate with other municipalities that adopted a similar resolution.

The Somerset County Business Partnership recommended to the state of New Jersey (Somerset County Municipal Managers Association, 2006) that the state should provide incentives to encourage sharing of services, such as:

▸ Funding for municipalities to continue existing programs, for implementation as well as, or in place of, feasibility studies that may waste money

▸ Funding for host municipalities to create new shared services

▸ Funding for seeking out privatization (which can be the ultimate result of a shared venture), and

▸ Funding for organized groups with a proven track record of facilitating shared services

The Partnership mentioned two other hurdles to sharing: health care costs and a lack of support for employees displaced by the sharing arrangement.

Displaced workers are a concern of trade unions, some of whom can mount powerful resistance even when there are few real disadvantages to offset the savings advantages of the shared service. The concern of trade unions in Scotland turned the displaced worker issue into a green argument. The unions perceive increased centralization of jobs draining them from more remote communities, which runs counter to the idea of being more environmentally-conscious by maintaining shorter commutes. (MacMahon, 2008)

In Massachusetts, barriers in the state law prevent municipalities from pursuing regional agreements easily—a problem that has hampered some communities' efforts to regionalize services. A proposed legislative package would allow communities to enter partnerships without having to engage in renegotiations with union groups, thus removing a significant barrier (Gunderson, 2008).

Union resistance may be coupled with public concern about loss of control over the delivery of the service. Gunderson continues in the newspaper article that local barriers to the plans to create a regional public-safety dispatch system for Maynard and Stow (Massachusetts) failed in the early 1990's. Towns could not agree on the specifics of a shared dispatch center, such as where the center would be located and how much actual savings would be realized. There was also a fear of losing personalized services, a common barrier to implementation of shared services.

> **Organized labor has been particularly effective in shared services involving public safety, arousing public concerns about security to derail attempts to contract police services to another government. Although there are many instances of a loss of political will on the part of an official confronted with an angry crowd at a public meeting (or the inability to summon the will in the first place, because of that fear), as more successful shared services for police and fire are implemented, the courage of our elected representatives is bolstered by the knowledge that public safety shared services can be accomplished. Some public safety experts are providing their expertise to right-size a merged department, given the dwindling resources that are available as local governments face budget crises.**

A *Boston Globe* article reported both successes and failures in regional collaboration efforts in Massachusetts. The article warned that union and community resistance might thwart a financially viable collaboration. It reported that although a consultant estimated a 1993 attempt to combine fire and police dispatch services in 13 western suburbs would have saved each community millions over ten years, a study by the Pioneer Institute for Public Policy Research noted that the attempt failed because "town and public safety officials didn't feel right handing over control of a system that is at the heart of local government. They also got flak from police and fire unions." (Bolton, 2008) Reportedly, although no jobs would have been lost, the unions viewed it as a "take-away" because dispatch duty was a safety net for older or injured police officers and firefighters.

A study of rural towns in Iowa confirms the importance of loss of local control. The authors report their "findings show higher citizen perceptions of quality with police services that are directly provided rather than those that are provided through inter-local agreements." (Morton, et al, 2008, p. 55) The study concludes that concerns with losing community identity and local control thwart collaborative efforts, because the public will "choose non-visible, routine portions of public services to share while directly providing those services that seem most important to their residents." (Morton, et al, 2008, p. 59)

The Australian Institute for Social Research notes barriers in addition to those associated with unions and employees. The complexity of a shared service agreement can create high costs for the research and development of a business case supporting it. The authors couple this with a fear that a hasty implementation of an inappropriate model might dissipate the accumulation of the human capital assets of corporate knowledge and skills (Spoehr et al, 2007).

Planning and preparing for the implementation of shared services can help overcome or mitigate the hurdles. A case study from the United Kingdom recommends a thorough examination of the business case and a comprehensive communication program from the earliest stages of implementation (Claps, 2008). This may be appropriate for a very complex agreement or in order to re-engineer a process perceived to be inadequate to deliver services efficiently. It also shows that the costs of feasibility studies can be high, as Spoehr suggested above.

Overcoming the barriers to entering into consolidated service agreements is important. Individual municipalities may not be willing to spend the effort and resources to tackle the issues and concerns elaborated above without external support and encouragement. There are increasing efforts from varied sources to provide a context of support, as the examples following show.

States have been creating programs to encourage shared services. New Jersey has programs to support shared services, including grants and a website full of information to help municipalities who want to enter into shared service agreements. New York State has been willing to make an investment of almost $30 million in local government efficiency, because they anticipate municipalities can save $245 million over five years (Cortes-Vazquez, 2008). The investment was in the form of grants to municipalities beginning in 2005. The New York State Department of State has increased its technical assistance and outreach capacity, has formed a partnership with the Albany Law School to augment its efficiency assistance and research capacity, and has formed a new Office of Coastal, Local Government, and Community Sustainability to deliver services to modernize local governments.

> **The strength of states' commitments to incentives to encourage restructuring of local government is weak, when times get tough. Ironically, in both New Jersey and New York, these grant programs, which are intended to save money, have been eliminated or reduced in the budget crises. New York cut funding by more than half and New Jersey cancelled all funding that was not yet committed, using the funds to meet FY2010 shortfalls in other areas. For FY2011, New Jersey did not appropriate these grants.**

The Southeast Michigan Council of Governments (SEMCOG) is a strong supporter of joint services (Davis, 2005). They have a detailed database with examples of success stories from the region. They recognize that there are concerns when entering such agreements, and have published pamphlets to aid local officials in the transition. In addition, they have recognized joint service programs and administrators with awards since 1998. They have also created a series of reports in conjunction with the Metropolitan Affairs Council (MAC) to assist communities with the creation of intergovernmental services.

In a chapter of the 2007 edition of *The Book of the States,* the authors "... recommend that in an effort to effectively encourage the development and implementation of shared services, states should: (1) provide financial support or incentives; (2) collect and disseminate concrete information regarding the benefits of shared service initiatives; (3) establish shared service performance measures; (4) develop a central point of information to field questions from communities who are in the process of developing, implementing, or sustaining shared services; and (5) work to ensure that the long-term interests of the taxpayers are paramount." (Holzer et al, 2007, p. 1)

Reported Benefits of Service Consolidation

The literature is full of examples of estimates of projected savings prior to implementation of a shared service, as well as savings that the authors state resulted from the implementation of the service arrangement. However, evidence of confirmed savings is seldom available. Success stories are largely anecdotal. Few studies exist that study shared services systematically and were able to gather verifiable information about cost reductions. Studies such as a report commissioned by the New Jersey Division of Local Government Services several years ago found that: "Concrete information about the benefit realized was seldom produced. The most common perception was that some savings has occurred, but that the larger benefit was in service to the community." (Holzer et al, 2003, p. 5) A report commissioned by the Public Service Association of South Australia to identify some of the key lessons from shared service arrangements in Britain and Australia (Spoehr et al, 2007) cast doubt on the credibility of the numbers that are produced:

▶ While cost savings can be achieved, projected savings targets are rarely met.

▶ The benefits of shared services are often overestimated.

▶ The costs of shared services are often underestimated because implicit costs and externalities are often not measured.

Despite the caveats we have expressed about reported cost savings, it is helpful to be aware of what the literature states about shared service successes. The numerical figures are affected by the year of the study, the currency used, and the scale of the jurisdictions involved. Hence, the figures below should not be evaluated for comparative purposes or used as a replacement for a careful analysis of a proposed agreement. The benefits of service consolidation suggested in the literature are substantial:

▶ One study projected that savings of over $64,000 a year could be realized for each community in an inter-municipal group in Niagara County (New York),and an additional $90,000 to $162,000 for the group if cost reduction strategies were followed in 12 areas of expense (Center for Government Research, 2006).

▸ The Shared Services Savings Report determined $13,695,962 in savings to Somerset County (New Jersey) taxpayers resulted because of local shared services initiatives by the municipalities, the schools and the county (Somerset County Municipal Managers Association, 2006).

▸ A study projected that merging the Village of Angola and Town of Evans police departments in New York State could achieve annual savings of $140,000 (Center for Government Research, 2006). The town of Evans (New York) agreed to create a dedicated policing zone with the Village of Angola, which could eliminate $350,000 from the Village's annual budget (Cortes-Vazquez, 2008).

▸ A newspaper article in the *Philadelphia Inquirer* reported the elimination of the court and police department in Audubon Park (New Jersey) would save $500,000 over five years, with Audubon providing the services for an additional $300,000 in revenue, less the costs of providing the service (Colimore, 2005).

▸ In North Redington Beach (Florida) the cost of law enforcement, now provided by the Pinellas County Sheriff's Office, was reported to be $100,000 less than was paid previously for the town's police department (Estrada, 1999a).

▸ When the county assumes the policing responsibilities, the *St. Petersburg Times* reported Bellair Beach (Florida) would save about $250,000 annually (Estrada, 2007).

▸ The annual savings in the first fiscal year for the City of Inverness (Florida) to hire the County Sheriff's Office to provide police services was estimated to be $108,206, but it will cost the City $6,523 in start up costs to realize the savings (Gonzales, 2004).

▸ Reportedly, Kenneth City (Florida) would save a half a million dollars a year if the county sheriff took over policing duties (Lindberg, 1999).

▸ A county publication promoting shared services stated that creating the West Side Police Department (Pennsylvania) would save about $73,000 in each of three communities every year and allow them to strengthen police presence during busy times (Luzerne County, 2005).

▸ A local Massachusetts newspaper reviewing plans for combining three part-time police departments reported the collaboration will not lead to cost reductions in the first few years, but might do so over a longer period, and it would provide better police service (Appleton, 2008).

▸ The *Boston Globe* reported on the efforts to improve police services in several Massachusetts communities. Police departments in Wrentham, Norfolk, Plainville, Franklin, and North Attleborough have been working the kinks out of a wireless data-sharing network. By linking databases, the communities hope to retain a law-enforcement edge (Bolton, 2008).

▶ Fire service from the Indian Rocks Fire District (Florida) will cost the town nearly $90,000 less than in previous years, according to a *St. Petersburg Times* article. Combined with the savings for eliminating the Police Department, there will be a 25% reduction in taxes (Estrada, 1999b).

▶ A newspaper article reported the estimates of savings to taxpayers to be $1.2 million after closing Fire Station 28 (Florida) without affecting the quality of service (Lindberg, 2008).

▶ According to a local news report, a county consultant projected that consolidating the county and city fire departments in Pinellas County (Florida) would save an estimated $10–$15 million a year (El-Khoury, 2005).

▶ Reportedly, officials expect to save $5 million in operating and equipment costs annually, since five towns joined in the North Hudson Regional Fire and Rescue Department (New Jersey). The number of firefighters will decrease from 332 to 307 through attrition (Smothers, 1999).

▶ Although there was debate about the cost savings and quality of service, it was reported that the consolidation of the Spring Hill (Florida) and county fire rescue districts could improve service. Two of the fire stations that sit next to the border of the Spring Hill Fire District could provide services in addition to those for life threatening situations, which are the only situations currently covered by mutual aid (King, 2004).

▶ A county publication credited combining the volunteer fire companies in Butler Township and Conyngham Borough (Pennsylvania) into the Valley Regional Volunteer Fire Company with allowing the purchase of a new ladder truck, which had been impossible before the merger (Luzerne County, 2005).

▶ Coverage of a budget workshop indicated the City of Brooksville (Florida) will save $195,564 per year by having the sheriff take over the dispatching of 911 emergency calls (Neill, 2007).

▶ Burlington County (New Jersey) projected $100,000 savings per year as the result of cooperative purchasing of electricity, if the 40 towns and other governments in the county participated in the bulk purchase program (Bewley, 2003).

▶ The Department of State in New York stated that when unsafe and inadequate water supplies necessitated creating a new water district, the Town of Cape Vincent formed a partnership with the Village, avoiding the $1 million cost for constructing a second water tank, and reducing the annual cost per household by $200 (Cortes-Vazquez, 2008).

The reader should note that most of these savings claims are not audited and many are projected. The academic literature bemoans the lack of concrete data. Unfortunately, unaudited claims of savings are the best information available. They are consistent with the belief that cooperation promotes savings, but the amount of the savings usually cannot be confirmed or relied upon.

Comments and Conclusions

Information in the academic literature on consolidation of specific services includes public safety functions, animal control, utilities and public works functions such as road maintenance, solid waste, and parks maintenance. The discussions are more descriptive than proscriptive, determining where restructured service delivery mechanisms are likely to occur, but not addressing where they should occur to maximize efficiency.

The literature provided no formula for success, but identified shared services as successful. Other successful arrangements in specific situations include two-tiered governments, privatization, special districts (particularly if regionalized), centralized services, and varied forms of joint policy making. The literature does not discuss which service delivery arrangements are optimal in relation to municipal characteristics, although it does relate some of the characteristics to the likelihood of adopting consolidated services, as discussed above.

The academic literature provides some empirical basis for evaluating shared service potentials. There is little debate about whether sharing services promotes efficiency in local government; the consensus is that it does. The literature far more consistently supports service consolidation than it does formal municipal consolidation. Despite many cost estimates and statements as to cost reductions and quality improvements achieved by service consolidation, the quality of this data is mixed. There is a great amount of variance in the savings estimates, far more than would be accounted for by a proportional relationship to population size or budget size. The literature on measuring efficiency provides possible reasons for apparent inconsistencies—varied accounting practices and the inclusion of different budget lines from one government to another. However, gathering more accurate or precise data will not likely change the overall conclusions of practitioners, consultants, or academics—who uniformly perceive shared services as effective in achieving efficiency.

Because of the informal nature of many cooperative agreements, and the informality of how they are developed, both the academic literature and government information sources probably underestimate the amount of cooperation. These sources may not count long-standing relationships as inter-governmental agreements and may not consider certain forms of sharing as shared service agreements (for example, in some states, mutual aid is not generally included as a shared service).

The literature supports the assumption that inter-governmental cooperation can provide cost and quality efficiencies. In addition to discussing the benefits of shared services and other forms of cooperation, the literature provides insights into how to increase the amount of service delivery consolidation:

▶ Benefits of Consolidated Services

The literature holds that consolidation of services leads to efficiencies in service delivery and improved service quality; but the extent of those gains is not clear.

▶ Quality Improvements

Quality of service delivery is an important factor in implementing cooperative agreements, although the literature emphasizes cost savings in describing successes. Some of these cases state that improvements in service delivery and quality should be the primary motivator in forming shared services, and, for some arrangements, quality issues were the sole motivation. Sharing seldom reduces quality of the service, and often sharing improves quality.

▶ Providing High Cost Service Improvements

There are functional service areas, such as information technology, in which local government has made only limited investments. Traditionally, this is because the government perceives the costs to be unpalatable to the citizenry. Sharing the cost for infrastructure development for improved service delivery, such as information technology and e-government, makes service improvements possible that would otherwise be too costly for an individual municipality and does so without incurring the skepticism of the public about expensive investments. There is a great deal of untapped potential in using large organizations to change the paradigm of service delivery.

▶ Case-by-Case Resolution of Obstacles

The literature demonstrates that municipalities can overcome hurdles to cooperation on a case-by-case basis. These hurdles are situation-specific, and should be assessed and resolved in forming an agreement. Fear of loss of local control and labor issues are among the most common obstacles to consolidation of service delivery. Appropriate planning and communication about the consolidation effort may bring forth other issues that need resolution to make the consolidation succeed.

▶ Public Safety Services

Reports from around the country indicate a reduction in public safety costs is possible. The transfer of police, fire, and dispatch services to other units of government are common potential efficiencies cited in the literature. Police and fire are difficult services to consolidate, because of the public's concerns with safety (in terms of response times) and organized labor's concerns with employment security. Governments must counter public concerns about loss of control, as well as concerns of organized labor, in order to realize the large potential savings in consolidating public safety services.

▶ State Encouragement

Evidence shows that local governments want to capitalize more fully on potential for cooperation and want to do more service sharing than they actually accomplish. States have provided incentives to encourage collaboration through grant and education programs. Some have tried to launch more of an outreach program, and others have tried to create databases of needs to meet through sharing.

▶ Need for Focus

Successful shared services require planning. Probably the greatest obstacle to doing what everybody seems to want—shared services that result in economies—is not spending the time and detailed effort to focus on it. The fact that most sharing arrangements come from informal networks and contacts is testimony to the fact governments do not spend enough time thinking about how to be efficient. They need to be encouraged to invest time and resources to do so. A more focused effort by elected and appointed officials to develop arrangements for consolidating service delivery will lead to increased cooperation and improved municipal efficiency.

▶ Incentives to Productive Organizations to Provide Focus

Grants, such as the State of New Jersey made available to develop county offices dedicated to promoting shared services in a local area, create an on-going local focus to uncover more cost-effective strategies. These state grants to counties are a good step in the general direction of funding effective locally based sharing organizations, but similar incentives to any organizations, even non-governmental or public/private, would uncover additional potentials and may be more effective in the long run than providing incentives for individual sharing projects.

▶ Positive Effects of Fiscal Stress

Fiscal and budgetary pressures also encourage a focus on cooperation between units of government. Conversely, aid or grants, which maintain specific services, are disincentives to increasing the focus on developing consolidated service delivery mechanisms. Municipalities that receive grants for services are less likely to consolidate service delivery.

Finding the right level of government to deliver a service is an important concern. The following chapter expands on the discussion of shared services and discusses some other mechanisms to move service delivery to the appropriate government, including centralized government, special districts, and regional delivery structures.

CHAPTER 4

Alternative Service Delivery Arrangements and Efficiency

Most municipal services are delivered directly by local government in the United States. The next most common form of delivering services is by contracting: with another government, with a non-profit organization, or with a for-profit private organization.

However, there is growing interest in other alternatives to promote increased efficiency in the delivery of municipal services. Many of these alternatives are not well defined or are defined differently in specific circumstances or in different regions and countries. They enhance the benefits and address the disadvantages of the more conventional forms of collaboration. In Chapter 4, we provide the groundwork for a basic understanding of several alternative structures, leading into the remainder of the book, which provides tools to align service delivery mechanisms with the characteristics of a service.

This chapter reviews five broad categories of alternatives to direct delivery of services:

▸ Contractual agreements

▸ Centralized services

▸ Special districts

▸ Joint boards

▸ Regional policy groups

There is promise in many of the models, but more work must be done to assess both the best way to configure them (or combine them) and estimate the cost savings or other benefits that will accrue. The discussion begins with the characteristics that the literature provides about each of the service delivery arrangements in the United States and elsewhere.

Analyzing the Literature on Alternative Service Delivery Arrangements

The notion of transferring services to the most appropriate level of government to deliver those services has begun to appear in the academic literature. It also appears in some government publications and in statements of the rationale for laws that address the optimal arrangements for delivering various public services from the standpoint of efficiency (or to achieve other benefits). This chapter focuses on service alternatives that are not directly provided by the responsible local government, but utilize another organization in some way to attempt to improve the quality and/or reduce the cost of the delivery of the service.

The literature has shown that alternative arrangements for service delivery are often investigated when an evaluation of consolidation has led to the conclusion that complete merger is not the best solution. Dollery and Byrnes (2005) state that even though it embraced consolidation in decades past, Australia is one source of the growing skepticism about the results of consolidation.

> **The high failure rate for implementing government consolidations is increasingly recognized. Recent studies of comprehensive sets of services are less likely to predetermine consolidation to be the end result.**

Consolidation ("amalgamation" in Australian parlance) is the ultimate relinquishing of all control to the larger government in a taxonomy of governance models introduced by Dollery and Johnson (2005). The taxonomy has two positive features that will advance our investigations. First, it uses governance models that have evolved in Australia as a reaction to the push for consolidation, but that are not common in much of the United States. Second, it differentiates the models based on the degree of political and administrative control over the service delivery, a concept we will use to help find optimal service delivery mechanisms.

> ...current small Australian councils represent both fully decentralized political and operational control, within the legislative confines of their respective state enabling acts. On the other hand, virtual local government enjoys full political control, but relinquishes a substantial degree of operational control to external organizations in service delivery. Area integration models, as exemplified by the proposed joint board model, exhibit lower levels of political control by constituent councils (since some power has been surrendered to the joint board) together with no operational control. By contrast, Regional Organizations of Councils (ROCs) maintain complete local political control and substantial simultaneous operational control. At the other end of the continuum, amalgamated councils concede all political and operational control to the larger new entity to which they belong.

This work, based on Australian local government, provides a jumping off point because the authors propose a range of alternatives, but it is apparent that potentials exist to define other structures that emphasize the benefits of different types and levels of government. The review that follows discusses these arrangements in terms more familiar in the United States, but the lines between the models are not rigid, and governments may mix the modes of delivery, sometimes with remarkable advantages. The real potential for increased efficiency in the delivery of local government services may lie in matching specific services to the best mode of delivery for that service, given the characteristics of the municipality.

An analysis of an ICMA survey from 1982 shifted the concern from what type of organization was delivering public services by stating the relevant issue was "whether governments have matched their service responsibilities with the appropriate method of service arrangement." (Stein, 1993, p.67) The study discusses a broader range of alternatives, even though direct service delivery was the modal form. There continue to be exciting examples of matching modes of delivery to the service need, even in the United States, but it still represents a relatively uncommon and evolving perspective.

Regional Policy Groups

Regional policy groups are uncommon in the United States, but a couple of examples show great promise and some positive results. The concept is based on the Australian

Regional Operating Councils (Dollery and Johnson, 2005), which constitute a formal regional group without any taxing authority. The ROC is governed by a board with two members from each constituent municipality, often the Mayor and a manager or another elected official. Specialist committees or an administrative structure support the board, so the staff can research issues and accomplish work to help the board develop policy recommendations. ROCs provide a formal mechanism for the free exchange of common concerns and potential solutions, engendering a sense of common purpose and destiny. They develop common policy positions based on the combined expertise of their members and facilitate the coordination and rationalization of their member governments. They have been successful in implementing cost saving programs of resource sharing, joint purchasing, and other mutually beneficial schemes that may create economies of scale, economies of scope, and enhanced capacities. They also represent a regional lobbying group for interacting with more centralized governments, enhancing the political power of the individual governments. In the United States, the most common term for regional policy groups is "Council of Governments (COG)."

Forty years ago, British Columbia established a network of regional districts throughout the province that remains in place today (Sancton, 2005). The regional districts are part of two-tiered governments that successfully provide consensual metropolitan leadership and a framework for voluntary municipal cooperation. Recently, the province of Quebec formed metropolitan communities to perform the same functions as British Columbia's regional districts. Sancton stated it was too early to assess the impact in Quebec.

Constituent governments have formed similar regional policy groups with local representation in the United States. Based on a report issued over thirty years ago (Masse and DiPasquale, 1975), a centralized agency was formed as a catalyst for change in Monroe County, New York. In 2000, Monroe County created the Council of Governments (COG) to continue the cooperative efforts of local government and address the convergence of three trends that may strike familiar chords (Center for Government Research, 2003):

1. the rising cost of government at all levels

2. a stagnating local economy

3. high local taxes

After evaluating a complete merger of governments, the 2003 report recommended focusing on functional changes that could result in cost savings in the foreseeable future, which is a result often seen in the literature when consolidations have been investigated:

> One topic that the Group discussed in detail was the question of the benefits of pursuing a complete merger of the city and county governments. Because together they represent over 80% of local government expenditures, it seems reasonable to speculate that substantial savings might be achieved by merging the two entities. Without more detailed study, it is not clear what level of savings might be achieved from such a merger in Monroe County. In any event, the substantial legal and political challenges to carry out a structural change of the size and scope required to merge the City of Rochester and Monroe County caused the Rump/COG Group to assume that the time horizon for such an event to occur would be much longer than the time horizon for more achievable changes. Therefore, the Group believes that the community would be better served by focusing on the functional cost savings proposed in this report at this time. (Center for Government Research, 2003, p. 11)

COG has already created substantial savings for its citizens. It meets on a continuing basis to look at common problems of its constituent governments and identifies solutions that fit the needs of the service to be delivered. "Cooperation and collaboration opportunities have been, and will continue to be, accomplished among groups of two or more governments, working together, to pool resources and achieve economies of scale, without requiring a change in any structure of government" (Center for Government Research, 2003, p. 10). However, COG (and the central agency that was its predecessor) has made incremental changes on an evolutionary basis, which was only possible because it is a central agency given the authority to act as a catalyst for change. Some of the specific mechanisms the central body has implemented or is considering include the following:

▸ Consolidating various functions into the Monroe County Water Authority, the Monroe County Pure Waters Agency, the 911/Office of Emergency Communications, and the Public Safety Training Academy.

▸ Developing a vehicle fueling facility used by six entities, a county highway materials bid to utilize volume pricing, and a proposed cooperative purchase of insurance.

▸ Recommending the development of a community-wide strategic plan to be implemented over a number of years for the provision of more efficient fire services.

▸ Recommending the development of a consolidated economic agency to reduce costs, but more importantly to determine a unified approach to marketing and economic development activities.

The Monroe County Water Authority and Office of Emergency Communications were new agencies created because home rule legislation, the desire to retain local autonomy and control, and the precedents created by laws and past practices restrict the ability to consolidate operations in New York.

The alternative service delivery options below describe many of these cost saving mechanisms. The importance of the Monroe County COG is that it seeks and achieves continual improvement by having a joint policy making body focused on continual improvements in service delivery. A total budget (not including education) of close to $2 billion annually for local government in Monroe County underscores the importance of COG. Most practical studies of cost savings due to increased efficiency estimate only a 2% annual return for their recommendations. Still, applied to the total budget in Monroe County, that would be over $34 million annually.

The Louisville-Jefferson County Compact required action of the state legislature as well as the participation of the city and county (Savitch and Vogel, 2000). Its resulting 23 member metropolitan council is comprised of city, county and small city representatives. A portion of an occupational tax funds this council and its small staff.

The Compact reviewed the management of a number of other joint city-county agencies that had evolved over the years. Although they retained four joint agencies, the city and the county divided responsibility for another eight. Either the city or the county assumed full operational and financial control, but they maintained countywide services in either case.

This regional group achieved greater efficiency and effectiveness in service provision through cooperative relations by eliminating duplication of services, realizing economies of scale and providing one voice to provide services coherently. Initially set up for 12 years in 1986, the members viewed it as successful and renewed it with minimal changes for another ten years. The Compact is justly proud of the fact that the tax-sharing formulas were kept intact and the moratoriums were continued on annexations and incorporations.

Regional planning boards and economic development organizations that reach across local boundaries are good examples of regional policy groups. They remove harmful competition between smaller units, which, left to their own vested interests, might hurt the region in an attempt to maximize their individual economy or revenue streams. Usually these organizations have no operational component, as opposed to a special district, such as a regional water commission.

Joint Boards

The joint board model of local governance represents an attempt to capitalize on the advantages of small and large governments, while mitigating the disadvantages associated with each. The work of Dollery and Johnson (2005) describes this mechanism as Australia implemented it. In Australia, the joint board, virtual government, and agency model are all mechanisms that put the preparation and delivery of the service in the hands of a larger administrative body, but retain the decision-making about the definition and funding of the service in the local government. Australia is concerned with effective representation, which is assumed more available in small governments, but the countervailing assumption is that larger governments are capable of using resources more effectively.

The literature refers to the joint board model as a cooperative agreement, inter-local cooperation, or network model. These cooperative agreements (ILC's) differ from inter-local agreements (ILA's) in the United States, in that ILA's are essentially contracts assigning the service responsibility to only one of the entities. The joint board resembles a special district, but it does not relinquish responsibility from the constituent municipalities for funding and defining the service. The literature in the United States does not emphasize this alternative, and it is not commonly implemented, if it is implemented at all. Chapter 8 delves into this more deeply and compares it to virtual governments, agency models, and joint meetings.

A joint board includes representatives from the constituent local districts so that the constituent governments closely monitor the board's actions. They are usually organized around a single function or related functions. They have features of both a shared service and a special district, but maintain control of the provision decisions in the constituent municipalities.

The *Sunday Telegraph* refers to strategic alliances, which are a part of a centralized government plan in Australia that reportedly could save millions of dollars for municipalities (Markson, 2005). Although there was no detail on how the alliances would operate, the article was noteworthy because of the proposal by the Local Government Minister that examples such as an alliance of two to eight councils to create centralized records storage could save $500,000. These alliances would also create contracts for joint purchasing and garbage collection and road maintenance services. They are joint boards with operating capabilities that are defined by the constituent municipalities.

Special Districts

Special districts are organizations created with specialized expertise in a particular service area. They may provide services only within the boundaries of a single municipality or serve several municipalities. These organizations have independent budgets and governing bodies. In most cases, they also have taxing (or rate-setting) authority. They are operational in nature. Examples are regional water commissions (authorities) or fire districts. Some states refer to them as special districts or service districts. Their advantages, no matter how they are configured, is the expertise in the specific service area and the focus of the organization on this single service, which provides scale efficiencies in the purchase of capital equipment and utilization of resources, in general. This chapter will refer to these organizations as special districts.

In some states, special districts have recently come under investigation, because poor management has allowed inefficiencies and abuses to increase. There is a lesson to be learned—a promising mode of delivery, which affords a specific focus and heightened expertise in a specific service area, can cease to provide the efficiencies that are possible due to ethical and managerial failures. When a local government has transferred the delivery of the service, it can retain the responsibility to ensure there is a good mechanism in place for monitoring the entity that provides the service directly. Special districts are often formed without practical mechanisms for accountability.

While there are examples of new districts being created, many are being dissolved, or evaluated with the intention of bringing the service under a more direct local government. An article which reviewed some of the changes in Great Britain suggested special districts got deserved attention: "Other reasons for restructuring were to ensure cost-effective delivery of local services and to counter the diminished accountability that resulted from the emergence of new inter-municipal special-purpose bodies." (Sancton, 1996, p. 273)

The concern is that these districts, often buffered from the direct view of the public, are inefficient fiefdoms that may provide inappropriate perquisites for their boards and members. The Louisville-Jefferson County Compact decided to disband two-thirds of the previously independent city-county agencies because they had become poorly managed and inefficient. A *New York Times* article which reviewed the final report of a New York State commission indicated concern with a profusion of "special districts" created to provide water, library and other services to the state's sprawling suburbs. The article reported that those entities are studded with appointive jobs and that many can levy taxes, helping give New York "arguably the most complex property tax system in the nation," according to the commission's final report (Confessore and Peters, 2008).

New York State's concern about Commissioner-run special districts is coming from many sides. Nassau County taxpayers would save about $17 million if towns took over the garbage collection operations from sanitation districts (Cassese, 2008). The Town of Hempstead, which controls its own collections, cost $229 less per household than surrounding commissioner-run districts. If they consolidated these districts under the Town, the report projected savings at over $13 million.

Nassau County homeowners who live outside of villages and cities receive water from private water companies, authorities and special districts (Weitzman, 2007). When analyzed by form of governance, it is apparent that town-run water districts are less expensive than commissioner-run districts. It is likely that private companies are not as reliable stewards of water resources as are governments.

There are no town-run fire districts in Nassau County, so there is no opportunity to compare costs between districts headed by commissioners and districts headed by a town board. However, Weitzman did find that fire protection districts, where towns negotiate the fire contract, were generally more cost effective for residents than commissioner led fire districts.

Despite concerns with special districts in some areas of the country, other areas are still creating new special districts. They are generally deemed cost effective. For example, a regional subsidiary established for the collection and disposal of domestic waste (garbage collection) was touted as saving over $50,000 per year in Fiscal Year 2004 in Australian dollars (Dollery and Byrnes, 2005). An explanation for this apparent inconsistency showing effectiveness of special districts in Australia and ineffective special districts in New York State and the Louisville-Jefferson County Compact is management issues. Management issues, which can occur anywhere and reverse the potential gains of an alternative governance structure, are more likely to go unnoticed in a special district, the governing body of which is appointed, not elected, and whose board meetings are sparsely attended. A governing body in a special district is more distant from public oversight than the governing body of a municipality.

New York State has 6,900 special taxation districts to provide municipal water, sewer and trash collection services, and some of these districts have more cars and supervisors than workers, as reported in the *New York Times* (Kocieniewski, 2009). This number is in addition to the layers created by a hierarchy of villages, towns, and counties that serve many residents in New York's smaller municipalities. Another *Times* article reports Governor David A. Paterson has called for abolishing salaries and perks for special district commissioners and having towns take over independent sanitation districts (Confessore and Peters, 2008).

There is nothing to prevent a special district from being well run and cost effective. The specific focus on the single service area suggests economies through specific expertise in the service area, if the district is well managed and there is proper oversight to assure good management. However, some efficiency may be lost in overall administration, which is not specific to the service focus. For example, the purchasing and finance functions in a utility authority are redundant with those functions in the municipality that formed the authority.

Centralized Services

Centralized service provision occurs when an existing government assumes the provision of a service for all the smaller governments within its boundaries. County-provided services are typical of these. This mode of service provision should be distinguished from an inter-local agreement between one or more municipalities and its county government. In centralized service provision, usually the larger government has determined that they will provide and deliver the service centrally. In an inter-local agreement, all parties to the agreement or contract can decide to terminate the relationship and return to direct service delivery or some other arrangement.

The main reason for centralizing services is to provide economies of scale or better resources to improve service quality or reduce the costs of delivery. The discussion below examines contracting with a larger government, through a mutual agreement. In this section, we review consolidations to a central government authority made available or mandated for all the local governments within the jurisdiction of the central government. This is not an easy form of alternate service delivery to investigate, because what would be an alternate model in one state may have been occurring for a century in another (for example, county provision of services in Maryland and Virginia), and, therefore, has not been studied recently.

The reliance on counties to provide local services varies from state to state. Although New Jersey does not have a tradition of local services provided by the county, we have observed growing interest in region-alization in that state. Several non-profit organizations are encouraging regional collaborations and a few counties have started to discuss providing services formerly provided by the municipal governments. Some of these counties, although not offering to produce the service at the county level, are facilitating the discussions.

A comparison between Long Island and Northern Virginia provides a good example of this (*Long Island Index,* 2007). As a starting point, despite the fact that the population of Long Island is only slightly over twice that of the Virginia counties, the number of government enti-ties in the Northern Virginia area totals 17, while Long Island has 239. Including special dis-tricts in this total, Virginia's total does not budge, but Long Island's jumps by an additional 200 governments to 439.

The report states it is more difficult to introduce efficiencies in Long Island because of the large number of governments:

> Northern Virginia makes budgeting and expense decisions on a county-wide basis. Certainly the complex form of governance that has evolved on Long Island as well as other older regions makes it difficult to achieve economies of scale or other efficiencies. With so many governmental units responsible for budgeting decisions of the same services, discussions of efficiencies or change are, at best, made more complicated and, at worst, stymied. (Long Island Index, 2007, p. 16)

The *Long Island Index explains* the complexity of governments that has resulted in Long Island by referring to three different sources. The New York State Comptroller's report (2006) states that New York devised its forms of general-purpose government in the 18th century. Although the functions of governments converged in the 20th century, the creation of single-function special districts and authorities increased layering and complexity. The *Index* quotes from the 1961 book *1400 Governments* by Wood and Almendinger (as cited in Long Island Index, 2007, p. 17), who described the New York—New Jersey—Connecticut metropolitan area's system of governance as "one of the great unnatural wonders of the world...more compli-cated than any other that mankind has yet contrived or allowed to happen." A further quote from political scientists Gerald Benjamin and Richard Nathan noted (as cited in *Long Island Index,* 2007, p. 17), "Because localism has significant political value, changes typically are made by adding on, not replacing, existing local governments...attempts to eliminate local units are just too costly politically. Adding on is easier and politically safer."

The *Long Island Index* study goes on to analyze the cost differences between the two areas, some of which are the result of bargaining unit gains in New York and some due to schools, which are not a responsibility of municipalities in many states. However, the basic concept is that a county-based centralized system is far more cost effective.

The researchers were concerned that Long Islanders, while concerned with the cost of government, might be more satisfied with the quality of service provided or the responsiveness enabled by more local units of government. The Index commissioned a study by the Stony Brook University's Center for Survey Research to investigate the satisfaction of the residents in the two regions with their respective governments. The survey showed that Virginians are happier with the quality of their government services and feel that they could trust officials—no matter at what level of government—to resolve a problem when it occurs. Not surprisingly, combining these differences in satisfaction with the higher taxes in Long Island, almost twice as many Virginians feel the value they receive from their property taxes is excellent or good.

When comparing fire services, the study also evaluated objective measures of service quality. Considering the insurance industry's ISO ratings, fire response times and number of fire and EMS calls, there was no discernible difference between the two regions. Although Long Island's population was a little over twice that of the Northern Virginia counties, it has almost six times as many fire and EMS vehicles as Northern Virginia. The personnel costs in Virginia are about six times as high as Long Island's, although Virginia pays its Fire and EMS staffs, and Long Island relies on volunteers. The authors express concern about the impact on overall costs when volunteers are no longer an adequate resource on Long Island.

The New York State commission that recommended ending compensation and perks for special district commissioners (Confessore and Peters, 2008) also recommended centralizing specific functions at the county level. Some of the functions included tax collection and emergency dispatch, as well as various back-office functions that support other services, such as the courts. According to *Newsday*, a consultant's report on the schools in Nassau County (Hildebrand, 2008) recommended coordinating at the county level functions such as telecommunications, computer services, and risk assessment and internal auditing, using the county comptroller's office. The concept is transferable to municipalities and included them in its recommendations for services that span both types of government.

Centralized services are often part of a two-tier approach to providing services. Indianapolis is another example of mixed service provision from different levels of government. The author describes the effort as including services delivered at a regional or county level, while others are delivered by the administration of smaller areas.

> For example, Indianapolis, through its centralized UniGov tier of government, provides street maintenance services for all residents of the consolidated city, but the independent cities (with far smaller populations) are responsible for their own streets and parks. Indianapolis provides police and fire services for the residents of its pre-UniGov service boundaries. Residents of areas beyond the old

city of Indianapolis retain the right to receive police services from the sheriff's department or to select another provider. Several of these areas contract with private companies for police patrols. Those areas that utilize private firms for police patrol functions rely on the sheriff's department for other policing services, including criminal investigations. The Indianapolis Fire Department also provides services to the residents of its pre-UniGov service boundaries, whereas fire departments with service boundaries matching those of their respective townships supply service to residents in areas that joined Indianapolis as part of the UniGov program. (Rosentraub, 2000, p. 182)

Contractual Agreements

The last form of alternate service delivery we will discuss is contracting. We have defined it to include any contract or agreement that transfers the full responsibility for the production of the service to another entity. It differs from centralized service provisions in this categorization because it does not include services provided by a larger government entity for all its constituent members, such as a county-provided service that is available for all municipalities in the county. Further, the decisions of provision—funding and level of service—are retained by the municipality, unlike a county-provided service.

Contracts include agreements with other governments, private for-profit firms, and non-profit organizations. When formed with other governments (shared services), the arrangements arise spontaneously and serendipitously and normally require no centralized directives or legislative changes. They are very varied and often can involve sharing skilled employees, capital equipment, information technology systems and equipment, or entire operational services. Because they do not compromise the independence of the governing bodies, they do not impinge on democratic representation or citizen engagement. If there are other alternative providers, the parties to these inter-local agreements can terminate them easily without significant cost, when they do not work as well as was expected. These arrangements have been discussed in Chapter 3 on *Consolidation of Service Delivery and Efficiency,* but are included here as one of the alternatives to direct delivery of service.

Contracts are the most common form of alternate service delivery in the literature. From an analysis of the 1982 ICMA (International City/County Management Association) survey of municipalities in the United States:

> The service contract is the main alternative to a direct municipal service arrangement. An average of 30.2 percent of all municipal service responsibilities was either totally or partially contracted out to other governments, private firms, or neighborhood associations in 1982. (Stein, 1993, p. 80)

While governments provide most services directly, the proportion provided through other institutional arrangements was growing through the 1980's (Joassart-Marcelli and Musso, 2005). Their study showed the domination of outsourcing by contracts with other governments and by totally relinquishing the service to other independent governments, such as in the creation of special districts, as opposed to contracting to private companies. However, in comparing these two forms of restructuring, there are some important differences. Contracts can be terminated, but it is more difficult to end the relationship with an independent government formed as a special district. It is also more difficult to provide oversight to a special district, because a special district has both the responsibility to deliver (produce) the service and to budget for its provision. One of the interesting findings in this study, which looked at a number of the conditions and factors associated with outsourcing, was that grants reduce the need to outsource, because they reduce the local tax-based cost to provide the services directly.

A survey of the chief elected municipal and county officials in New York State in 1997 concerning municipal restructuring (Warner and Hebdon, 2001) reveals that inter-municipal cooperation occurs in 55% of the cases, privatization in 28%, reverse privatization (returning an outsourced service to direct service delivery) in 7%, governmental entrepreneurship in 6% and cessation of service in 4% of the cases. Inter-municipal cooperation in Warner and Hebdon's context (other authors use it differently) refers to shared services achieved through a contract with another government to provide a service for a fee. Privatization is a contract with a non-governmental organization, either for-profit or non-profit. The reverse of that occurs when a government has decided that privatization was not as effective as was projected. Both reverse privatization and governmental entrepreneurship (also referred to as competitive contracting) provide new motivations and increased empowerment to municipal departments by allowing them to contract and compete, but they do not involve different organizational structures than those represented by direct services or inter-local contracts.

The literature has also studied the conditions that lead to contracting and the utilization of contracting. Not all studies agree on the existence or direction of the relationships. Furthermore, the terminology used by different authors muddles the distinction between contracting and cooperative relationships between governments.

According to an analysis of the 1992 ICMA survey data by Michael Nelson, *Municipal Government Approaches to Service Delivery: An Analysis from A Transactions Cost Perspective,* conditions leading to increased contracting are high relative salaries of municipal workers, homogeneity of age and education in the population, and smaller population size (Nelson, 1997). Contracting increases if the municipality is in a more populated county or a metropolitan area.

Warner and Hefetz (2002a) use the data from the ICMA 1992 and 1997 surveys to look at restructuring in general. Larger townships and counties are more likely to restructure. Yet larger metropolitan places are less likely to restructure. Furthermore, although contracting is related to lower expenditures per capita, this effect is greatest in the suburbs. Perhaps density is a confounding factor in these findings. Contracting is more common in higher income municipalities and in municipalities with more poverty. Lastly, although council-manager forms of government were more likely to contract in 1992, they were less likely to do so in 1997. The simple explanation that the contracting fad had run its course is appealing, but not proven by these findings.

Using the 2002 ICMA data, another author finds no correlation between population size and the joint production of services at the county level (Jeong, 2006). Jeong defines joint production mainly as governments contracting out to vendors. Other findings include that having elected county executives is related to increased joint production of public works projects, and that having robust fiscal resources encourages joint production of services.

The most common services contracted were public works, public safety, and administrative support. Governments select the private sector for the contracts for public works, transportation, and administrative support. Awards of contracts for health and human services and contracts for parks and recreation are more often to non-profits (Warner and Hebdon, 2001). Feiock, et al, made similar observations. Direct provision of the service in-house is much less likely for both public works services, as well as health and human services, than for other services (Feiock, et al, 2004).

Contracting allows municipalities to achieve economies of scale while retaining some control over service provision. Contracting with other governments increases the chance of contract success because it mitigates the risk involved in contracting with private firms or even non-profits (Brown, 2008). Hence, inter-governmental contracts are preferred for those services that are more likely to risk failure in a private contract. The cost of monitoring the contract can be high with private vendors. When failure does occur, it can be difficult for the government to extricate itself from the contract.

In a study of large cities in the United States between 1990 and 1999, it was found that governments are not as concerned with monitoring the contract with another government. Past cooperation is a very important factor in maintaining inter-local cooperation. When there is established trust with the providing government, the municipality becomes more concerned with the investment cost of developing the capacity to provide the service directly. The analysis also indicates that inter-local cooperation is more efficient than solutions developed by a centralized government because of lower transaction costs for inter-local cooperation (Shrestha, 2005).

The choice of for-profit vendors can be very limited for some services. Governments contract services with high asset specificity (i.e., investments to produce the service are not readily adaptable to other services) with other governments (Brown and Potoski, 2003) or with non-profits, because they are willing to provide services that do not have as general an application, but may fit their agenda.

Contract failure was common in a study of the ICMA data from 1997 and 2002 (Lamothe and Lamothe, 2006). The most common reason for returning to direct service delivery was that service quality was not satisfactory (about 70% of the cases of reverse contracting), but insufficient cost savings was mentioned in almost 50% of the cases, and political pressure was cited in 20% of the cases.

A study of almost 15,000 nursing homes compared quality of the service delivered (Amirkhanyan, et al, 2008). The study found no difference in quality between non-profit and public run nursing homes. For-profit ownership correlated with significantly higher regulatory violations, that is, lesser service quality.

Comparing the data from the ICMA surveys in 1997 and 2002, services that were in-house tend to stay in-house (Lamothe, et al, 2008). Some services previously contracted out, however, move back in-house over the five years between the two studies. Cities with greater ability to manage contracts are more likely to prefer contracting. Where there are greater levels of competition, more contracting occurs, yet non-profits tend to be less involved. This is the corollary to the finding that governments choose non-profits more for services of high asset specificity.

Another study confirms these results (Feiock, et al, 2004), but with some additional specificity. Almost as many services were brought in-house in the five years (12.3%) as were contracted out (13.1%). The author also observes that contracting to other governments (which he terms vertical integration) is almost as common a method of outsourcing as privatization.

Contracting can promote efficiency (See Figure 1). Although the most expensive method for residential trash collection was private provision contracted by the resident, the least expensive was private provision contracted by the municipality. It is most cost effective for the municipality to have responsibility for the provision, but not the delivery of the service (privatization).

A study of Buffalo suggested that re-engineering the delivery of services could reduce the local tax levy by 9%–13% (Center for Government Research, 2006). The proposal was for a two-tiered approach wherein the city would provide core governance and administrative services, but contract out for other services to the private sector or other governments.

1998 Average Annual Cost of Residential Trash Collection by Service Type in Onondada County
(Per Household)

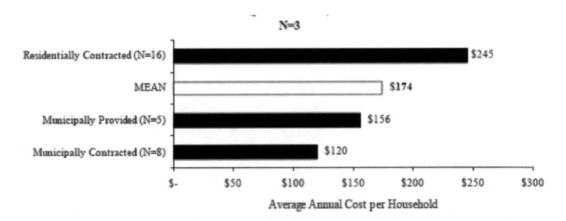

Source: Community Benchmarks Program. (1999, p.13).

Cheung (2008) has studied private governments in California in planned developments and condominiums. Local governments lower spending in response to private government activity. The services affected include police, fire, parks and recreation, solid waste disposal, and housing and community development. Generally, a private government has less potential to leverage economies of scale, so one anticipates that the overall costs might rise. From the government point of view, concerns include whether tax revenues might be reduced or whether costs would be shared by the local government, which would make direct payment to the private government.

Hybrid Government Structures

The traditional approach of government is to provide most services directly at the most local level. Providing and producing a service at the appropriate level of government that can best perform that service may offer an improvement.

This chapter categorized alternative service delivery into five different mechanisms in addition to direct service delivery by the municipality. This simple categorization made it easier to describe the options, some of which may be uncommon in the United States. The literature provides some analysis of the relative benefits of each of these mechanisms, which the following chart, "Characteristics of Different Alternative Service Delivery Arrangements," (see next page) summarizes.

The categorizations in the chart are ideal types, that is, categories that make it easier to understand the relative benefits of each delivery strategy. The reality of government often blurs the lines between these service delivery arrangements. In some cases, governments have formed useful government structures with combinations of the features of different arrangements

That is certainly true of two-tiered governments, one of the promising alternatives found in Monroe County, New York; Jefferson County, Kentucky; and Indianapolis, Indiana. The two-tiered government links service delivery to the appropriate level of government, but maintains local control or oversight over the service. Hence, it is both more responsive than centralized services and yet works more efficiently than directly provided local services. Joint boards and regional policy groups have achieved this by requiring local representation on a governing body that has access to greater and more efficient resources. (Dollery and Johnson, 2005)

Sancton (2005, p. 321) reviews two-tier governments in Canada over the last fifty years:

> The basic theory of two-tier metropolitan government is simple: a metropolitan level of government is established for those functions of local government that require a metropolitan-level solution, usually metropolitan-wide land-use planning and major inter-municipal physical infrastructure; local municipalities remain in place to provide such local-level services as zoning and recreational facilities. As in a federation, the metropolitan (or upper-tier) level is not hierarchically superior to the local (or lower-tier) level. Each level has full autonomy to act within the legal authority allocated to it by the provincial legislation.

Characteristics of Different Alternative Service Delivery Arrangements

Characteristics of Service Delivery Mechanism	Regional Policy Groups	Joint Boards	Special Districts	Centralized Services	Contractor Provided Services	Directly Provided Services
Policy—making authority	Yes	No	Yes	Yes	No	Yes
Operational responsibility	No	Yes	Yes	Yes	Yes	Yes
Taxing or rate-setting authority	No	No	Yes	Yes	No	Yes
Availability of staff for policy research	Yes	Depends	Yes	Yes	N/A	Yes
Availability of other resources	From constituent municipalities	Transferred from constituent municipalities	No	No	No	No
Potential benefit of economies of scale	Yes	Yes	Only if regional	Yes	Yes, depending on contractor	No
Prevention of additional fragmentation	Yes	Yes	No, and adds a government	Yes	Yes	No, but does not add a government
Retention of local control	Through representation	Yes	No, but through appointment	No	Yes, through monitoring	Yes
Simplicity of terminating arrangement	Yes	Yes, must rebuild capacity	Difficult	Difficult, only with agreement	Depends, must rebuild capacity	N/A
Number of municipalities served	Multiple	Multiple	Varies	All	Varies	One
Breadth of service focus	Multiple	Single, but with exceptions	Single	Varies	Single	Multiple

The detailed definition of the configuration of the tiers varies with each implementation. Further, the perception of success or failure also shows little consistency. An optimist may see this as indicating that, done right, very positive benefits will accrue.

On the other hand, Sancton (2001a) lists the European cities in which a two-tier metropolitan government has been "at best controversial, at worst, unstable." In his later work reviewing two-tier governments in Canada (Sancton, 2001b), he observes that in three of four two-tier governments with a directly elected upper-tier, the constant conflict between the two levels has led to consolidation into a single tier. Constant questioning of the slow and cumbersome system has beset the remaining government.

While there have been difficulties with two-tiered governments because of the political conflict that (almost) inevitably results from the very definition of the form, two-tier governments have attractive features that are hard to obtain in non-hybrid structures. In the same era that three other Canadian provinces created two-tiered forms that were later abolished, British Columbia made a conscious effort to avoid the political conflict by creating an upper-tier of regional districts that was not a government. The regional districts continue to thrive.

British Columbia took pains to define the regional districts so they would not be perceived as another level of government (Sancton, 2005). Indeed, they replaced many existing special purpose bodies (special districts) and acted as an institution encouraging increased inter-municipal cooperation. They have flexible relationships with the constituent municipalities, allowing them to opt out of regional services. A Board of Directors, whose members are not directly elected, governs the regional districts. The Board consists of members of municipal councils who have varying numbers of votes on the Board proportional to the population they represent.

Sancton (2001a) presents the opposing views of advocates of consolidation and public choice in an article which analyses how urban growth leads to concerns about the most appropriate government structure. Many consolidationists consider a two-tier system superior to complete consolidation because it creates one government to manage the entire urban area. The size of the upper tier is a concern because different size governments best deliver different services. Public choice proponents provide evidence that some services, such as policing, are best provided over smaller areas. The two-tier approach at least provides two options within the same structure. In addition, it meets another concern of public choice theory, because it maintains a layer of local government that can continue to provide competing service and tax packages to prospective residents and businesses. Sancton remarks that the structure bifurcates the activities of existing governments, requiring coordination of two governments.

Some hybrid forms give up local control, but the hybrid can contain mechanisms of oversight built in to the service arrangement. Joint boards and regional policy groups are structures that attempt to provide that oversight for the benefit of local residents. One can meld these structures with some of the arrangements utilizing central or regional providers. Centralized services at the county level are effective and efficient and are the norm in some other states (for example, dispatching, fire, and emergency medical services). Regional forms of special districts (for example, water utilities) take advantage of economies of scale for services that benefit from larger providers. Mechanisms such as joint boards and regional policy groups can properly manage these services with adequate oversight on behalf of local residents.

Regional districts are often a centralized component of a two-tiered governance model. The Greater Louisville Economic Development Partnership resulted from an agreement to share revenue collections from the occupational tax to ensure that the city will benefit from suburban growth, eliminating a source of unhealthy competition (Savitch and Vogel, 2000). The Louisville-Jefferson County Compact formed this public-private partnership for economic development, which includes the chamber of commerce, dissolving the former joint city-county office of economic development. They set up a new city-county office of business services to carry out functions that they did not transfer to the partnership.

UniGov in Indianapolis is a good example of an effective two-tiered government structure. "Structurally, UniGov is a multilayered local government system under which authority for economic development, public works, parks, transportation, and some elements of public safety is transferred to the county (or regional) level—the first layer in a multi-tiered structure" (Rosentraub, 2000, p. 181).

Consolidating Indianapolis with its surrounding suburban areas inside Marion County offered the potential for financing the public costs of the redevelopment plan across a diverse and affluent tax base. Although UniGov provided for tax integration, it actually maintained some separation between important components of its property tax base. Failure to integrate property taxes into the consolidated government's fiscal structure could have produced a set of regressive and unfair or unbalanced outcomes with regard to the burden of financing the redevelopment program.

A consolidated governance structure can be an asset in terms of preparing, executing, and managing a downtown revitalization plan endorsed by an appropriate constituency. Although other downtown areas have seen a renaissance without a countywide consolidation program, in the context of Indianapolis's politics and culture, UniGov established a framework to accomplish something that had not taken place before.

Hybrid forms of service delivery have potential, if the coordination and political issues can be resolved, while providing oversight for the local citizens. The discussions above suggest jurisdictions such as British Columbia and Monroe County may have accomplished that. The literature indicates that in both of these situations, the development of a regional solution was consensual. A coordinating body comprised of representatives of the constituent municipalities maintained the on-going focus on local concerns combined with regional efficiencies.

Comments and Conclusions

Some of the literature includes only contracted arrangements as types of alternate service delivery, at best giving only a brief mention to other forms. In addition, the literature concentrates far more on cataloging which governments are more likely to contract than it does comparing the efficiency of the results.

The description of the literature on alternative service delivery by Dollery and Byrnes (2005, p. 2) uses the term "nascent" and refers to an "embryonic body of research". However, this is in contrast to the multiple studies our research found on contracting and the comparison of contracting to direct service delivery.

The literature provides little information on some service delivery structures, such as centralized provision of service. Yet centralized structures, in which services are provided and produced by the county level of government, have been the norm for a very long time in some states. Studies are infrequently conducted of structures that have existed for some time, despite the possibility for comparative analyses to other states in which these structures are not common.

The literature was disappointingly skimpy on estimating cost savings for different service delivery options. The most that can be drawn from the literature is that specifics of a situation will dictate what efficiencies are possible and how they are best achieved.

One of the biggest problems in the literature for alternative service delivery is the use of terminology. There is confusion between terms such as inter-local cooperation, inter-local agreements, and joint production. The discrepancies between Nelson's (1997) findings and Warner and Hebdon's (2001) findings demonstrate this problem. Nelson concentrates on contracting, but Warner and Hebdon use restructuring, which includes contracting, as well as municipal aid and joint production. Jeong (2006) uses joint production as a term including contracting out. The discrepancies between the authors appear in the relationships with a variable as basic as size, so there is evidence that there are differences in what is defined as restructuring and joint production of services. This review was not always able to resolve the inconsistent use of terms.

For some of the arrangements that are not common in all areas of the country, the states or countries that have implemented such arrangements have laws that allow the forms to exist. For example, an article discussing options for a joint services model for streetscape services compared the legal basis for joint boards, joint committees, management boards, and Companies Limited by Guarantee. This chapter tried to avoid these legal distinctions in favor of discussing concepts.

In summary, while there is no reason to doubt the findings of the literature, in general, there is a concern about the inconsistent use of terms to describe alternative service delivery. This chapter reviewed varied approaches to service delivery arrangements. However, it is not obvious how to compare these approaches from what appeared in the literature, much less propose an optimal array of service delivery arrangements. This area of alternate structures for service delivery is new and evolving, which makes the task of developing concrete conclusions more challenging.

The literature describes these different service delivery arrangements and highlights their strengths and weaknesses. It does not compare their relative efficiencies or give comprehensive direction about how to choose an optimal service delivery arrangement to use in specific situations. The literature seldom addresses specific service types in examining service delivery arrangements, but we can glean some information from the literature on optimal size and municipal consolidation.

The literature on consolidation indicates that the political desire to use a suburban tax base to finance the maintenance and restoration of deteriorating infrastructure may be a factor in consolidations. This could also affect any regionalized or centralized arrangements, including joint boards, regional policy groups, and special districts, if they are regional.

The consolidation literature did note that the desire for equity in service delivery has an impact on the desire to consolidate (depending on the policy goals) and the success of the consolidated government. Equity concerns are most noticeable when the parts of the area being consolidated have vastly different valuations. This can affect any form of service delivery arrangement that is supported by a tax base from the entire service delivery area, including parts of the area with disparate valuations. It can affect any regionalized or centralized arrangements, including joint boards, regional policy groups, and special districts, if they are regional.

For services that show economies of scale, such as infrastructure based services (water utilities, for example) or specialized services (crime labs, for example), contracting with a regional provider (including shared services), regionalized special districts, centralized services, joint boards, or regional policy groups may all be more efficient and effective than directly delivered services. If regional coordination is beneficial to the delivery of the service, such as land use planning, regional arrangements are more appropriate than local efforts. This could take the form of regional policy groups, joint boards, regionalized special districts, or county or other centralized services.

Regional policy groups and joint boards primarily serve the function of representing the interests of all the constituent municipalities, while taking advantage of economies of scale or other benefits from services delivered over a broader area. Both these structures require an operational producer to deliver the service, if it is transaction based, rather than a purely administrative implementation of policy, such as regional economic development. Municipalities form these groups because they fear the loss of control when they transfer service delivery to a regionalized or centralized entity. They function both to make policy decisions about service delivery that are best for the entire area represented and to provide a monitoring function to assure that the services are delivered effectively and efficiently. Successful regional policy groups, joint boards, and two-tier governments most often seem to be formed by consensus and created voluntarily.

It is difficult to defend the logic of the benefits of non-regionalized special districts. The literature has identified these structures as being under attack in a number of states and other countries. They are a source of fragmentation and duplicate the administrative services of the municipality. In essence, special districts represent added governments serving the same geographic area. Only the service delivered is different.

The literature highlights the following arrangements as providing efficient and effective solutions for delivering public services:

▶ Contracted Services

Shared services are a contract with another government to deliver a service and are generally agreed to improve efficiency. Shared services can increase efficiency while retaining local control. The numbers show that a private contractor may be more efficient, but only if the municipality has the capacity to monitor the contract adequately. The need for contract monitoring exists with non-profit contractors, also, but the specifics may vary with the interests of the non-profit organization.

▶ Special Districts Provide Specific Service Expertise

Special districts (authorities and fire districts, for example) provide a focused area of expertise, but possibly at the cost of greater fragmentation, redundancy of general administrative functions, and loss of accountability. They reduce accountability by creating a new government, usually with oversight by the municipality only when it makes appointments to the governing board. In most cases, the appointed governing body has authority to levy taxes or create user fees as well as incur debt. In fact, it is this autonomy that often motivates the creation of a special district, duplicating the administrative structure of the municipality, including additional appointed positions to support the staff necessary to produce the single service. Regionalized special districts can provide economies of scale for targeted delivery systems, such as infrastructure-based services, in which a larger entity may be more efficient. Compared to special districts operating only within a municipality's boundaries, regionalized special districts mitigate the increase in fragmentation and administrative redundancy, but make accountability more distant.

▶ Centralized Services Provide Scale Economies

County or regional service provision is attractive for those services (infrastructure related or highly specialized) that show economies of scale, but there may be a need to provide representation of the constituent municipalities in order to assure local input or control in service delivery policy making.

▶ Joint Boards for Specific Functions

Joint boards are effective for unique services that require coordination over a broader geographical area (for example, land use planning and economic development) and may provide local representation for policy decisions that determine how the service will be delivered.

▶ Regional Policy Groups Increase Local Control for Varied Services

Regional groups that are policy setting are very effective in providing local representation in an effort to collaborate and cooperate in providing services, but they depend on other structures to deliver the service directly. The Council of Governments in Monroe County, New York is an example. Constituent members usually form these regional policy groups to increase their local involvement in regional services. Most often, they control multiple services provided regionally through a separate regional or county organization.

▶ Hybrid Arrangements to Promote Efficiency and Provide Local Control

Arrangements that combine adequate local representation with an array of service delivery mechanisms applied appropriately to each specific type of service may optimize the benefits of different delivery arrangements. Two-tier governments are a hybrid form. They often combine a regional board, composed of representatives of constituent municipalities, with local delivery for services such as police patrols and regional or county delivery for services like economic development and land use planning. Governments form hybrid arrangements to obtain the benefits of particular service delivery arrangements, offsetting potential disadvantages by combining one delivery arrangement with the features of a different service delivery arrangement. For example, the constituent municipalities may form a regional policy group in combination with a county provided service to provide local representation in service delivery decisions. Without this representation at the regional level, there may not be any local input in decisions about a county delivered service.

The literature indicates there is potential in each of these approaches. It is important to fit the mechanism for delivery to the service type. In his review of fifty years of evidence on the relationship between the structure and performance of local governments, Bish (2001) suggests:

...given the diversity of communities and local services, no single organization can perform all the tasks demanded of local government. Metropolitan areas composed of a multiplicity of local governments and production arrangements are more responsive to residents' needs and generally provide local government services at less cost than monolithic amalgamations.

CHAPTER 5

Measuring Municipal Performance

The preceding chapters have made use of measurements of municipal efficiency to determine what forms of restructuring of municipal service delivery are best. When a direct comparison of the new form or mechanism to the prior one is appropriate, the studies use a simple reduction in costs as the indicator of success. This is fine for determining the simple "yes/no" answer to "Is it better?" However, the ability to compare different results or different existing structures requires standardization. To evaluate the relative performance advantages of different mechanisms for municipal service delivery, it is essential to develop a methodology for assessing efficiency. When comparing municipalities, efficiency usually is expressed in terms of cost per capita. Doing this in a simplistic fashion results in greater inconsistency in the results due to the noise in the system created by the underlying inconsistencies in definition, categorization, and data measurement. Performance measurement systems represent a comprehensive alternative for measuring efficiency and offer many other potentials for improving how government delivers services to citizens.

Although centralized performance measurement systems have been in place and continue to evolve and improve in other countries, they are generally absent at a state level in the United States. States are beginning to recognize the value of such a system and some have started efforts that could result in implementation. Any state that wants to encourage reorganization of local governments or their mechanisms for service delivery would be well advised to develop a method to be able to determine what structures and mechanisms are best and to evaluate the results when changes are made.

This chapter provides an overview of performance measurement systems in the United States and throughout the world. It goes far beyond investigating a simple measurement of efficiency to determine the best mechanisms for municipal service delivery. It may have information particularly appropriate to a state or other centralized government that is attempting to help its local governments find ways to cut costs and maintain service quality. According to the Public Performance Measurement and Reporting Network (2009), performance measurement and reporting serves three purposes:

▶ Informs government policy and management practices and should lead to: performance improvement and policy development that results in better practice and alignment of governmental services to community needs.

▶ Provides data that enables accountability and transparency.

▶ Enables informed communication between citizens, government, and not-for-profit organizations to foster trust.

Analyzing the Literature on Measurement of Municipal Efficiency

The literature on performance measurement in local government is vast. "From New York City to government entities of all shapes and sizes, performance measurement continues to gain in popularity. Robert Kaplan's Balanced Scorecard, David Osborne's Reinventing Government, the success of the New York Police Department's COMPSTAT process, and the ever-increasing public pressure to report performance have made the practice of performance measurement commonplace in the public sector." (Page and Malinowski, 2004, p. 29)

To provide insight into how to measure the efficient delivery of municipal services, our review describes types of efficiency measures, surveys some of the techniques for analysis of the resulting data, discusses the important methods of targeting and comparing results, and highlights some of the benefits resulting from performance measurement. The final section attempts to describe a performance measurement model that could be implemented by a state at the crossroads of increased interest and limited experience in performance measurement. Although the review highlights the best practices in the field, this discussion recognizes that getting to that level will require time and a process of educating and training local government officials and staff.

A Primer on Performance Measurement

Since this field has evolved so quickly in recent decades and can be quite complex, it is useful to introduce some terminology and an overall model of performance measurement. Over the years, there have been many categorizations of performance measures, and there has been accompanying disagreement about what the categories should be and what is really important. For the purposes of this review, the following types of indicators provide the framework of the discussions that follow (Julnes and Holzer, 2008; Fry, 2004):

- **Workload**—indicators of the amount of work that must be accomplished, such as the number of patients requiring treatment or the curb miles that are required to be swept.

- **Inputs**—indicators of the resources used, such as budgeted dollars or FTE's.

- **Outputs**—the work completed, such as patients treated or curb miles swept.

- **Exogenous or explanatory variables**—factors that affect the work process but are not a part of it, such as the education level of the population served or the number of days without snow cover.

- **Outcomes**—the results of government service delivery, such as infant mortality or cleanliness of the streets.

A simple model of service delivery views the workload as the amount of work to be done, which is a variable determined by the conditions or the population served. The inputs are determined by government executives or high-level managers. Outputs are affected by these input decisions, as well as by the effectiveness of the operational management and the productivity of the employees. Outcomes are the ultimate result of all the other indicator types, including factors over which government does not have direct control, such as workload measures and exogenous variables.

The following concrete example is from Project Scorecard (The United States Conference of Mayors, 2000), a street and sidewalk litter rating system begun in the 1970's in New York City and now part of the Mayor's Management Report. In a given sanitation district, the workload was the curb miles to be swept and the frequency of sweeping that was required. The input was the sweeper hours or a budget figure based on manpower and equipment allocated to the service. The output was the curb miles swept. Exogenous variables could include the number of days with winds over ten miles per hour, the percent of commercial land use (litter creating), or the education level of the population. The outcome was the cleanliness of the streets as measured by the city or its contractor through a trained observer rating of cleanliness on samples of streets in the sanitation district.

The more sophisticated model recognizes that the real workload is the amount of litter generated on the streets, which drives the frequency of sweeping that is necessary. If the workload increases and resources are adequate to the task, the output of curb miles swept will increase, but the outcome of street cleanliness may not be affected. Enlightened government will look for ways to reduce the workload, that is, the amount of litter generated. New York City used Sanitation Police to reduce the workload by writing tickets for improper containerization of garbage (reducing spillage onto the street and sidewalk), for littering, and for alternate side of the street parking (to increase the effectiveness of the sweepers). One of the results of the enlightened examination of the Scorecard outcome measure of street and sidewalk cleanliness was the civilianization of the Sanitation Police, which allowed more enforcement effort at less labor cost, a direct attack on workload, while maintaining or improving the desired outcome.

The literature discusses indicator types in addition to the five presented. The basic five indicator types yield efficiency, productivity, and effectiveness measures from simple calculations. Among the many sources for examples of specific indicators is the Public Performance Measurement and Reporting Network website (www.ppmrn.net), including lists of indicators. Many of the references in the annotated bibliography list other indicators. (Braadbaart, 2007; Garcia-Sanchez, 2006; New South Wales Department of Local Government, 2008; Drake and Simper, 2000; Sun, 2002)

Efficiency Measures

Measurement of efficiency is not an easy task. Attempts to do so have been going on since at least the 1920's (Ridley, 1927), but the growth in the literature over the last fifteen years (Government Accounting Standards Board, 1994; International City/County Management Association, 2008) is a testimony to the overwhelming increase in the interest in measuring performance and, it appears, to the belief it can promote improvement. The experts know the difficulties, as well as the potential:

> In the face of these complexities, too many local governments resort to reporting "FTEs per 1,000 population" or "cost per capita" for services overall or for the services of a particular department. These are extremely crude measures of efficiency, if they can be called efficiency measures at all. (Ammons and Rivenbark, 2008, p. 310)

Outcomes are reasons governments produce. Outcomes are the crime rate, the cleanliness of streets, and the economic vitality of the community. However, outcomes are not totally under the control of municipal government, or any government for that matter. Behn, who writes a monthly management report, largely on performance measurement and managing for results, states in one of his articles:

> The standard measurement mantra is: "Don't measure inputs. Don't measure processes. Don't measure activities. Don't measure outputs. Only measure outcomes." Unfortunately, in city government (indeed, in any government) this is often difficult. Sometimes it is impossible. Consequently, a CitiStat strategy may have to rely more on output data than on outcome data. (Behn, 2007, p. 17)

The implication of Behn's comments is that the use of the data determines what one needs to measure. From an internal management perspective, the use of the data is to increase allocative efficiency, that is, to reallocate resources, to modify processes, and to reconfigure budgets to get the results desired. Outcomes, such as clean streets, are more important to the public. Outputs, such as curb miles swept, are more important to line managers (department heads) and supervisors. Elected officials and CAO/CEO's need to be concerned with all the types of measures and the interrelationships among them.

The discrepancy between larger goals and measures over which managers have control is more severe when one considers workload measures. Some department managers use workload based indicators as a measure of productivity, but workload only describes the amount of work that needs to be done. A classic example is using tons of garbage collected as a measure of productivity. The New York City Department of Sanitation traditionally used tons of garbage collected as their main output measure, their view of the department's productivity. If the tons-of-garbage indicator declines, it does not indicate the Department of Sanitation is slacking off. (Missed or late pick-ups are alternative indicators that are measures of performance.) Tonnage is not productivity. In fact, if recycling is effective, the workload-oriented measure of tons will decline, which, in the traditional perspective of the department, would indicate a reduction in productivity. However, it is clear that reduced tonnage is a result of improved productivity of the solid waste program as a whole.

Ammons and Rivenbark (2008, p. 314) comment on the use of workload indicators:

> Officials taking the narrow view of accountability are less likely to venture beyond workload measures and are unlikely to try to incorporate performance measures into key management systems. For them, it seems rational and prudent to collect only the simplest measures and to divert as few resources as possible from service delivery to the measurement of performance. Given their narrow view of accountability and the minimal value of raw workload counts for management or policy decisions, they are unlikely to use performance measures meaningfully in strategic planning or management systems, performance contracts, departmental or individual work plans, performance targets, performance audits, program evaluations, service improvement strategies, cost—benefit analyses, annexation and other special studies, or budget proposals.

Practitioners and empirical studies have often distinguished between controllable and non-controllable inputs to explain results or outcomes. Controllable factors include management systems and capacities, while factors that are often beyond the control of a local jurisdiction may include economic, environmental and demographic factors. In his description of Project Scorecard, Mayor Rudy Giuliani states:

> The cleanliness of New York City is not determined by the performance of the Department of Sanitation alone. Many factors contribute to the cleanliness of streets in neighborhoods. Weather conditions and the collective behavior of pedestrians, motorists, homeowners, tenants, landlords, building superintendents, shopkeepers, commercial establishments and private carters are all major factors affecting street and sidewalk cleanliness. Scorecard is designed to measure actual litter conditions that are the product of the millions of "sanitation transactions" that take place every day. (The United States Conference of Mayors, 2000)

Project Scorecard does not measure all of these exogenous variables, but it includes some, like weather, that provide additional credibility to the results, when managers are held accountable for performance.

Other articles reference the use of socioeconomic or other conditions outside the control of the government unit (Ouellette and Vierstraete, 2005; Stevens, 2005; Worthington and Dollery, 2002). An alternative approach is provided by incorporating the exogenous variables in a profile of the government and categorizing the governments based on the profile before comparing them (New South Wales Department of Local Government, 2008). Accounting for these exogenous variables, in one way or another, can reduce the estimated level of inefficiency and make it more palatable for managers to focus on outcomes over which they do not have complete control.

The Balanced Scorecard approach (Eagle, 2004; Ho and Chan, 2002) is a methodology that was developed to counteract the over-reliance on bottom line, profit-focused indicators in the private sector. The Balanced Scorecard used other measures that were related to performance and were part of the production process prior to the final determination of profitability. This allowed organizations to see problems before they hit the bottom line. The concept is used in the public sector to encourage a broad view of different parts of the process of producing municipal services.

Data must be comparable, particularly if the organization intends to use cross-jurisdictional comparisons. One author blames the demise of one system on self-reported data and their inconsistencies (Coe, 1999). To ensure different organizations in a benchmarking consortium provide comparable data, some form of auditing can be helpful, including even the inexpensive device of asking the manager to certify that the data is correct (New South Wales Department of Local Government, 2008).

The North Carolina Local Government Performance Measurement Project had difficulty in its early stages because of comparability problems (Rivenbark and Carter, 2000, p. 125). "The lack of generally accepted criteria to compare service costs for local government has hindered benchmarking initiatives." Led by the Institute of Government at the University of North Carolina, the project now contains a "full cost-accounting model developed to ensure that localities employ the same methodology to collect and report cost data associated with performance measures." The author states further that the "accuracy and comparability of performance and cost data are the fundamental ingredients of a benchmarking and performance measurement project." The Institute engages in a rigorous data cleaning process and returns drafts to the participating units for their review. Without the centralized resource represented by the Institute of Government, the comparability of the performance measures would be suspect and the entire project would suffer.

Analysis of the Measures

Both reporting and service improvement can be products of performance measurement systems. "Perhaps it is axiomatic that performance measurement systems designed strictly for the former [i.e., performance reporting], especially when a premium is placed on ease of data collection, are unlikely to yield much of the latter" (Ammons and Rivenbark, 2008, p. 308). The authors concern is that service improvement is not the priority of such systems driven by the ease of data collection. This is not to say that the performance measures that municipalities are already collecting are of no use. At the present time, they are the only data available on which decisions can be made. However, looking past that short-term time-frame, the systematic collection of more meaningful data for all municipalities would drive better management decisions.

The basic steps in a performance measurement system include the following (United States Office of Personnel Management, 1974; Hatry and Wholey, 1999):

1. Begin with a simple measurement system and draft performance measures.

2. Collect the data on performance measures.

3. Analyze the data.

4. Interpret the data, using comparisons where possible.

5. Identify functions, units and procedures that are "ripe" for performance improvement.

Performance measurement is a routine and iterative process. Once the five steps are completed, the steps begin again. Since performance improvement is an on-going process, sometimes the steps do not appear so distinct. In particular, analyzing, comparing, and reviewing the data may occur simultaneously or, at the very least, in iterative phases.

The literature has recommended a number of different ways to analyze performance over the years, often touting the relative capability of an analytic method to identify types of efficiency or to segregate pure efficiency, thus improving management insight into the effectiveness of prospective changes in operations or policies. One—Data Envelopment Analysis (DEA)—has become the standard for relatively advanced systems, first internationally, but now with growing widespread acceptance in the United States. DEA calculates performance indicators based on multiple inputs and outputs and distinguishes between types of efficiency, such as scale, technical, and allocative efficiency (Drake and Simper, 2000; Sun, 2002; Ouellette and Vierstraete, 2005; Williams, 2005; Woodbury et al, 2003; Chalos and Cherian, 1995; Moore et al, 2005). DEA also separates out the effects of exogenous variables. Woodbury, et al (p. 77) state: "... the present reliance on partial measures of performance is inadequate and should be heavily augmented by data envelopment analysis" and "the obvious analytical route seems to be an industry-wide adoption of DEA methodologies."

According to Worthington and Dollery (2002, p. 454), "The use of DEA as a technique for measuring the efficiency of government service delivery is now relatively well-established in Australia and several other advanced countries." DEA assesses any municipal service, including the efficiency of courts of law (Pedraja-Chaparro and Salinas-Jimenez, 1996), municipal water services (García-Sánchez, 2006), public schools (Mante and O'Brien, 2002) and municipal police services (Drake and Simper, 2002; Barros, 2007).

The analyst or manager must be watchful of confounding effects when measuring efficiency. In a study of health care, it appeared there was distortion in the estimates of inefficiency and the comparisons of hospital units because of the manipulation of indirect data (Barretta, 2008). This health care study breaks the total costs into sub-categories in an analysis of the variations found in efficiency, concluding that accounting differences are masking the real rates of efficiency. It suggests removing the costs allocated from internal subunits in the hospital (indirect costs) because the hospitals manipulated them in order to increase perceived efficiency.

While interest in complex analytic techniques has increased, so too has interest in techniques that quickly get to the point and exhort managers to act. Dashboard analysis, emphasizing very visual presentation more than analytic comprehensiveness, has become popular. Like the automobile device of the same name, it shows indicators of performance, including an alarm status, when appropriate. Writing about the Washington State Transportation Improvement Board, the authors claim: "The Intranet-based dashboard has been the key to restoring financial stability to an agency in dire need of a new approach." (Gorcester and Reinke, 2007, p. 56) The authors state the dashboard supports an active management approach, which has helped avoid problems by analyzing and responding to the warnings the data presents.

We would make the argument that focused visual displays that encourage managerial action may be supported by sophisticated analytic efforts that result in seemingly simple results. This is a good solution, but it requires resources that may not be available to all jurisdictions. When priorities must be set, it is helpful to remember that the goal is improved management and efficient service delivery; improved measurement and analysis supports these goals, but should not supplant them when resources are constrained.

Standards and Comparisons

Comparison of performance data with targets is the key step in assessing performance. A twenty-year-old recommendation of the United Kingdom's Audit Commission of five comparisons for local government gives a good starting point to understand the range of possibilities and the particular advantages of other comparison types (Palmer, 1993):

▶ **Temporal**—for example comparing this year's performance with last year's.

▶ **Standards**—comparing performance with some standard, which may be derived from local or national statistics or standards.

▶ **Intra-service**—comparing the performance of a number of units or sections within a department that provide the same service, for example homes for the elderly.

▶ **Private sector**—comparison with provision in the private sector, for example in legal and architectural services.

▶ **Inter-authority**—comparisons with all other authorities, all authorities of the same type, or specially selected authorities, which have similar characteristics or with neighboring authorities.

Comparisons to similar units within a department are not always possible, although they do promote competition when appropriate. Comparison of one's own performance on a timeline has been criticized as not capable of "raising the bar," thus not encouraging significant improvement in performance, but it does address self improvement by changing performance compared to prior achievements.

Managerial Goal Setting

Comparison to a standard or target determined by management is easy to implement and is not fraught with comparability issues. It requires strong management to work well. The management-derived targets can be set with an eye on past performance, or on other jurisdictions, or on where an agency or program wants to be. Most importantly, it requires the manager to take an active role in the goal setting represented in the target. The setting of the target is a policy choice based on the resources available and the commitment to a specified level of performance (Behn, 2008).

The disadvantage is that it is inherently a management perspective and an internal one, at that, because of the lack of firm footing in anything outside the government unit. When the effective manager sets managerially determined goals, he/she encourages improvement but keeps the goals attainable, periodically evaluating the performance measure and the goals. "To be truly effective, standards should be set at a level of performance well above average, but within the bounds of what has been achieved with current best practices and technologies. That is, they should require that agencies and contractors strive for excellence without setting a goal that cannot be achieved." (Richter, 2004, p. 22)

Several major cities in the United States have developed statistics-based operational "command centers," based on the police model. One version, CitiStat, is a popular form of managerial goal setting and performance monitoring used throughout the country. Key to a CitiStat approach is comparison, as Behn (2007, p. 21) states:

> It may be the comparison of the city's data with similar data from other similar municipalities. It may be the comparison of the data for one city unit with the data for another similar unit. It may be the comparison of the data for one city agency with some ideal—an ideal expressed in a general mayoral aspiration or in a specific performance target. Whenever the CitiStat staff reaches any conclusion about the performance of a city agency—positive or negative—they do so based on some kind of comparison.

Most critical to a CitiStat approach is the review process, with many of the governments using CitiStat actually devoting an entire room to the review. They outfit the room to create an air of managerial monitoring and use the room solely for that purpose. The literature reports the Stat models as being very successful, although they are often less analytically sophisticated than other techniques.

Behn (p. 41) continues about how the implementation in Baltimore progressed:

> Baltimore launched CitiStat in the summer of 2000. Two years later, Baltimore's approach to producing results was only beginning to collect real data on results and only beginning to have an impact on its Department of Transportation's ability to fill potholes quickly. This, however, is not surprising. After all, changing the

behavior of any large organization (public, nonprofit, or for-profit) is very difficult. Nevertheless, within two years, Baltimore's CitiStat was beginning to have the desired impact. Six years later, the impact was significantly bigger.

Queensland saw benefits in performance with CitiStat's Operational Performance Reviews. A subsequent section of this chapter on the benefits of using performance measurement provides more details on the Queensland implementation.

The MIDAS system is notable in the literature (Plumridge and Wynnycky, 2007). Like CitiStat, flexibility is exercised in the nature of the comparisons. Ontario implemented the system with a top-down approach, but the users have requested enhanced abilities to be able to compare performance to other municipalities. The system affords year-to-year comparisons, comparisons to other municipalities for a specific set of results, and comparisons to aggregated performance statistics. Users want the ability to specify the level of comparison and the ability to choose comparable municipalities.

Inter-jurisdictional Comparisons

Benchmarking, or inter-jurisdictional comparison, is a well-accepted system. In the last twenty years, there has been an increase in the number of governments measuring their own performance, the number of governments measuring performance using indicators from a central source, and the number of governments mandated to use indicators as a group. All of these factors have made inter-jurisdictional comparisons easier, but they remain less common than comparisons over time. Much of the literature examines the additional benefits available through benchmarking

The increase in the ability to do it practically is not the only reason for the rise in the popularity of benchmarking. There is also an inherent desire to compare oneself with others. However, Keehley and MacBride (1997, p. 77) suggest it offers something no other comparison can. "Any organization can use outcome measures to monitor its internal improvement quarterly, but new horizons can be discovered only through unconventional ideas. This factor is key to benchmarking; without it, breakthrough improvement is impossible." This is echoed with: "By challenging the status quo, the benchmarking process provides public utility managers with a tool that can be used to provide meaningful assessments of an organization's competitive position and point the way to productivity and customer service improvements." (Meszaros and Owen, 1997, p. 22)

"Local officials would be well advised to face this fact: inter-jurisdictional comparisons will be made. Those comparisons can be anecdotal, pseudo-systematic (for example, "quick and dirty" studies that often sacrifice precision, consistency, and validity for simplicity and speed), or systematic. The first two types—anecdotal and pseudo-systematic comparisons—rank highest on the cringe-factor scale." (Ammons, 1997, p. 15)

Unlike managerially set targets, benchmarks are externally determined and unaffected by the power of management. One author finds the automatic nature of the benchmark freeing: "... it serves to create a point of common reference that is based neither on opinions nor on values, but on factual measurements of productivity." (Triantafillou, 2007, p. 839)

These comparisons are still not without problems, such as those alluded to above in discussing the measures themselves. "The problems with superficial comparisons are numerous. Such comparisons often ignore differences in the nature, scope, and quality of services from place to place." (Ammons et al, 2001, p. 101) Some of the sources of the problem include the differences in the array of services included in the budget line, cost accounting rules, which costs are included in a budget line, and differences between appropriations and expenditures.

One also needs to account for exogenous factors, which the section on measurement discusses. The reason they are measured is to permit comparisons absent of the effects of these external variables, which government does not control. In addition, governments do set different goals, which specific performance indicators will reflect. The use of profiles captures differences in both environment and goals. New South Wales Department of Local Government (2008, p. 10) explains how they are used:

> When assessing or comparing the performances of councils, it is important to remember that local circumstances can influence how well a council provides its services. There are often good reasons why it is harder or more costly to provide certain services in some local government areas than in others or why a different mix of services may be delivered. In some cases, councils may have made conscious decisions to provide lower or higher levels of services depending on local needs. The council profiles will help you assess the comparative performance information.

In an article on the construction of performance standards, one author also emphasized the concept of standards that are within the manager's control. "...only state and local program efforts—not characteristics of their populations or economic conditions that were beyond program managers' control—should explain why they met, exceeded or fell below their negotiated performance standards." (Courty et al, 2005, p. 340)

The literature addresses methods for comparing performance between jurisdictions. Performance measurement systems are different from isolated performance measurement initiatives in that they permit comparisons with outside entities. Benchmarking is the act of using outside comparisons. Benchmarking is a management tool to identify better practices (Raaum, 2007). These comparisons with other practices provide a real "base line for performance improvement" (McAdams and O'Neil, 2002, p. 454).

With comparative data, benchmarking produces a reference that is based on factual levels of productivity, rather than historical performance in a single organization. This enables managers to make more meaningful assessments of an organization's performance, using information about its relative performance (Meszaros and Owen, 1997). Triantafillou (2007, p. 839) reports that benchmarking "urges the organizations, which are the target of the comparison, to act." Comparisons "help to establish a performance-based culture in the public sector" (Kouzmin et al, 1999).

Using solely internal historical assessment of performance is not as satisfactory for performance improvement purposes as external benchmarking comparisons (Boyne et al, 2002). However, in the United States, because there are few performance measurement systems, historical comparison is still the main benchmark level found in budget reporting (Willoughby, 2004; Julnes and Holzer, 2008). In a 1999 study of local governments in the U.K., researchers (Bovaird and Davis, 1999, p. 310) concluded, "internal benchmarking activity (sharing ideas around a single authority)[49] appears to be relatively inefficient in many cases." Others (Keehly and MacBride, 1997, p. 77) went as far as stating that benchmarking has to go further than internal comparisons, otherwise "breakthrough improvement is impossible."

Generally, the literature states that comparisons between similar governments are best. In the empirical results from a nationwide Norwegian benchmarking study, organizational learning is demonstrated as a result of benchmarking (Askim et al, 2008). A key finding of this study conflicts with much of the literature and assumptions of practitioners. Municipalities learn more from dissimilar benchmarking partners. The study found greater learning occurred in networks in which there was more fiscal heterogeneity among the municipalities.

Comparing performance and costs for different activities with a statewide average is not the best way to identify possible gains in efficiency. Unless professional standards, like police or EMS response time, validate an average, the average is just that (Woodbury et al, 2003)—it tells little about how good or poor the performance is. Moreover, to identify factors public managers can manipulate to produce better results or services that municipalities might share, one should examine not the typical average case, but the high performing ones to see how they manage differently.

The Best Value approach receives support in some of the literature. A cluster of units comparing their results among themselves seems more effective than a comparison of each unit to the best practice (McAdams and O'Neil, 2002). The study identified mutually supportive programs within the cluster and good guidance material from the government as the causes for the effectiveness of the cluster.

A study of the use of Best Value Performance Plans in Wales finds disappointing results in the improvement in accountability using this approach (Boyne et al, 2002). Pre-existing conditions led to the failure to improve accountability. These included a lack of prior performance indicators and limited staff expertise in performance measurement.

---

[49] The literature uses benchmarking in two other ways in addition to the most common, comparisons against the performance of other jurisdictions. Some authors use it to refer to examining operational differences of other, high-performing organizations and incorporating those changes. It is also used, although infrequently, as any general method of comparison. This is the meaning used by Boivard and Davis in declaring internal benchmarking inefficient.

In the North Carolina Project, Winston-Salem was the top performer as a benchmarker, not because it was the best performing municipality in the delivery of services, but because it used the project information to improve its operations to the benefit of citizens. In response to the disappointing result that showed Winston-Salem was most inefficient in providing residential refuse collection service, the city took several steps to reduce its operating cost. As a result, the city was able to reduce the inefficiency factors, and expects to achieve cost savings in upcoming years. (See Figure 1) "True benchmarkers, however, realize that benchmarking is a management tool, not a beauty contest. Benchmarkers select benchmarking partners in hopes of discovering ways to improve their services, not simply as a public relations ploy. They seek out high performance organizations." (Ammons, 2000, p. 122)

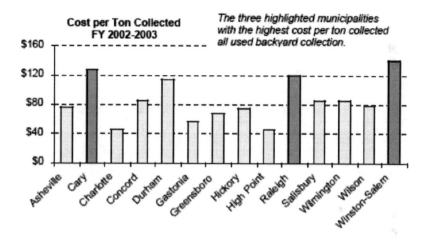

Estimated Impacts				
Households	Changes in routes	Changes in personnel	Changes in trucks	Estimated savings ($)
5,000	-1	-3	-1	$29,000
10,000	-1	-3	-1	-$14,000
15,000	-2	-8	-2	$104,000
20,000	-2	-8	-2	$61,000
25,000	-3	-12	-3	$144,000

Figure 5A.
Source: North Carolina Local Government Performance Measurement Project. (2005).
Benchmarking for Results.

Another author reviewing the results of the North Carolina Project sees benchmarking as resolving conflicting pressures on public administrators (Williams, 2005). The author perceives the pressure to perform at a high level as being in conflict with the incentives to avoid risks leading to failure and negative publicity. Leveraging performance data to improve program outcomes yields both a high level of performance and avoids risks in performance outcomes.

Factors Affecting Benchmarking

There is considerable discussion about how visible benchmarking should be. Early on, it was commonplace to espouse voluntary participation; self-directed analysis; and internal use for management purposes. These and other devices would protect the participant. Now the consensus is that benchmarking is more effective when management makes the results available to the public.

Braadbaart (2007) states publication of performance achievements promotes performance improvement, For example, media coverage and praise from various sides prompted water utilities to develop internal targets, to begin discussing performance at industry seminars, and to swap performance tips. The confidential benchmarking that was taking place between 1989 and 1995 did not even produce any improvements over non-benchmarkers When the benchmarking became public in 1997, the economic performance of the utilities was enhanced and the performance converged.

An article in the *Government Finance Review* states that government officials were initially apprehensive about reporting some programs had performed below standard (Berman, 2006). Not only did nothing untoward happen to the sitting administrations, but at least one favorable newspaper editorial praised the honesty and forthrightness of the administration. The author suggests "listening" to the public about services to help align government programs to the needs and desires of the citizens whom government serves. The recent literature echoes these sentiments about public communication (Gelders et al, 2008; Page and Malinowski, 2004).

Another issue about the use of benchmarking is whether the effectiveness of the tool in promoting program improvement varies along the continuum of voluntary to mandated benchmarking programs. This relates to the discussion of the publication of benchmarking data because of the force behind published materials, but it is also deserving of a separate discussion because a central government can mandate benchmarking, while keeping it as an internal management tool, without external publication.

Despite the trend toward transparency and the evidence that public benchmarking is more effective in encouraging improvement in service delivery, many officials continue to fear releasing data publicly. New Jersey, where there is not a strong tradition of performance measurement for local government, enacted a law in 2007, which required the New Jersey Local Finance Board to establish performance measures to promote cost savings in the delivery of services by municipal governments and award state aid to municipalities that meet those performance measures. Nothing has happened in over three years since the law was signed. The prior Director of the Local Finance Board (who was removed after a change in governors) spoke at several public seminars about the impracticality of developing comparable performance measures for the 556 municipalities. Yet, there are individual municipalities that have been trying to implement performance measurement systems, some using voluntary benchmarking. None of the attempts made the measures public.

In Norway, where the political environment is quite different from that in the United States, highly competitive comparisons offer the most improvement in management and performance (Askim et al, 2008). The opposition will use the information on poor performance to wrest power from an opposing party. The use of managed competition to improve performance is not a necessity (Braadbaart, 2007). Collaborative benchmarking can enhance both transparency and performance.

With the Best Value approach to benchmarking, compulsory and defensive modes of benchmarking result from the external accountability that is required (Bowerman et al, 2001). This reduces the focus on tangible improvement. The author's conclusion is that management of the benchmarking by local government needs to balance the centralizing approach.

Australia found it necessary to mandate performance measurement throughout its local governments (Woodbury et al, 2003). Using the "average municipality" statistic, each state determined what specific service areas should be included for its municipalities. In Ontario, Canada, municipal governments are required to report financial and non-financial information on thirty-five measures of performance in nine core service areas (Chan, 2004).

Proof that voluntary benchmarking does not work is provided by the lack of consistent improvement in the municipalities participating in the North Carolina Project (Williams, 2005). Although there were stars, efficiency gains were not uniformly distributed across all program areas, leaving a great deal of unexplained variance. From a study of health care: "... it is not enough to make use of voluntary benchmarking models to obtain an orientation toward improvement." (Barretta, 2008, p. 364)

Successful benchmarkers plan how to use the tool and implement those plans. The less successful incorrectly assume benefits will accrue from having the tool. Hence, in the early stages of the programs for three projects the authors examined in North Carolina, they reported relatively few cost savings or program and service improvements (Ammons et al, 2001).

Best practice efforts are dependent on comprehensive benchmarking and, therefore, may require a mandated system (Bretschneider et al, 2005, p. 309). The author defines best practice as preferable to any other course of action to achieve a deliberate end. It involves a comparative process, an action, and a linkage between the action and an outcome or goal. If a complete range of comparisons is not available, the notion of a best practice is not defensible, because the comparison was not made to "any alternative course of action."

Benefits Derived from Performance Measurement

It may seem frustrating to some, but obvious to others, that citizens may not recognize government efforts in performance measurement, benchmarking, and best practices. Furthermore, there is little evidence that service productivity enhances the satisfaction of citizens with their government (Moore et al, 2005). Although Behn (2007, p. 41) illustrates the cost savings from the control and reduction in the use of overtime due to the CitiStat system in place in Baltimore, he comments:

> If you walked through downtown Baltimore and asked individual citizens, "What do you think of CitiStat?" the most honest answer you would get is "Huh?" Citizens don't pay attention to government's management strategies. But they care about the results of those strategies.

CitiStat is a system for improving performance of all departments in a local government. In the initial implementation in the Police Department of New York City, it was called CompStat. CompStat has had documented benefits in a number of police departments. A recent implementation of CompStat in Queensland provided some detailed documentation of net program benefits (Mazerolle et al, 2007). Queensland documented the cost savings from reduced crime and compared the savings to the costs of over $1.5 million to conduct the OPR's (Operational Performance Reviews) since the inception of the program. The overall savings were close to $1.2 million, after accounting for the costs of running the program. Most of these "costs" were not added costs. Rather, they were the salaries of the participants, which, prior to CompStat, paid for the other management activities they engaged in. The overall savings of $1.2 million are conservative.

The exciting thing about the Queensland study is the other benefits. Queensland attributed to the OPR's a reduction of 3,200 crimes of the 11,700 that could have been expected without the introduction of the OPR's, according to historical trends. This significant decrease in crimes was strongest in the reduction of unlawful entry into properties.

A group of utility providers in the Netherlands reduced costs due to benchmarking (Braadbaart, 2007). Both novice and experienced benchmarkers showed similar pricing behavior, although the novice bench markers had the advantage of operating in a mature system.

The results from the North Carolina Project showed a significant reduction in the cost per ton of refuse removal. The officials had been aware of a need to change the recycling and refuse collection systems before they had comparative data, but the hard evidence made the case clearer and provided a needed impetus for change. Data also smoothed the internal negotiations that accompanied the required operational change (Ammons, 2000).

A State Performance Measurement Model for Local Government

The literature shows a range of different implementations of performance measurement. Academics generally agree that other countries have done more, and there is more sophistication abroad than in the United States. No state has mandated a performance measurement system, but there are many centralized governments outside of the United States which have mandated or promoted a centralized system, usually with benchmarking comparisons inherent to it.

One of the most sophisticated and transparent systems is the British Comprehensive Performance Assessment (CPA) system, which has been in place since 2002. Under the CPA systems, British municipalities have to report on a vast number of indicators to the central government, where the data is then fully accessible to citizens. The oldest systems in place are Ontario's Municipal Performance Measures Program (MPMP) and Nova Scotia's Municipal Indicators, which both started in 2000. A third Canadian province, Quebec, started a province-wide municipal performance measurement system in 2003. Different states and territories in Australia and the central government in Norway have mandated municipalities to provide information on certain key service areas. However, there are not as elaborate as the systems presented above.

There are important individual and group implementations in the U.S., including New York City; Worcester, Massachusetts; Portland, Oregon; North Carolina; and Fairfax County, Virginia. For any state that chooses to implement the systematic collection of standardized performance measures from all its local governments, the effort would be considerable. However, it could avoid pitfalls that previous performance measurement system implementations encountered: hastiness of implementation; no or little practitioner outreach in the design phase (Davis, 1998); lack of comparison subcategories (Foltin, 1999); and the absence of shared accounting practices (Coe, 1999).

Most performance measurement systems evolve from their initial implementation. Behn (2007, p. 11) proposes the low hanging fruit approach for a beginning effort: "In this situation, the mayor might well choose to focus on a few smaller but easily corrected, if not eliminated, problems. Faced with skepticism inside and outside of city government, a mayor could elect to demonstrate some quick wins that can silence the critics and convince others ...." Picking key service areas to begin with and indicators of performance in these areas where improvement is easy to attain would maximize the chance of early success and start a learning process in any state that wishes to venture into state-defined performance measurement.

The literature has considered the North Carolina approach to be a good model, but its results in performance improvement are mixed. The key point is that it is a voluntary model that has sought to achieve consensus as it has evolved. Specific suggestions from this project would include using steering committee meetings to discuss new areas of study, building consensus, and ensuring comparability (Rivenbark and Carter, 2000). A state could use this process to evolve a beginning system into a sophisticated system that would improve local government and provide a means to measure performance continually. However, if there are not effective incentives and disincentives present, it may have the same mixed results as North Carolina experienced.

It is easier for a state to emphasize standardization of a performance measurement system and provide a practical audit capability to assure the standardization of the implementation. This is where a state government should place its emphasis. However, the real payoff is in the management and policy use of the information. That is not easy for a state to regulate, and may even have negative implications. One of these is the squelching of creativity and breakthrough improvements. Regulatory actions are good at preventing the worst behaviors or, at least, identifying them. They are not good at raising the bar and achieving better overall performance.

If a state were to create and implement a good standardized data collection and reporting tool, it will have positive results. It will more easily detect the worst performance. If the comparisons are public, it will create increased attention on municipal government performance and create an environment in which the discourse between the public and its representatives is about the same issues with the same information. Like the North Carolina consortium, some municipalities will use the information more productively than others will.

The state cannot tell municipalities how to manage based on the data or what decision-making process to use, although both of these are important aspects of increasing municipal efficiency. It can set up mechanisms that maintain a focus on the performance results, that reward improvement and discourage inertia (or worse), and that encourage learning from the most improved performers. It can also provide technical assistance in implementing on-going management review systems, like the "Stat" models. A public review draft of a performance management framework for state and local government includes a warning for anyone who thinks this is an easy fix. "Simply superimposing a performance management process onto a traditionally managed organization is not likely to produce expected benefits. Organizational culture issues must also be addressed." (National Performance Management Advisory Commission, 2010, p. 2)

Comments and Conclusions

The data in the literature are thorough and comprehensive. They are a good reflection of the state of our knowledge. The academic community writes extensively on performance measurement. In addition, academics are often the consultants to or creators of systems that have been implemented.

The literature has evolved in this field, because it is, as they say, "Hot." What was written twenty years ago formed a base for the conceptualization of the field and a roadmap to the investigations that followed.

The literature on performance measurement is extensive, but culling out what is most appropriate from the volume is challenging. It is wise to consider the work recently done in other countries when considering what the final model for any state in the United States should be. However, because these international systems have already evolved from the initial implementations, a state may need to look elsewhere to find the initial steps it should take to get to a final model.

Behn, who is cited in this review and writes a monthly management series with a performance measurement focus, states that what you need to measure is determined by what you are going to do with it. Determining how the information will be used is an early stage in developing a performance measurement system. Once that decision is known, specific parts of the literature become more appropriate and the designers can formulate a specific model.

No state has centralized a performance measurement system. Countries and sub-units of countries have done so, but the literature only covers what they require to be measured and reported. It is silent on how to manage using such a system.

Based on the components found in the systems the literature describes, a performance measurement system of local governments in any one state should include the following:

▸ A system of benchmarking among the local governments in the state in order to facilitate improvement and best practices.

▸ A system of different types of performance measures including workload, input, output, and outcome indicators.

▸ A system of management review that encourages management action and monitors its effectiveness.

▸ Reporting to the state on performance measures and management initiatives resulting from the analysis and review of the performance measures.

The most difficult decision for a state is not what the overall system should look like when it has matured. The most difficult decision is how to get there from the current situation. Since no state has implemented a centralized performance measurement system for its localities, the context of this research should provide an appropriate basis for further action. More specific findings from the literature should guide an implementation of a performance measurement, reporting, and management system. Although they are elaborated in the body of the chapter, they deserve emphasis here:

▸ Performance Indicators

There are many models and techniques for measuring efficiency. The commonly used "cost per capita" measure of efficiency has issues of comparability and usefulness. The literature provides a number of different indicator types used in a performance measurement system in order to provide useful data to managers and others. Performance measures should cover the range of the processes monitored, from workload and inputs to outputs and outcomes, with a consideration for external variables, which may affect performance potential. Outcomes measure those conditions that are concerns of the public and help managers, who accept their responsibilities for outcomes, to think outside the box. One also needs to focus on inputs, internal capacities, and outputs. The literature contains many good measures. The body of the chapter contains references to other resources, which list specific indicators.

▶ Measurement Considerations

Basic information can now be collected, but the highest and best use of the information will require changes in record keeping and data collection. If users or stakeholders are to make inter-jurisdictional comparisons, then measurements must be standardized. The literature states that it is easier (and most common) to measure efficiency if comparisons are only historical within the same unit, but such comparisons have limited usefulness. Measurement of outcomes requires changes in record keeping, since the focus, where performance has been measured, is typically on workload or output measures.

▶ Analyzing the Data

Analyzing performance data has advanced in recent years. The most powerful tool appears to be Data Envelopment Analysis, which accounts for multiple inputs and outputs and distinguishes between technical, scale, and allocative efficiency. DEA requires sophisticated analytic expertise to use appropriately. However, good management can occur with simple, even basic, forms of data analysis, if it is informed by an understanding of the processes being monitored.

▶ Managing with the Data

Internal management is the primary use of the data, and less frequently public reporting and accountability. Stakeholders should use the data for diagnosis of efficiencies and improvement of services. CitiStat is an example of a successful data review and performance management system. Since it relies more heavily on management review than on sophisticated analysis or benchmarking, it is hard to replicate throughout an entire state. CitiStat does not preclude sophisticated analysis, but it does not rely on it to achieve its internal management goals.

▶ Benchmarking

Local governments should make comparisons in order to maximize improvement in the delivery of services. Benchmarking against the performance of other governments is often a popular choice, but there are difficulties in creating comparable cost-based data. When data is available, stakeholders and managers will readily benchmark. This chapter provides examples of systems that utilize inter-jurisdictional comparisons, including an example from the North Carolina Local Government Performance Measurement Project, which utilized benchmarks as a catalyst to performance improvement in solid waste efficiency.

▶ Transparency

Managers and local officials debate whether they should publicize all performance data, but the literature considers the benefits of transparency and critical analysis as overshadowing the concerns of those who fear public reaction.

▶ The Bottom Line

The literature rarely links examples of actual cost savings to tax savings. Cost savings, not tax savings, are documented, but not that frequently and with suspicions about reliability. The literature promotes quality of service delivery as a major, perhaps even primary, benefit of performance measurement, although most evaluations rely on cost savings.

Performance measurement, and the general attempt to measure efficiency of local government, is an increasingly important concern. Both internationally and with increasing frequency in the United States, local governments are implementing performance measurement systems to improve efficiency and outcomes. Overall, the literature points to promising tools or approaches.

CHAPTER 6

Overview of Municipal Efficiency

The preceding chapters reviewed what is known about five subject areas related to municipal government efficiency. This chapter integrates the results of those reviews of municipal cost-efficiency in service delivery as affected by municipal size, municipal consolidation, service consolidation and alternative service delivery arrangements, as well as the review on the measurement of municipal efficiency.

In presenting what we know from the literature as a base, this chapter sets the stage for applying this knowledge to the realities of service delivery in local government. It begins by reviewing the advantages that the literature has attached to the different delivery arrangements that the literature discusses. The chapters that follow use this base to look more deeply into the details of services municipalities provide, to investigate less common delivery arrangements and compare their advantages, and to consider the best matching of the varied arrangements to the details of the services.

The major findings of the five preceding chapters are these:

▸ Consolidation of municipalities has not been effective in increasing efficiency of municipal service delivery.

▸ The relationship between the size of the population served and efficiency is not consistent for the delivery of different service types.

▸ Size is associated with economies of scale for capital-intensive services and highly specialized services, resulting in greater efficiency in larger governments.

▸ Size is associated with diseconomies of scale for labor-intensive services, suggesting greater efficiencies in smaller governments.

▸ The most common measure of municipal efficiency is cost per capita.

▸ The literature considers the cost per capita metric greatly flawed due to inconsistencies of measurement and accounting in different jurisdictions.

▸ Performance measurement systems have addressed inconsistencies in measurement and accounting in order to provide valid comparative benchmarking.

▸ Benchmarking between jurisdictions has been effective in identifying performance improvements and cost savings.

▸ Data-based management review systems, such as the "CitiStat" or "CompStat" models, are effective at improving operational efficiencies.

▶ The perception is that sharing of services is effective in promoting efficiency of service delivery.

▶ The literature promotes sharing and other forms of service consolidation, even for services that demonstrate no economies of scale in studies of size and efficiency.

▶ Of the several modes of delivering municipal services, the most common is direct delivery by the municipality; the next most common is shared service delivery.

▶ Privatization and regionalization, provided by special districts or centralized governments, such as counties, provide increased efficiency in some implementations.

▶ Hybrid delivery arrangements, such as regionalized service delivery combined with a regional council or policy group, are appealing as alternatives to reduce the potential loss of local control that might result from consolidated service delivery arrangements.

▶ Hybrid forms of delivery foster the matching of different service delivery arrangements to the characteristics of specific service types, such as labor-intensive or capital-intensive services. For example, two-tier governments may provide regionally based water services through a special district, police patrol through the local municipalities, and economic development through the county.

▶ No service delivery arrangement is universally efficient, suggesting that a municipality always needs to complete a realistic, full cost evaluation of the projected results of an alternative service delivery arrangement before implementation.

These highlights are a summary of the detailed conclusions from the five preceding chapters. To make it easier for the reader to understand the complexity underlying the sixteen highlighted findings, we have reproduced the conclusions from each of the preceding chapters.

Conclusions of the Five Studies

We examined efficiency in municipal government, reviewing other alternative mechanisms, including municipal consolidation or the use of other local governments to deliver municipal services to the public. The goal was to study the most appropriate allocation of service delivery and to determine the optimal level and configuration of government or its contractors from the standpoint of efficiency of municipal service delivery. We expected our insights might range from suggestions to share specific services to the realignment of local government units, including possible municipal consolidations, the merging of specific existing autonomous agencies into parent municipal or county governments, or the sharing of services between or among municipalities and other public entities.

We were aware that many government practitioners believe that there are inefficiencies associated with the multiple municipal governmental units and that municipal consolidation, particularly directed at the smaller municipalities, will result in more cost-effective government. Further, we understood that a belief in the effectiveness of economies of scale dominated much of the thinking about municipal efficiency.

We therefore conducted a systematic review of what is actually known about these aspects of municipal efficiency and queried how that knowledge fits with these beliefs of practitioners and elected officials. Below, we have listed the detailed conclusions from each of the five preceding chapters, in order to provide an easy reference for the reader.

Conclusions on Optimal Municipal Size and Efficiency

Although the literature does not reveal strong and consistent relationships between size and efficiency in the delivery of local government services, some relationships are evident. The first relationship describes the overall effect of size of government on efficiency. The second and third statements show that the general relationship does not hold when specific services are considered. The fourth point, about the difficulties of measuring efficiency, is very important in the determination of what promotes municipal efficiency:

▶ The Inverted U-shaped Curve

There is an inverted U-shaped relationship between size and efficiency on a general level. Efficiency increases with population size up to about 25,000 people, at which point it is stable until size is about 250,000 people, and efficiency declines with increasing population size after that. The inverted U-shaped curve that describes the relationship between municipal size and efficiency offers two opportunities for improvement: the very smallest and the very largest governments. The literature defines the smallest as populations less than 20,000 to 25,000. The largest are municipalities with populations in excess of 250,000. The literature suggests states should examine their largest governments as well as their smallest governments for ways to increase efficiencies.

▶ Service Specific Relationships

The most important finding other than the inverted U-shaped curve was the difference in the relationship between size and efficiency in capital-based services as opposed to labor-intensive services. Efficiency gains are related to size for capital or infrastructure intensive services such as sewer and water. The literature supports the finding that this same concept is operative for seldom used and specialized services, such as a high technology crime lab. This suggests that contracting, sharing, or receiving specialized services from a larger entity can make selected services more efficient.

▶ Labor-Intensive Services

Labor-intensive services are more efficient in smaller governments. The literature only offers burdens of management control and excess administration in larger governments as an explanation for such inefficiencies. Reduced levels of services and expectations in smaller towns may also be operating to reduce costs. This finding of increased efficiency in smaller units is an important conclusion, because the literature attributes over 80 percent of governmental cost to labor-intensive services including police, fire, and education.

▶ Complexity of Measuring Efficiency

An additional finding from the literature is the difficulty in determining one measure of efficiency that works well at the level of a municipality or even for a service area. The most common basis for a measurement of efficiency is expenditure data, which is the numerator in the cost per capita indicator used throughout the literature. Varying definitions of expenditure measures across jurisdictions are the culprit in the comparability of this indicator. It is surprising that no state has used its municipal expenditure data to examine efficiency and the factors that promote it. While a difficult task, this makes a great deal of sense, because of the ability to control some of the confounding influences, where there is knowledge about the accounting categories typically used in a specific state.

Finally, we must recognize that there are many inconsistencies in the literature. Even the most consistent findings of the inverted U-shaped curve and the relationship for capital-intensive versus labor-intensive services have variations supported by some authors. For example, we could not reconcile the debate over police responsiveness and inefficiency in small versus large units. Different authors observed greater managerial efficiencies in small units, but others saw relative efficiencies in large units. The literature does not provide a high level of confidence for further action on a systematic and broad basis.

Conclusions on Municipal Government Consolidation

If the question is "Do we consolidate and where?", the literature shows there is not adequate information for an unqualified "yes" or "no," and there are certainly not concrete criteria to follow through on a "yes" answer. The literature indicates that governments have achieved only a small portion of the attempted consolidations, and the results of those achieved are mixed.

▶ Cost Savings Are Not Assured

The literature does not consistently support the general belief that increasing the size of municipalities will lead to cost savings. The overall inverted U-Shaped curve relationship between population size and costs per capita masks the details of size relationships that vary with the nature of the service being delivered.

▶ Implementation of Consolidation Is Costly and Time Consuming

Transitional costs can be substantial if the consolidated government requires new facilities or infrastructure. It will normally take years to complete a consolidation.

It is a complex task to achieve. Simply assuming a better organizational culture and better procedures in the merged government does not provide an accurate estimate of the results.

▶ Savings Only Result from Reductions in Resources

There is a tendency (at times, a legal mandate) to create a wage and benefit structure that rises to the highest wage levels of the pre-merged governments. The merger must be evaluated as to how positions, equipment, or facilities can be reduced, if not immediately, then in the long run, so that these savings will balance the costs of the transition. The on-going costs resulting from higher uniform service levels and wage and benefit structures among merged municipalities are another major consideration.

▶ Most Consolidation Attempts Fail

Governments have not achieved the majority of recent voluntary attempts at consolidation. Of those that have been achieved, the results, measured in terms of costs savings or improved quality or responsiveness of service delivery, are mixed.

▶ Politics Is an Obstacle

The literature most often cites political considerations, running the gamut from multiple concerns of the public to concerns of political parties about shifts in the balance of power, as the most significant obstacles to consolidation

Evaluations of potential mergers must be specific to the needs and situations of the communities involved. The mere attempt to consolidate often focuses an evaluation on ways other than consolidation to achieve increased efficiencies, even when the merger of governments does not result. This "unintended consequence" has led to better arrangements for service delivery in many situations.

Conclusions on Service Delivery Consolidation among Municipalities

The literature supports the assumption that inter-governmental cooperation can provide cost and quality efficiencies. In addition to discussing the benefits of shared services and other forms of cooperation, the literature provides insights into how to increase the amount of service delivery consolidation:

▶ Quality Improvements

Most shared services success stories assess cost savings, but some of these cases state that improvements in service delivery and quality should be the primary motivator in forming shared services. Sharing seldom reduces quality of the service, and often improves quality. Quality issues are the sole motivation for some arrangements.

▶ Providing High Cost Service Improvements

There are functional service areas, such as information technology, in which local government has made only limited investments. Traditionally, this is because the government perceives the costs to be unpalatable to the citizenry. Service sharing offers the potential for quality improvement in areas such as this, without incurring the skepticism of the public about expensive investments.

▶ Case-by-Case Resolution of Obstacles

Although there are hurdles to implementation of shared services, they are situation-specific, and should be assessed and resolved in forming an agreement. There are a great many successful shared service arrangements that have overcome the typical obstacles. Even the most common concerns, loss of local control or loss of local delivery of the service, are infrequently mentioned as obstacles in the literature.

▶ Public Safety Services

Reports from around the country indicate a reduction in public safety costs is possible. The transfer of police, fire, and dispatch services to other units of government are common potential efficiencies cited in the literature. Despite successes, police and fire are difficult services to consolidate, because of the public's concerns with safety (in terms of response times) and organized labor's concerns with employment security.

▶ State Encouragement

Evidence shows that governments want to do more service sharing than they actually accomplish. States are trying to encourage collaboration through grant and education programs. Some have tried to launch more of an outreach program, and others have tried to create databases of needs to meet through sharing.

▶ Need for Focus

Successful shared services require planning. Probably the greatest obstacle to doing what everybody seems to want—shared services that result in economies—is not spending the time and detailed effort to focus on it. The fact that most sharing arrangements come from informal networks and contacts is testimony to the fact governments do not spend enough time thinking about how to be efficient. They need to be encouraged to invest time and resources to do so.

▶ Incentives that Support Productive Organizations

Grants, such as New Jersey made available to develop county offices dedicated to promoting shared services, create incentives and the focus to evaluate more cost-effective strategies. These state grants to counties are a good step in the direction suggested by the Somerset County Business Partnership's proposal to fund effective sharing organizations in order to continue their successful work.

▶ Positive Effects of Fiscal Stress

Fiscal and budgetary pressures also encourage cooperation between units of government. Conversely, aid or grants, which maintain a service, are disincentives to finding alternative service delivery arrangements.

Finding the right level of government to deliver a service is an important concern. The conclusions from the analysis of *Optimal Service Delivery Arrangements and Efficiency* discuss some other mechanisms to move service delivery to the appropriate government, including centralized government, special districts, and regional delivery structures.

Conclusions on Optimal Service Delivery Arrangements and Efficiency

This chapter reviewed varied approaches to service delivery arrangements. However, it is not obvious from what is found in the literature how to compare these approaches, much less propose an optimal array of service delivery arrangements. This area of alternate structures for service delivery is new and evolving, which makes the task of developing concrete conclusions more challenging.

The literature highlights the following arrangements as providing efficient and effective solutions for delivering public services:

▶ Contracted Services

Shared services can increase efficiency while retaining local control. The numbers show that a private contractor may be more efficient only if the municipality can monitor the contract adequately.

▶ Special Districts Provide Specific Service Expertise

Special districts (authorities and fire districts, for example) provide a focused area of expertise, but possibly at the cost of greater fragmentation, redundancy of general administrative functions, and loss of accountability. Regionalized special districts mitigate the increase in fragmentation and redundancy, but make accountability more distant.

▶ Centralized Services Provide Scale Economies

County or regional service provision is attractive for those services (infrastructure related or highly specialized) that show economies of scale, but there may be a need to provide representation of the constituent municipalities in order to assure local control.

▸ Joint Boards for Specific Functions

Joint boards are effective for unique services that are best provided over a broader area (for example, land use planning and economic development) and may provide local representation in determining how the service will be delivered.

▸ Regional Policy Groups Increase Local Control for Varied Services

Regional groups that are policy setting are very effective in providing local representation in an effort to collaborate and cooperate in providing services, but they depend on other structures to deliver the service directly. The Council of Governments in Monroe County, New York is an example.

▸ Hybrid Arrangements to Promote Efficiency and Provide Local Control

Arrangements that combine adequate local representation with an array of service delivery mechanisms applied appropriately to each specific type of service may optimize the benefits of different delivery arrangements. Two-tier governments are a hybrid form. They often combine a regional board, composed of representatives of constituent municipalities, with local delivery for services such as police patrols and regional or county delivery for services like economic development and land use planning.

The literature indicates there is potential in each of these approaches. It is important to fit the mechanism for delivery to the service type. In his review of fifty years of evidence on the relationship between the structure and performance of local governments, Bish (2001) suggests:

... given the diversity of communities and local services, no single organization can perform all the tasks demanded of local government. Metropolitan areas composed of a multiplicity of local governments and production arrangements are more responsive to residents' needs and generally provide local government services at less cost than monolithic amalgamations.

Conclusions on Measurement of Municipal Performance

Performance measurement, and the general attempt to measure efficiency of local government, is an increasingly important concern. Both internationally and with increasing frequency in the United States, local governments are implementing performance measurement systems to improve efficiency and outcomes. Overall, the literature points to promising tools or approaches:

▸ Performance Indicators (Measures)

Performance measures should cover the range of the processes being monitored, from workload and inputs to outputs and outcomes, with a consideration for external variables, which may affect performance potential. Outcomes are most important because they measure those conditions that are concerns of the public and help managers, who accept their responsibilities for outcomes, to think outside the box. One also needs to focus on inputs, internal capacities, and outputs. The literature contains many good measures.

▸ Data Envelopment Analysis

Analyzing performance data has advanced in recent years. The most powerful tool appears to be Data Envelopment Analysis, which accounts for multiple inputs and outputs and distinguishes between technical, scale, and allocative efficiency. DEA requires sophisticated analytic expertise to use appropriately. However, good management can occur with simple, even basic, forms of data analysis, if it is informed by an understanding of the processes being monitored.

▸ CitiStat

CitiStat is an example of a successful data review and performance management system. Since it relies more heavily on management review than on sophisticated analysis or benchmarking, it is hard to replicate throughout an entire state. CitiStat does not preclude sophisticated analysis, but it does not rely on it to achieve its internal management goals.

▸ Benchmarking (Inter-jurisdictional Comparisons)

Local governments should make comparisons in order to maximize improvement in the delivery of services. Benchmarking against the performance of other governments is often a popular choice, but there are difficulties in creating comparable cost-based data. When data is available, stakeholders and managers will benchmark.

▸ Transparency of Performance Data

Managers and local officials debate whether they should publicize all performance data, but the literature considers the benefits of transparency and critical analysis as overshadowing the concerns of those who fear public reaction.

An Integrated Analysis of the Conclusions

The conclusions of the literature do not support consolidation as an avenue for reducing property taxes. This is demonstrated both by the difficulty in obtaining approval for consolidation attempts and in mixed results in efficiency for those attempts that are implemented. In addition, the underlying logic— economies of scale—rests on an assumption not proven by the data.

The common backbone of the support for consolidation is a belief in economies of scale, which is borne out when looking at the costs for the total of all municipal services. Looking at the total costs of providing all municipal services, the smallest municipalities (under 20,000–25,000 population) appear to be inefficient (although efficiency is also lower in very large municipalities over 250,000 population). However, at the next more detailed level of analysis, segregating the effects by type of service, the literature is clear that economies of scale do not exist for labor-intensive services (most of the day-to-day service efforts of municipalities are labor intensive) and, in fact, appear to indicate diseconomies of scale. That is, larger municipalities have reduced efficiencies for labor-intensive tasks, such as police patrol. Economies of scale do exist, but, according to the literature, only for capital-intensive or specialized services that are relatively infrequent at the local level.

Although the literature shows that consolidation, or the full merger of municipalities, is not a favored option, other mechanisms for consolidating services are in common use. Consolidation of specific services does not draw the negative reviews attributed to formal consolidations that result in the dissolution of a municipality. It is worth noting that attempts at formal consolidation, when they are not completed, often lead to other forms of consolidation of services that are more acceptable. Several of the studies of consolidation point to increased sharing of services between governments, transfer of service to a county or regional level, and, on some occasions, to the development of a regional group with constituent representation from the participating municipalities that encouraged cooperation and sharing of services among the members.

What accounts for the acceptance of consolidation of services but not the consolidation of municipalities? Transition costs are greater and the disruption more complex when consolidating whole municipalities. Clearly, the legal and political hurdles of formal consolidation are great. The literature shows that "politics" is a major obstacle. Hence, it advises consideration of costs in terms of what the merged governments realistically can achieve in the face of potential changes caused by harmonizing wages and benefits, increasing uniformity of services, and merging of different facilities and cultures.

An "obvious" conclusion from the consolidation literature is that savings only result if there is a reduction in resources required. Successful reforms must use fewer employees, less equipment, or less costly facilities than were used in total in the pre-reformed governments. Some examples in the literature demonstrate the increased efficiency in the resulting governmental unit based on clear prior understandings about how they would achieve desired results. Those understandings are regarding employee reductions and compensation packages in the reformed government.

The literature describes alternative arrangements for delivering services, but the comparison of these alternatives is not comprehensive and consistent enough to choose one or another mode of service delivery. Further, there is no common identification of a set of general conditions and factors one should use to point to a better choice in a situation. There is a broad menu of choices, but no concrete basis on which to make the decision. The literature frequently states that quality and cost of services must be evaluated in terms of the specifics of the situation.

Direct service delivery by a municipality is the most common form of service delivery. The next most common is shared services, which is the "apple pie" of alternative arrangements for service delivery. The literature is not clear on why this is such a popular alternative to direct delivery, although it clearly is. In fact, the literature expresses concern that the impact of sharing services is not more carefully measured. There are estimates of the impact of sharing, non-quantified statements of the success of the cooperative arrangements, and even after-the-fact assessments of cost reduction or avoidance, but there is little that provides enough confidence to say how much cost saving can be achieved under any general set of conditions. Possible results must be evaluated for each situation.

Although examples exist of sharing arrangements that are not beneficial, the literature indicates that, all else being equal, sharing is beneficial in service quality and cost. The literature also states that local governments want to cooperate to a much greater extent. States have developed grant programs and technical assistance mechanisms to encourage cooperation, municipalities have created regional groups to promote shared services, and fiscal stress has led to increased sharing. The common thread in the attempts to increase sharing is to focus attention on it. The literature reports that informal mechanisms are the most common sources of sharing. However, regional groups that are formed largely to find common solutions to local problems have reported considerable success in fostering cooperation.

These regional groups are not, however, that common in many states. The effectiveness in some states of formal county offices to promote collaboration and state organizations that provide technical assistance offsets the lack of informal private-public partnerships and informal county or regional associations. The climate of fiscal stress also contributes to elected and appointed officials talking to each other about how to do more with less.

> **Fiscal stress can be a powerful motivator for increased efficiency. Continued fiscal stress is resulting in more shared services, as well as considerations of greater reform, such as regionalization and centralization.**

Evaluating Service Delivery Arrangements for Efficiency

Cost per capita is by far the most popular metric used. On the other hand, the literature is largely negative about the validity of cost per capita as a measurement of efficiency. The problems with this measure include the inconsistencies of cost allocations and differences in how individual jurisdictions define a service.

These inconsistencies will be present in any analysis of existing models of service delivery in different jurisdictions, and may distort the results. A careful analysis of costs can control some of these inconsistencies.

The review of performance measurement systems demonstrates that the comparability issue remains, but efforts to measure consistently across different jurisdictions can reduce many of the sources of inconsistency. If such a system is in place, comparisons can be made between different delivery arrangements. This would be in addition to the other benefits of a performance measurement system, including the capability to evaluate and monitor the quality of service delivery in an on-going fashion.

In general, the literature review indicates that decisions based on data are possible and more practical when there is a measurement system. Furthermore, that availability of information has led to continual improvements in performance and the development of a culture of rational decision-making.

The Building Blocks of Service Delivery Optimization

The literature about alternate arrangements for service delivery can be confusing because of definitions and semantics. Terms like regionalization and consolidation of services are very general. This discussion will use these familiar terms, but when we match delivery arrangements with specific local government services, specific terms are helpful in order to understand the options and how local governments can combine them. We will start by defining the general terms used to evaluate the efficiency of service delivery.

"Scale" is a term that appears frequently in the literature. Changes in geographic scope determine scale. The common method of enlarging geographic scope (and, therefore, scale) is to increase the area in which a service is delivered by a single organization. Municipal consolidation, shared services, centralization, or the creation of a special district that serves multiple jurisdictions can achieve greater scale. The logic is that the needs for some resources, such as administrative personnel and equipment, do not grow as quickly as the scale of services being delivered, resulting in increased scale efficiency.

There is also functional scope, or scope of services. Functional scope refers to how many different services are offered by the same organization. A municipality usually delivers a full complement of services. By having a large scope of services, some general government functions become more efficient than in a single service organization. A single service provider duplicates administrative efforts and, therefore, administrative and overhead costs. A competing view is that this specialization of focus and expertise provides greater efficiency through singular attention to one service. The literature points out, however, that specialization often leads to higher wage costs to pay for the specific expertise in the service area.

The literature also defines service as both service provision and service production[50]. Provision is the responsibility to budget for and make decisions about the amount of service to be delivered, or provided. Production is the actual act of bringing the service to the user or public. Production is a direct act or transaction, which is driven and defined by the budget and other policies of provision. A municipality retains responsibility for provision of a service when it contracts the service production to another government or the private sector. But

---

[50] Chapter 8 *Characteristics of Service Delivery Arrangements* provides greater detail and further breaks down the distinction between provision and production.

when a service is centralized to the county, or a special district is formed, the municipality transfers the entire service responsibility.

When the municipality no longer provides for the service, it no longer has control over the service and it no longer needs to budget for such service provision. An implication of not budgeting for the costs is that the municipality no longer needs the source of revenue to support the service. The municipality can reduce or eliminate those fees or taxes (depending on how the service was funded), but those costs will be transferred with the responsibility to the special district or county. Some governments, through the concomitant creation of regional policy groups or joint boards, counteract the concern about loss of control caused by relinquishing the responsibility for provision. Conversely, policy setting and budgeting may rest solely in the hands of the county or special district, with no input from constituent municipalities.

Advantages of Different Service Delivery Arrangements

Direct Service Delivery

Direct service delivery is the baseline method of service delivery. It is also the most common method. Its advantages include local control and local response, ability to set appropriate service levels on a uniform basis, the development of local expertise in the service, and the availability of resources (employees, equipment, and facilities) that the municipality can use to provide delivery of other service types during periods of weak demand in the original service type.

The disadvantages of direct service delivery revolve around cost and efficiency. The logic is that scale reduces unit costs; the reality, however, may be different. A smaller organization may attempt to keep costs down based on policy and operational decisions. The implications for quality may or may not be important.

For example, response and availability are essential for crime response and prevention, or any service with unscheduled demand, but not for trash collection and tax assessment, services that the municipality schedules. Resource levels in a small operation may need to be higher to meet peaks in demand (and to counteract unscheduled leave), leading to excess capacity that is not used efficiently in weaker demand cycles. Policy and budget decisions may sacrifice this excess capacity, and therefore response effectiveness, to attain overall efficiency.

> The impact of uneven service demands is magnified in small governments. We have observed several collaborations in police services that were effective in reducing the excess capacity that existed, but had been underutilized in the government prior to collaboration. Department sizing, particularly in small departments, cannot be based purely on average service demands. The need for officer safety, as provided through adequate backup, may result in over-staffing relative to the public need for the service. Collaboration can address minimum staffing requirements without creating underutilized excess capacity.

On the other hand, service levels in a larger scale operation may be inappropriate for some parts of the area, especially if service levels are made uniform across the entire service area. A larger service area is more likely to lack homogeneity of service demand throughout the area, perhaps related to varying population densities, a rural-suburban-urban mix, or some other factors affecting service needs.

Small communities will use the same personnel resources to provide a range of services. Wearing many hats, the employee of a small jurisdiction providing a service may not be as expert as a specialized employee in a larger entity. Citizens may find their service needs met and may be happier with the transaction simply because a familiar face has provided the service. On the other hand, the larger organization, which contains more expertise, may be better at meeting the uncommon needs of the public and will be more likely to avoid serious errors based on lack of experience with unusual situations (e.g., tax lien calculations and redevelopment financing). The benefits of greater expertise also apply to internal administrative services available to municipal operating departments. Specialized expertise available in a larger government may support internal offices in being more efficient when that expertise is needed, but the larger administrative department may result in slow, bureaucratic response to routine internal service needs.

Most, but not all, alternative forms of service delivery are intended to provide efficiencies of scale. Although the literature was mixed on this point, efficiencies of scale were seen to apply uniformly only for capital-intensive services, such as infrastructure development and maintenance, or highly specialized services, such as a police crime lab. Most authors hold that diseconomies of scale were in evidence for labor-intensive services such as police patrol. Against that background, the next sections review delivery arrangements that take advantage of efficiencies of scale, if they do exist for the specific service type.

Shared Service Delivery

After direct delivery, the next most prevalent service delivery arrangement is shared services. A shared service is a contract between two or more governments. It is usually contracted for one service at a time, but multiple service type arrangements can be made between the same partners. Typically, one municipality (or other government) acts as the lead agency, directly producing the service for all the partners and supplying the administration necessary to support the service production. Joint production of the service is uncommon, but mutual aid in fire and EMS response is an example where there is no lead agency. Joint production agreements are often more informal.

The provision of the service remains the responsibility of each municipality in which the shared service is delivered. The providing agency must budget for the service as well as make policy about the level of service delivery. Usually the providing agency compensates, through the budget allotment, the producing agency. Policy decisions about the service delivery and service levels made by the providing agency must be consistent with the agreement between the partners. Terminating the agreement is usually straightforward, if policy choices create an inconsistency or performance of the producer is considered inadequate.

> Although termination of a shared service may be easy to achieve, it can be more difficult for the producer to adjust to the downsizing of service needs. One such termination of a police services sharing left the producer with excess resources following the termination. The provider stated they were shopping for a better deal at the end of their original agreement, but the producer maintained that a newly elected mayor was unhappy with his inability to control the police chief. Agreements should be of sufficient duration to weather the transition period and should contain a sufficient time-period from announcement of termination until termination occurs, to provide both a cooling off period and a preparation and planning period. On the other hand, these issues must be balanced with concerns about entering into the agreement in the first place. If termination is too difficult, it provides a disincentive to collaborate.

The logic is that the service will be delivered over a larger service area, which is comprised of all the municipalities included in the agreement. If economies of scale exist for the service type, all partners should realize efficiency gains. If the scale is great enough, it may be practical to recruit specialized expertise and to acquire specialized equipment to provide the service. An example is the hiring of sophisticated computer experts and the purchase of high-end network servers and communications equipment to provide records storage and retrieval for a consortium of municipalities.

The partner responsible for the service provision typically loses some control over the actual operation of service delivery, perhaps causing the citizens of this municipality to expect the new service deliverer will not address their needs. In a good shared service relationship, either staff of the municipality responsible for providing the delivery, or a citizen, will contact the delivering partner when there is a service delivery issue (for example, a missed trash pick-up). Because all partners are governments, the relationship usually shows sensitivity to public demands.

Privatized Service Delivery

In theory, the only difference between a shared service and privatization is that in the latter case the contractor is a for-profit or non-profit organization, not a government. The evidence of the cost savings of privatization in the literature is so mixed that the determination of relative efficiency is not useful on a general level, but can be assessed when entering into a contract. This suggests there are at least three potential comparisons of costs for most services: direct delivery, shared services, and privatized delivery. In theory, the advantages and disadvantages of privatization, compared to direct delivery of the service by the municipality, are the same as for a shared service.

However, some differences are more likely to occur with a non-government contractor. The most serious is that the contract is often harder to terminate, even in cases of poor performance. In a related manner, monitoring the contract is more expensive. The contractor may not share the sensitivity to public demands that a government does, but may have more of a business motive for contract performance.

The contractor may have more expertise, in both personnel and equipment, for the service type because it may be an area of business concentration. On the other hand, if the contractor is only providing the service type for the one municipality (more likely with a non-profit contractor), economies of scale will not exist.

Special District, Non-regionalized Service Delivery

A special district, whether regional or based in only one municipality, is formed to provide one, or perhaps two, related service(s). On the surface, it is difficult to make a case for a special district serving a single municipality, unless there are other factors. At a regional level, the numbers might be more attractive.

A special district serving only the residents of the municipality, or only a part of the population, if there are multiple special districts providing the identical service type within the same municipality, provides no economies of scale. The logic of the advantage of a special district is the concentration of expertise on one service type. A special district duplicates much of the administrative resources and, therefore, administrative costs that are already part of the municipality that the special district serves.

Compared to the direct provision of service by a department of the municipality, the sole difference in a non-regionalized special district is the formation of a new government, perhaps with authority for taxing, setting rates, and incurring debt. A special district requires the creation of an additional governing body, elected or appointed, for the delivery of the service type. At best, the special district operates at arm's length from the municipality, and, usually, the public it serves. The literature is clear that special districts are increasingly under scrutiny and are being disbanded, although they are still being created in some localities. The literature is silent on the benefits of a non-regional special district.

Compared to a shared service, it is very difficult to terminate this type of delivery arrangement. There must be a legal act to dissolve the special district entity. The assumption of debts and assets is a difficult issue. In addition, an assumption of mismanagement may accompany the dissolution.

Regionalized Service Delivery Using a Special District

Like any regionalized service, there is a potential benefit from economies of scale in a regionalized special district. Compared to a non-regional special district service, opting out of the regionalized service is easier for an individual municipality, because the dissolution of the special district is not necessary. However, the distribution of debts and assets remains an issue.

Otherwise, the discussion above applies, but the difference of scale, when a special district serves several municipalities, is a very significant consideration affecting efficiency results.

Centralized Service Delivery

Regionalized service delivery can also be accomplished through centralization. Most centralization occurs at the county level of local government. In the literature review, we differentiated between a shared service and centralized service by determining whether the constituent municipalities had the option to maintain their own service production for the service type being centralized.

> **Of course, the lines blur throughout the taxonomy of alternate service delivery mechanisms. One case that bends our definition of centralization occurred in a county that decided to deliver a service previously provided and produced by its constituent municipalities, but without requiring the municipalities to utilize the county-produced service. Cleverly, the county put the cost of the service in the county tax rate, essentially forcing a municipality that chose to opt out of the county service to pay for it twice. The truly reluctant may continue to produce the service locally, but eventually the "free" service will be more attractive than keeping the costs in the municipal budget.**

In a shared service, the municipality and the county enter into a contract, which either entity can terminate under the conditions of the agreement. The municipality maintains the responsibility for service provision, turning over just the responsibility for service production to the county. It continues to budget for the service and make policy decisions about service levels and delivery, although the county must agree with the amount of compensation it receives and the service it delivers.

In a centralized service, the municipality transfers both provision and production responsibilities to the county. The municipality removes the service from the municipal budget and has no formal control over service delivery. It becomes a county function.

The county service offers economies of scale, if economies exist for this type of service. Because of scale, there is potential for increased expertise. In a centralized service, uniformity of service delivery across the county will usually result. This can lead to service equity (a positive) or inappropriate service levels (a negative), depending on the homogeneity of service needs. Local control is absent, except informally. Responsiveness and quality are dependent on the effectiveness of the operation the county establishes, as the literature shows. Whether the service is delivered locally or centrally does not directly determine the responsiveness and quality of the service.

Hybrid Service Delivery: Regional Policy Groups and Joint Boards

The arrangements covered above are reasonably comprehensive as a discussion of modes of service delivery. However, the field is evolving as governments seek better methods of service delivery, sometimes developing new forms of government to offset disadvantages arising from an existing service delivery arrangement. Regional policy groups and joint boards are two such forms. They may take other names and have variant implementations throughout the country and abroad, but their essence is a mechanism to re-introduce local control into a service delivery option in which the municipality has relinquished some of its responsibilities for service provision or production.

Regional policy groups counteract the loss of control that ensues when a municipality transfers service delivery responsibilities to other entities, most often counties or regionally operating contractors. The focus of their concern is both policy setting for provision and oversight for production. The chapter on *Optimal Service Delivery Arrangements* describes the Council of Governments in Monroe County, New York as a regional policy group. A regional policy group is usually formed when the county or a large city has taken over production for many service types. The group provides input from the constituent municipalities to the organizations actually delivering the service. The literature notes examples of regional policy groups that have been very effective in encouraging innovation and cooperation in restructuring how to deliver services when widespread consolidation of services was seen as necessary.

Regional policy groups are often part of a two-tier government structure. Although this is nothing more than a combination of local and regional delivery of services, it appears that the recognition of the need for a two-tier government is accompanied by an increased focus on the best way to deliver each service. From the statements in the literature, this is exactly what will be most effective in maximizing efficiency of government service delivery. Some two-tier governments cited in the literature have:

▶ Moved services needing a regional perspective (economic development) to a regional level

▶ Maintained labor-intensive and citizen responsive services at a local level

▶ Provided a regional council to encourage collaboration and cooperation, identifying optimal methods of service delivery, and providing local oversight of regional services

▶ Dissolved special districts that were poorly managed, moving the functions to a central or local level, as deemed appropriate

▶ Consolidated infrastructure intensive services previously delivered by multiple entities into single regional district authorities

▸ Developed revenue sharing schemes to finance services of regional importance

▸ Developed central facilities (such as vehicle fueling), taking advantage of bulk purchasing to service individual local departments

The joint board is a mechanism that combines the economies of scale in the production of the service without relinquishing local control over the decisions about providing the service. The joint board is a regional mechanism to control the preparation and distribution of a service, based on the provision decisions of the individual constituent municipalities. In that sense, it is the opposite of a regional policy group, but formed for the same reasons of keeping local control while increasing scale. It combines aspects of a regional special district with those of shared services.

The lines of the distinctions between service delivery arrangements are not rigid, and, in fact, the legal authorities vested in a government in a particular state create variations. Because the literature so often states that specific conditions foster specific service delivery responses, hybrid service delivery arrangements should be encouraged, particularly the customization of hybrid forms that are suggested by careful evaluation. Hybrids appear to be effective and usually result from an evaluation of specific issues and conditions. They are appealing because they utilize the advantages of an efficient delivery arrangement, while mitigating the disadvantages that are observed or anticipated in the non-hybrid service delivery arrangement.

Section II:

Details of Service Delivery

CHAPTER 7

An Inventory of Service Delivery Types

The examination undertaken in this book uses the existing literature on municipal efficiency and service delivery to determine if there are more optimal ways to do the business of local government. It appears the characteristics of service delivery types may be key to understanding how municipalities can increase the efficiency of delivering services. However, the literature lacks a comprehensive inventory of service delivery types and the characteristics that define them. Following is an attempt to assemble this inventory with characteristics that might provide insight into service delivery alternatives, leading to an understanding of which alternatives might optimize municipal efficiency.

To best summarize details about services and their characteristics, Table 1 that follows organizes all common municipal services and assesses the characteristics that define each one. Not all municipalities provide these services, although the fact that a municipality may contract out the service, determine not to provide it as a governmental function, or transfer it to a more central government, such as a county, is part of this overall examination. The intention is to provide the most complete base for further examination, noting the characteristics that distinguish the service from the norm of direct municipal production.

The service characteristics are those which may be important to consider to determine how best to provide the service. They involve the source of costs of the service, the types of skills required to deliver the service, the timing of the service, and whether factors outside the municipality are important to design the service. The specific definitions follow for the characteristics used in the table. The table displays "Y" if the characteristic is very evident for the service, "M" for moderate importance, and blank if the characteristic does not apply significantly.

Sources of Cost

The basic distinction is between personnel costs and other than personnel service costs. These may be termed Salaries and Wages, Other Expenses, Personnel Services (PS), or Other than Personnel Services (OTPS), depending on the region of the country. Personnel costs should include all costs related to employment, including benefits, payroll taxes, and pensions. In order to make good decisions about how to deliver municipal services cost effectively, it is also important in an evaluation of the service costs to be certain to include capital costs, which may not appear in a budget tied to the service area, and overhead costs, particularly related to the development and maintenance of the facilities to deliver the service. The table considers the total cost of delivering a service in three ways, which together should constitute all the costs to deliver the service.

▸ **Labor-intensive**—If personnel costs are the great majority of the costs of delivery of the service, the table displays a "Y".

▶ **Infrastructure-intensive**—If the majority of the costs are for facilities, expensive equipment, and infrastructure, the table displays a "Y".

▶ **Equipment-intensive**—If the majority of the costs is other than personnel services, not due to expensive equipment or infrastructure, but the service requires considerable equipment or supplies, the table displays a "Y". Note that costs of equipment, such as trash trucks, will seldom be the primary cost, but may be at about the same proportion to total costs as the salary and wages for the personnel to operate them.

Skills Required

The need for specific skills or equipment is the basis of these characteristics. Unlike the cost-oriented characteristics above, these characteristics are independent of each other. The service may require considerable amounts of more than one of the different characteristics.

▶ **Public Interaction**—If the majority of the time expended for this service involves interaction with the public, the table displays a "Y". The location for delivery of a service that requires public interaction affects the convenience to the public in need of the service.

▶ **Special Expertise**—If special expertise or a certification or license is required to deliver the service, the table displays an "M" or a "Y". The high expertise required may also be associated with specialized equipment that the personnel must be qualified to operate.

Timing of Delivery

Whether the municipality can control the timing of the delivery of a service and has flexibility in doing so may be an important factor for efficiency. The characteristics involving the timing of delivery are defined to be independent of one another. They may all be operative for the same service type.

▶ **On-Demand**—If the service requires an immediate response and the occurrence of the need cannot be predicted, the table displays a "Y". A service that can be scheduled by the municipality is the opposite of an On-Demand service.

▶ **Concurrent Demand**—If the service requires delivery at the same time by almost all municipalities but it does not require delivery at all times, the table displays a "Y". Leaf pick-up is a seasonal version of this characteristic and snow removal is an event-driven version. This characteristic limits the ability to share equipment because all municipalities need it at the same time.

▶ **Infrequent Demand**—If the service is rarely required, the table displays a "Y". The implication for efficiency of this characteristic is the need to have the capability available despite limited use.

External Perspective

The literature notes that coordination with surrounding municipalities in the design and delivery of some services produces better results for the region. The concept is that the vested interest of a municipality acting individually may produce a result less efficient or effective for the region and all the municipalities contained in it. For example, competition between municipalities can increase costs or decrease revenue for each of the municipalities.

▶ **Regional Outlook**—If the service will be better if a regional perspective is utilized, the table displays a "Y".

Table 7A: Service Characteristics

Service Types	Service Function	Costs			Skills		Timing			
		Labor Intensive	Capital Intensive	Equipment Costs	Public Interaction	Special expertise	On-demand	Concurrent Demand	Infrequent Demand	Regional Outlook
Public Works	Trash Collection	Y		Y						
Public Works	Roads—maintenance, sweeping	Y		Y						
Public Works	Snow removal	Y		Y			Y	Y		
Public Works	Leaf removal	Y		Y				Y		
Public Works	Buildings Maintenance	Y								
Public Works	Parks—grounds maintenance	Y								
Public Works	Storm Water and pollution control systems maintenance	Y		Y		M				M
Public Works	Waste Water systems maintenance	Y		Y		M				
Public Works	Water distribution systems maintenance	Y		Y		M				
Public Works	Forestry	Y		Y		M				
Public Works	Engineering					Y				
Public Works	Infrastructure replacement and development		Y			Y			Y	Y

(continued on next page)

(continued from previous page)

Service Types	Service Function	Costs			Skills		Timing			
		Labor Intensive	Capital Intensive	Equipment Costs	Public Interaction	Special expertise	On-demand	Concurrent Demand	Infrequent Demand	Regional Outlook
Police	Patrol	Y		M		M				
Police	Call response	Y		M		M	Y			
Police	Communications (equipment)			M		Y	M			Y
Police	Investigation					Y	M		M	
Police	Laboratory analysis			Y		Y			Y	
Police	Traffic control	Y		M						
Police	Records									
Police	Local ordinances	Y		M		M				
Dispatch		Y		M		M	Y			
Fire	Prevention									
Fire	Response			Y		M	Y			
Fire	Investigation					Y	M		M	
Fire	Inspections, regulations, records					M				
Fire	Equipment Maintenance				M	M				
EMS	Response			M		M	Y			
Public Health	Clinics, immunization	Y				M	M			
Public Health	Residential Inspection—infestations					M				
Public Health	Commercial Inspection					M				
Public Health	Environmental and sanitation					M				
Public Health	Animal Control	M				M	Y			
Public Health	Animal Shelter			Y						
Cultural/ Recreation	Children's programs	Y						M		M

Cultural/ Recreation	Adult Programs								M
Cultural/ Recreation	Senior Programs	M							
Management	General	Y			Y				
Management	Human Resources	Y			Y				
Management	Grants, insurance	Y			Y				
Tax Collection	Payments, customer service, records	Y			M	Y	M		
Tax Collection	Liens & bankruptcies	Y			Y	M			
Tax Assessment	Field work	Y			Y				Y
Tax Assessment	Records, customer service	Y			M	M			
Finance	Accounting, records				Y				
Finance	Purchasing, A/P	Y			M				
Court	Traffic records, pay, inquiries, trial	Y			M	Y			
Court	Criminal warrants, trial				Y	Y			Y
Court	Municipal Fines - pay, inquiries, trial	Y			M	Y			
Court	Neighbor disputes				Y				
Court	Records and other administration	Y			M				
Licensing, certifications	Dogs, Vital Statistics, mercantile	Y			M	Y			
Municipal records (clerk)	Minutes, Agendas, Ordinances, Resolutions	Y			M				
Municipal records (clerk)	Archiving and retrieval		Y		M				
Municipal Information	General and reception	Y			Y				
Elections					M	Y	Y	M	Y
Construction	Permitting and records	Y			M	Y			
Construction	Inspection	Y			Y				
Planning	Land use				Y				Y

(continued on next page)

(continued from previous page)

Service Types	Service Function	Costs			Skills		Timing			
		Labor Intensive	Capital Intensive	Equipment Costs	Public Interaction	Special expertise	On-demand	Concurrent Demand	Infrequent Demand	Regional Outlook
Planning	Development					Y				Y
Planning	Zoning	Y				M	Y			
Planning	Code Enforcement	Y				M	Y			
Technology	network, phones			M		Y	M		Y	
Technology	Public (web, e-commerce)			M		Y			Y	
Legal						Y			Y	
Transportation	Parking, buses, airports	M	Y							Y

Clearly, different types of services have different characteristics, and these characteristics may have implications for the most optimal manner in which to deliver the service. For example, police patrol is a labor-intensive service. As such, the literature suggests it does not provide economies of scale.

The explanation for the statement that labor-intensive services are not susceptible to economies of scale depends on the amount of service that can be produced by a unit of resources, such as a police officer. If one police officer can produce a given quantity of service, two officers must produce more than twice the original amount of service if economies of scale are operating. Alternatively, and more appropriate to the potential for cost-effective consolidation of services, doubling the total service can be accomplished with less of an increase than doubling the entire force, if economies of scale are operating. If a service is completely labor-intensive, the ratio between the number of units of resource and the number of units of service remains constant as an organization increases resource levels, resulting in no economies of scale. In fact, it is possible that the ratio of service to resources will decline with increased resource levels due to other factors, such as a need for proportionately more management resources.

Let us examine how economies of scale can operate to reduce costs per capita. One mechanism is through resources that are allocated in the budget that are not fully utilized or not utilized at their highest value in the pre-consolidated departments. This is not usually the result of poor planning. To the contrary, it is necessary to have resources beyond what is necessary for non-peak service needs so the municipality can respond to peaks or unforeseen service demands. A cooperative agreement is more efficient when it reduces the proportion of total resources that must be available for peak demand, but which are under-utilized at periods of non-peak demand.

When towns cooperate to deliver a service, they broaden the service area beyond that which was served by either of the original departments, individually. If the cost stays the same but the population served increases, it reduces the cost per capita. In practical scenarios, for the department taking over the cooperative service delivery, the cost will increase, but not proportionately as much as the service increases. Like any delivery option which benefits from economies of scale, there must be the potential for excess capacity in the pre-consolidated department due to the allocation of resources serving the original area, which can be used to advantage in a larger service area. The causes of the excess capacity may include equipment without adequate demand for full utilization, personnel with specialized skills without adequate demand to use those skills on a full-time basis, or staffing to meet peaks in service needs leading to the excess capacity during non-peak periods.

> **Excess capacity is a powerful factor in the efficiency of service delivery. We have found examples of implemented collaborations in which the pre-consolidated department had sufficient excess capacity to serve the post-consolidated area without adding resources of the service producer.**

A service which a municipality can schedule provides a good opportunity for sharing expensive equipment and spreading the costs over a larger population. Because the service is scheduled, conflicts arising from needing to use the equipment at the same time can be avoided. Alternatively, if personnel are not fully utilized by the one municipality, sharing those personnel may provide full use and, therefore, more total service for the same cost. This works well for specialized personnel, who, for example, have the training to operate complex equipment, but when that equipment is not in use, perform tasks other, less highly compensated, employees can perform. Using the specialist skills as fully as possible increases efficiency.

> **Services that are scheduled are easier to produce efficiently, but other factors can work against efficiency. In one case, a labor agreement required a full day's pay even if there is not sufficient work to be done throughout the day. Although this clause in an agreement is not unique, the practice had become to have the workers report for the day, even though the schedule was always light, and leave when the work was completed, about three hours later. Worse, there was more than one day in the week that was defined as light. In the face of the difficulties in changing the practice, the mayor sold the service production to a**

neighboring town at a very favorable contract price in order to utilize the excess capacity. The result was increased revenue to offset the artificially high costs of the service for the original town.

An example of such an arrangement is the use of trained personnel and equipment for tree removal in neighboring towns. By contracting for the employees and equipment to remove and trim trees, a smaller municipality does not need to incur the cost of owning the equipment used or to pay higher wage rates for the more skilled employee even when they are performing other tasks requiring less skill.

On-demand services are the opposite of services the municipality can schedule. Snow removal is an example. It would be attractive to be able to share expensive snow removal equipment, but this obviously is not feasible. In addition to the inability of the municipality to schedule the storm event and therefore the service reaction to it, snowstorms create a concurrent demand. That is, all nearby towns will need to perform the service at the same time. This difficulty is apparent with leaf collection, also, but over a longer period. It is difficult for towns to share a leaf vacuum, but not a street sweeper.

The fact that a service is scheduled is not the only criteria for effective cooperation, such as through a shared service. For an opportunity to exist to be more cost-efficient through cooperation, there must be a situation in which the workforce or equipment is not fully utilized at its highest use.

Even though police patrol is scheduled, it is required at all times, although with varying intensities to meet the perceived needs created by periods of varying illegal activity. On the surface, it is not practical to create a cooperative arrangement with another town because patrol cannot be limited to only certain times in the first town and to opposing times in the second town. In addition, although the municipality schedules police patrol, the component that is not scheduled, that is, response to criminal or other illegal activity, creates an on-demand service. The municipality needs to staff adequately to respond to this unpredictable activity, but without creating continual excess resources, which would be wasteful. We return to discussing police patrol in detail, after discussing labor-intensive services, and investigate the mechanisms that have made cooperation efficient.

Separating the sub-tasks in patrol and assigning targeted patrol activities to portions of the shift has reduced the number of officers that is perceived as required in well-managed operations. One such success used the CitiStat performance management model to identify targeted operations and reduce staff needs.

Labor-intensive services not only do not provide economies of scale, but several authors actually observed labor-intensive services producing diseconomies in larger towns. The logic is that merged police departments do not produce economies of scale because increased call volumes create a proportional increase in needed resources. Large police departments actually may be more inefficient than small ones because of the need to maintain appropriate supervisory span of control combined with the lack of economies of scale due to the labor-intensive nature of police patrol. As department head count increases, the need for administration grows. Although task-related work accomplished will increase proportionately with increasing staff to address increased service needs, the larger number of employees may require new layers of administration to manage the workforce. This results in a loss in productivity per employee, or increased cost per capita. This can lead to larger forces requiring proportionately more management staff.

Yet, many mergers of small police departments appear to have saved money and even improved the quality of service. The reality that makes this possible is the excess capacity that existed in the pre-consolidated departments that needed to provide minimum staffing levels. Even these minimum levels often were short of the recommended levels for appropriate backup and response. "Donut" and "donut-hole" towns are the best, but not the only, examples of successful mergers. The pre-merged "donut-hole" department may have scheduled at least one officer for patrol on all shifts, and may have used over-time personnel or leaned on its "donut" for backup and to provide coverage for vacation, sick days, court time, trips to the county jail, or other essential, but non-patrol, tasks. The merged department may adequately cover the "donut-hole" area without adding to its staff because they had excess capacity on the shift, which they now use to patrol the additional area and that is available for backup or coverage.

> In most right-sizing models of police patrol, once minimally adequate patrol levels are reached, needed patrol levels vary only with call volume, or service need. Small departments benefit from collaborations because minimally adequate patrol levels can be realized cost-effectively without creating excess capacity.

A careful evaluation of the feasibility of reducing costs and maintaining quality of service after the consolidation will reveal the ability to take advantage of excess capacities. Considering both scheduled patrol and on-demand response activities, a cooperative arrangement may work, if adequate coverage is possible while broadening the patrol area. The merger provides a better quality service if response and backup are improved by the cooperation, even as total staffing is reduced.

> In addition to a service consolidation providing better backup and response, some police departments that have merged have been able to justify specialized services, such as a detective bureau, without increasing the cost of the total police service. These specialized services benefit all the municipalities involved, unlike improved training and backup, which may be of prime benefit to the smaller of the merged departments.

This combination of an on-going scheduled activity and a response-oriented activity are found in other services in addition to police patrol. For example, public works employees are re-allocated for seasonal tasks and specific events, such as storm clean up. In Fire and EMS, mutual aid is a formalized mechanism to provide equipment and personnel when a neighboring town needs it, essentially responding to peaks in demand. This spreads the peaks in demand in one municipality over a broader area, which tends to smooth out the peaks. Mutual aid is usually provided without compensation on the assumption that every town is staffing adequately, making the cooperation "mutual." If this is the case, the use of other towns' resources will even out in the end.

Capital-intensive services, whether related to infrastructure or expensive equipment, can provide economies of scale. This is because a cooperative arrangement can use the same expensive equipment and facilities to serve a larger population.

Some types of service require specific employee skills, for example, a high level of expertise, licensing, or certification. Employees with specific training or experience often are paid more than general skill employees. There may be infrequent demand for this level of expertise, particularly in a small municipality. If these highly paid employees are used for tasks requiring lesser skills, cost per capita will be higher than if the general skill employee performs the same tasks. In essence, it represents an excess capacity because the skilled employee is not being used in tasks that represent the highest use of the employee. A cooperative arrangement between municipalities can reduce the amount of time spent in performing tasks not of highest use.

Services that require public interaction as a large part of the delivery process present different issues. Location of the delivery of the service can create inconvenience for the public or create a feeling of loss of local control. An example is a tax collection office providing assistance to seniors in the filing of forms for other tax payments or for reduction of tax obligations. This extra service can be performed in a larger municipality as well as a smaller municipality, but when the service is centralized this effort is often not available, or not available in a friendly, non-bureaucratic setting. The decision to provide this additional service is a policy decision, and is a decision that involves increasing costs, but it is a factor in evaluating service delivery options.

A quite different characteristic is present in services that benefit from a regional, or broader, outlook. Economic development, redevelopment, revitalization, and many land use planning services benefit a larger area than an individual municipality. These services should be evaluated differently for determining the best service delivery arrangement. Competition for tax ratables can have unhealthy consequences for every municipality in the region, raising the cost of attracting these ratables for all. The cost of financing large-scale revitalization or redevelopment may be prohibitive for an individual municipality, but the benefits of the investment may accrue throughout the region. The classic example of an urban revitalization appears throughout the literature, often in a depressed urban area that cannot finance the work without help from the suburban communities that surround it. The suburbs will realize the benefits of the revitalization, or, perhaps more pointedly, the disadvantages of a depressed downtown core will continue to affect the suburbs. This issue represents a policy decision that is frequently contentious and unstable.

Understanding the characteristics of the services a municipality delivers is a start to developing the optimal arrangements for service delivery. The discussion of the characteristics sometimes reveals immediate implications. In practice, the current situation in a municipality is a factor, as well as the existence of the potential for utilizing excess capacities more efficiently through cooperation or consolidation with other governments. Service delivery arrangements offer different features and benefits. Examining these is the next step to understanding optimal arrangements.

CHAPTER 8

Characteristics of Service Delivery Arrangements

Service delivery arrangements have different characteristics. These characteristics can represent advantages for government in some situations and disadvantages in others. To optimize how government delivers services to its public, it is important to examine these different characteristics to determine in which conditions the characteristic increases efficiency or effectiveness of the service to the public.

The literature describes most of these arrangements, but sometimes uses different terms or definitions (Stein, 1993; Dollery and Johnson 2005; Advisory Committee on Intergovernmental Relations, 1987; SEMCOG, 2003). Further, and most important, the literature does not detail the links between the service delivery arrangements and the types of service that benefit from those arrangements. This chapter provides a definition of each service delivery arrangement and then lists the features associated with it. There may be implementations of the service delivery arrangement that vary from the definition we provide, but it is important to use the same starting point so a reader in other regions or countries is not misled by different terminology.

Responsibility for Service Delivery

The literature makes an important distinction about the responsibility for service delivery. Where the responsibility lies can have important impacts on the service delivered because the locus of the responsibility determines the organization that is making decisions about the service and the organization that utilizes its resources to deliver the service. "Provision," the responsibility for the definition of the service, and "production," the responsibility for the actual delivery, is a straightforward distinction between policy and operations (Advisory Committee on Intergovernmental Relations, 1987). Policy decisions involve budgetary allocations and the related determinations about the quantity or frequency of the service to be delivered. These are governing body or council decisions. Operating decisions are the province of the department head or manager. They implement policy decisions through department operations.

Service Delivery Arrangements for Municipal Services as Defined by Delivery Responsibility

Service Delivery Responsibilities	Responsibility for Production	No Production Responsibility
Responsibility for Provision	Direct Delivery	Contract
No Provision Responsibility	Local Unit Production (uncommon)	Service Transfer

The combinations of responsibilities are a good starting point for understanding all the alternatives available to a municipality. The most common means of municipal service delivery is direct delivery (Stein, 1993). The municipality retains responsibility for both provision and production. The council determines how much will be delivered and adopts a budget to carry out the necessary tasks. The department head assures that the municipal staff performs tasks within the budget parameters established. Using an example of trash (solid waste) collection, the council may have determined that collection will take place once a week, with curbside pickup only, and only for residential properties. The council ordinance or law will probably be specific about what day is reserved for pickup in each area and what types of materials the town will pick up. The council will annually determine a budget to pay the employees and their benefits, provide the necessary equipment and facilities to perform the work, and maintain the equipment and facilities. This budget will be a combination of operating and capital costs, as determined by council.

Based on the definition of the service in the ordinance, and the personnel and equipment made available through the budget, the department head will schedule and direct his or her employees to complete the task. The department head will need to address missed pickups, equipment failures, weather conditions, employee absences and all the other realities presented by the task on a daily basis. Essentially, it is the responsibility of the department head to assure that the municipality delivers the service as described.

After direct delivery, the next most common form of service delivery is by contract (Stein, 1993). The council retains responsibility for provision, making all the decisions about the parameters of the service delivery, but it contracts the production to another entity that is not part of the municipal government. That is, none of the municipality's departments is involved in the service delivery.

The council will select a service producer and contract with that producer to deliver the service, as defined by council, compensating the producer. The producer may be another government, a private for-profit firm, or a non-profit organization. The contractor will have all the same responsibilities for assuring delivery of the service that the municipal department has in direct delivery of the service.

If a municipality relinquishes both the responsibility for provision and the responsibility for production, it has completed a service transfer. The service is still delivered to the municipality's public, but the municipality has no control over the amount of service, the cost of delivering the service, or the operations in the delivery of the service. If the service is not being delivered to the satisfaction of its citizens, the only recourse for the municipality (other than an informal request for resolution or political pressure) is to take back the responsibility for provision and production. This entails beginning to budget for the service delivery and developing the capacity to deliver the service. The municipality could take back responsibility for provision, but not production, allowing it to make the decisions about the parameters of the delivery of the service but contracting with another entity for the actual delivery.

It is not common for the municipality to retain the responsibility for service production to its municipal citizens but transfer provision to another organization, such as the county. Local unit production is another potential response to the hypothetical dissatisfaction with a total service transfer discussed in the prior paragraph. Operating decisions would then be in the hands of the municipality's employees. Snow plowing of county roads by the municipal public works staff is a common example of local unit production, although the agreement is informal, because logistics dictate it is more efficient and responsive to local needs.

Perhaps local unit production has a useful potential in a service such as policing. Efficiencies might be obtained by moving the budgeting and planning for police services to the county level along with administration and specialized investigations, but allowing the county to contract for neighborhood patrol with the local municipality. The question the municipality should ask is whether there would be either a perceived or a real advantage in the patrol officers being municipal rather than county employees. This is the type of question that the governing body should ask whenever it examines alternative structures for delivering a service.

> **Local unit production is an intriguing delivery mechanism that is not often considered in an evaluation of restructuring. Local people are involved in the service production, particularly the delivery, which in a function such as police patrol will please the citizens who want a police officer they know to bring their child home after an unfortunate event. The central level of provision and administration of production will lead to more efficient resource allocation decisions and the availability of greater expertise, when it is needed.**

Service transfers are far more common than they may appear to be. What one state or country might consider a service transfer is an institutionalized and accepted way of providing a public service in another. For example, Virginia has long provided and produced fire services at the county level, but New Jersey considers fire protection a municipal service. These differences afford opportunities to analyze the relative efficiency of services located at different levels of governments. Such an analysis, although not the subject of this book, could provide direction about potentials for service transfers that might increase efficiency.

> **We have heard very different numbers sometimes quoted for the cost of specific services in different states, but they sometimes do not hold up as comparable numbers when they are scrutinized further.**

Why is it important who is responsible for delivering a service and what resources the organization has available? Most simply, it may affect the cost of delivering the service. In addition, there are many other criteria for evaluating service delivery. Some are more or less important depending on the type of service the organization is delivering. The organization responsible for the service delivery makes the decisions about the characteristics of service delivery that are important and determines the public benefits it will emphasize through the mode of service delivery it chooses. It makes these decisions in the context of the resources it has available and can reasonably provide through its budget.

The four general service delivery arrangements defined above by the responsibility for provision and production of the service are important because they determine what decisions the municipality must or can make. In the details of municipal practice, the responsibility for provision divides further into planning and funding. For some services, the municipality may plan the service and determine the level of service, but it may transfer the funding responsibility. (One such mechanism is a franchise arrangement such as cable TV.) Service production divides further into the actual production or preparation of the service and the distribution of it. (Stein, 1993) Delineating the responsibilities this finely may maximize the benefits of the service delivery arrangement in specific situations and for specific service types.

In addition to distinguishing the components of responsibility for service delivery, other considerations about service delivery expand the options. Service delivery arrangements have different characteristics and, therefore, different advantages and disadvantages depending on the conditions and factors present in the municipal situation. Looking further at the characteristics of service delivery will provide us with criteria that we can use to evaluate any proposed model of service delivery.

Characteristics of Service Delivery Arrangements

The examination of the characteristics of the service delivery options begins with two primary factors that change the characteristics of service delivery by modifying the breadth of resources used to deliver the service. The first is the size of the service area (scale), which is related to the quantity and cost of resources that can be efficiently devoted to the service area. The second is the multiplicity of services delivered by the same entity (scope), which promotes the efficient use of internal capacities. The conventional wisdom is that there are economies of scale in larger size service areas. Economies of scope get less attention, because most municipalities use their internal capacities to deliver a full range of services, thereby maximizing economies of scope. However, examination of service delivery mechanisms affecting both economies of scale and economies of scope is appropriate.

In service delivery, size matters. However, size does not always matter in the manner conventional wisdom suggests. A government should always consider the optimal scale of the operation producing the service. In some cases, there are economies of scale, but in others, there are diseconomies. One should compare other delivery alternatives against direct delivery of service by the municipality to determine how scale operates for the service type and the conditions of the service.

Although the literature suggests that labor-intensive services show diseconomies of scale, we have not examined alternative delivery methods that might reduce scale in a large municipality to increase efficiency in labor-intensive services. Little has been written on mechanisms for reducing scale in a large municipality. The authors have limited this book to structural alternatives for delivery that involve other organizations, rather than techniques for achieving efficiency within an organization. Organizational or management techniques that reduce supervisory and administrative efforts should help reduce the inefficiency of a larger organization.

> There are factors beyond the structure of a delivery mechanism, such as culture and management of an organization, that determine efficiency. Both in New Jersey and New York, for example, local officials express concern about county governments and their ability to support local municipal service delivery efficiently. Yet, some counties have proven their ability to produce services more effectively or coordinate production for the municipalities. These conflicting views occur because the structural benefits of centralized (i.e., county) service delivery are sometimes offset by management variations in structurally similar organizations.

For labor-intensive services, the number of employees required producing the service and their compensation is the primary cost driver. Supervisory and administrative tasks require additional employees, but do not produce additional service, decreasing the efficiency of the service. In other words, for each unit increase in resources, the amount of increase in service is smaller than it was for the prior units of resources, due to management factors, such as added supervision. This is a diseconomy of scale.

There is a need for a conclusive study of the diseconomies of scale in labor-intensive service delivery types in order to avoid the tendency to operate on the erroneous "bigger is better" philosophy. Policing is the most prominent example of a labor-intensive service and is the largest cost driver among municipal services. The prior chapter discusses police patrol as a service type and then examines the underlying explanations for why economies of scale may or may not deliver increased efficiency. However, a definitive study of policing costs related to municipal size would be helpful to those who must make decisions about optimal service delivery arrangements. Conclusive results would mitigate the tendency to make decisions based on the conventional wisdom of economies of scale even when addressing labor-intensive services.

If a service becomes less labor-intensive because of the introduction of specialized technologies, economies of scale may make a difference. For example, introducing information technology to back office processing can result in significantly reduced labor needs required to perform repetitive and routine tasks. Collaborative efforts that increase the scale of the service production may be required to fund and implement the specialized technology. (Dollery, et al, 2009) The discussion of scope of services indicates that technology improvements to support other services are more readily justified when the technology costs are spread over more services.

While the argument based on diseconomies of scale has been effective and has had an impact on the emphasis on municipal consolidation, it has not been effective in mitigating the instinct to propose sharing police services and other scale increasing mechanisms even for these labor-intensive services. It is important either 1) to use the finding of diseconomies of scale to refute the conventional wisdom or 2) to demonstrate the inappropriateness of the interpretation of those studies showing diseconomies of scale, so that practitioners can revisit the notion of consolidation with new "facts." Succinctly put, it is inconsistent to argue against municipal consolidation on the grounds of diseconomies of scale and for consolidation of police services on the grounds of economies of scale.

For services that benefit from economies of scale, several different delivery structures increase the scale of the service producing organization. They include shared services, regionalization, and centralization. Privatization may also increase scale, if the contractor chosen provides the specific service to other governments or to a larger population. It is important to compare the other implications of these different arrangements, because, although they all increase scale, they have different characteristics. Only through a specific analysis can a municipality determine what provides the best array of features for its particular situation and goals.

Economies of scale may produce efficiencies for some services, but consolidating service delivery to achieve these economies can lead to the loss of local control in service delivery. The municipality should evaluate the specific mechanism proposed to achieve economies of scale to determine if it reduces local control, if the loss is important, and if there is an alternative mechanism or variation to mitigate the loss.

Scope of services is another technique to use resources more fully. Unlike scale, the increased use is not through servicing a bigger population, but by providing more and broader services to the same population. The increase in efficiency is a result of overhead and internal administrative capacities that the government uses for multiple, rather than individual, services, thereby spreading some of these costs over more services. Most municipalities provide a range of services, so the use of the facility and of the capacities for information technology, management, purchasing, and finance are spread through all of the public services the municipality provides. The cost, as well as the use, of the facilities and internal capacities is spread through all of the public services, also.

The efficiency gains realized by increasing the scope of services are not usually available to municipalities, because the common use of direct service delivery by municipalities creates a large scope of services, usually encompassing all public services that are provided locally. That is, municipalities generally have optimized their scope of services. Increase in the scope of services is possible if the municipality has created separate special districts in the past. Reducing the scope of services, which occurs when the municipality forms a special district to carry out a specific function, leads to increased fragmentation. Since special districts provide only one or two services, the cost of their facilities, other overhead resources, and internal capacities are borne by only these services. Here we must ask the question, "Does the focus on a specific service or other particulars offset the potential redundancy in overhead and administration from the formation of multiple service delivery organizations?" Scope can be increased by consolidating these districts back into the municipalities, by contracting back for administrative services from the municipality, or by creating regional service entities that provide a multitude of services. The latter two are not common, but the dissolution of special districts is getting increased attention in some states.

The two basic ways to change the characteristics of service delivery involve changes in scale and scope. However, there are a number of ways to increase or decrease both and there are many other characteristics of service delivery that are affected when these or other changes are made. Discussing the characteristics and then examining their relationship to these arrangements will help reveal the benefits of different arrangements. However, the initial discussion should concentrate on these characteristics or features and relate them to the different service delivery mechanisms, avoiding the determination of what is a benefit or what is a disadvantage. Describing them as benefits or disadvantages requires value judgments, an important aspect of policy decisions and politics. It is best to leave those judgments for the final analysis by the municipality when it determines the optimal arrangement in its specific context. We have attempted to help in the final analysis by presenting different sides of each feature.

Broadening a service area, either through increases in scale or scope, has a number of implications. Because more resources are available while maintaining the cost per unit served (per capita, per household, or another unit appropriate to the service), greater expertise in the production of the service is available. Although increased expertise is useful, it can lead to unnecessary specialization. Specialization is not only costly, but it can lead to a more bureaucratic response to the public.

Homogeneity of services often is affected by consolidating into a larger service area, through techniques such as regionalization or centralization, in which the provision decisions are made by a larger organization. Service delivery options such as contracting, whether to a non-governmental organization or a shared service, put service production in the hands of a larger organization, but keep the provision decisions at home. The natural tendency, within any organization making provision decisions, is to provide equity, that is, the same level of service to all constituents or the areas in which they live. Hence, consolidating provision decision-making will usually create homogeneity of service over the entire region consolidated.

Equity is a good thing. Or is it? In public health, we consider equity beneficial because it indicates adequate health services are provided to all parts of the population, rich and poor alike.

But if the population has varied service needs, equity concerns may waste scarce resources. It is easier to see this in a service type like street sweeping. Commercial areas need frequent sweeping to maintain cleanliness because of the use of the area. Providing street sweeping with the same frequency to residential areas would be equitable, but it would be a waste. In heterogeneous populations, one needs to look at the fit of the service level to the service need.

A broadened perspective can be effective for service types like economic development. Left to their own devices, individual municipalities have been known to compete against their neighbors for ratables, giving larger concessions than necessary to a developer in order to win the ratable chase. Yet a broadened perspective, even in land use planning, can lead to ignoring important differences in needs. This is reflected in concerns of small commercial centers, when they evaluate a consolidation with suburban townships. The regional outlook must factor in the local concerns of the constituent municipalities, but balance them for the good of the region as a whole.

A related benefit of a broadened perspective is spreading the tax burden over a larger area. A downtown revitalization project in an inner city may not be possible if the costs must be raised from the inner city tax base alone. The wealthier suburbs can contribute to the revitalization and may be seen as benefitting from the revitalization of the urban core. On the other hand, this strategy has led to conflict when not all stakeholders have perceived the same value in broadening the tax base.

Broadened perspective is achieved by service delivery arrangements that site the responsibility for provision decisions in a more centralized or regional organization. Contracts do not have that effect, since the decisions on the type of service to provide remain with the municipality. Centralization, regional special districts, joint boards, and regional policy groups do.

Competition is a characteristic of service delivery options. Proponents of increased competition feel there are two primary benefits. First, competition will lead to better performance and reduced costs. The primary mechanism to increase competition is privatization, but increased competition results from any attempt to solicit bids or proposals for the production of a service from a range of producers. The market of bidders may include private firms, not-for-profit organizations, or other governments.

Service types that have a high degree of asset specificity decrease the competitiveness of the market. That is, where the expertise and resources used to produce and distribute the service cannot be used for other clients, vendors (particularly for-profit organizations) are less likely to respond to a request for proposals, decreasing the competition. A reduced market of competitors will tend to increase the cost of the contract and make it harder to terminate the contract because of limited ability to find another producer (Brown and Potoski, 2003).

A second perceived benefit of competition is the result of intergovernmental competition. It has no impact on efficiency in the operational sense. Competition between municipalities creates an environment in which municipalities can create their own unique tax and service packages in an attempt to attract businesses and residents (Sancton, 2001a). Some service delivery alternatives increase this form of competition. Fragmentation increases inter-municipal competition; consolidation decreases it. This is a result of the impact of fragmentation or consolidation on the number of governments, which relates to inter-governmental competition. Inter-governmental competition is implicit in the consideration of the attractiveness of the mix of services and tax costs for residents and businesses. Alternatives that promote greater competition between municipalities provide more choices for the public. This is directly opposed to a broadened perspective, which attempts to reduce competition seen as unfavorable.

Defining Service Delivery Arrangements

Service delivery options are often defined or restricted by the laws of the state or country in which they exist. The laws can constrain and define the authority granted to some of the entities formed to deliver services and may restrict the flexibility of the arrangements between entities. Further, conditions in a specific government may alter the potential benefits or disadvantages of the concept.

Because of differences in what state law allows or different histories of municipal services and levels of government utilized to deliver services, the same term may be defined differently in different states, regions, or foreign countries. In order to minimize confusion that could result from different regional use or even different use by different authors, it is important to have an agreed upon definition of each of the terms for service delivery arrangements. The resulting list will help to analyze and compare the concepts and prepare the reader by providing a flexible menu from which to choose in configuring an optimal delivery mechanism for specific conditions. The following is the base inventory of service delivery arrangements and a definition of each term this book uses:

Direct Delivery

The norm is direct delivery of services. The municipality plans, funds, prepares, and distributes the service using its own facilities, equipment, and personnel. No other entities are involved. All other service delivery alternates should be compared to direct delivery as a baseline option for municipal service delivery.

Shared Services

Shared services, or inter-governmental agreements, are a contract from the municipality, which retains responsibility for provision of the service, to another municipality or other government, which takes responsibility for the production of the service. The government that produces the service, sometimes referred to as the lead agency, is compensated for delivering the service according to the agreement. The personnel used to deliver the service are employees of the lead agency, and the equipment and facilities used customarily belong to the lead agency. The benefits are those of economies of scale for services in which they obtain. Although the contracting municipality retains responsibility for providing the service and makes the decisions that determine the quantity and quality of the service (which must be part of the agreement with the contractor government), the contractor government controls the service distribution within the agreement. Residents of the contracting municipality will see the logos and personnel of the contractor delivering the service.

Shared services are no different from privatized services, except for the empathy of the service provider. Whether the costs are different is a matter of analyzing the proposals from both government and private providers. Because of the lack of collegiality with a private vendor, it may be more difficult to monitor the services of a private provider and more difficult to terminate the contract. Hence, services that are more likely to risk failure when contracted are more likely to be awarded to a government provider through shared services, even if a private provider might be less expensive (Brown, 2008).

The benefit of the economies of scale will vary with the specifics of the situation and service type. Governments acting as contractors will have a more restricted geographic range of service delivery. A private provider may deliver the service nationally and, therefore, be able to justify the acquisition of better resources (expertise and equipment) to get the job done more efficiently.

Not-for-profit entities are another possible source of contracted service delivery. Again, in theory, there are no actual differences from shared services or privatized services. In reality, the type of service and the nature of the non-profit organization may make the contract more or less advantageous. If the non-profit has the service type within its mission, it may bring to the contract expertise, passion, and willingness to share in the cost of the delivery. Passion is a two-edged sword. It is important for the contracting municipality to be certain the service will be produced in a manner consistent with its provision decisions, particularly if those decisions are in conflict with the mission of the non-profit.

Joint Services

Joint services are very similar to shared services. An agreement between two or more governments creates a joint service, but there is no lead agency, and the distinction between the contracting municipality and the contractor government is not appropriate. All partners are involved in the production of the service. This type of contract is not common, but examples are found in New York State, both in terms of some of the agreements in place and in the state-provided information that encourages both shared and joint services, distinguishing between the two terms.

The practical implication of the distinction between joint and shared services is that employees and equipment will be from all the partners. This can be done by an agreement that provides for each partner to pay a specified percentage of the costs for labor, equipment, facilities, and operating costs. The actual ownership (or employment) of the resources will be attached to one of the partners. However, all partners may make decisions about the resources.

The New York State Commission on Local Government Efficiency & Competitiveness (2008) elaborates on joint services, comparing the implications of alternative arrangements. The personnel can be employed separately by all the parties or by only one of the governments. The latter removes variation in pay scales but may be more difficult to construct so that the agreement remains a joint venture. Debt provides another issue in a joint agreement. It can be incurred individually or allocated among the constituent members with joint liability. The debt statements will only contain the portion allocated to the individual municipality, however.

An example that existed for eighteen years was constructed to maximize the joint nature of the agreement. The joint services agreement for public works in New York between the Village and Town of Cobleskill signed in 2007 indicates both governing bodies must appoint the same Superintendent (personal communication, S. Veith and K. Hotopp, , governing body members, May 22, 2009). The Superintendent receives two paychecks, since he works for both governments. The Town pays the benefits and any other costs, such as training, and vouchers the Village for half of these costs. In a similar manner, the Town invoices for the costs of maintaining the facility and equipment used to provide public works services. The employees are employed individually by either the Town or the Village, but no vouchering occurs.

The Superintendent has authority to make operational decisions, including purchasing supplies and equipment. A Highway Committee, comprised of two members of the Town Council and two members of the Village Board, reviews the overall performance of the Highway Department and recommend adjustments to the agreement to each governing body. As with any agreement between two parties, each body individually must approve these adjustments. The Superintendent reports to the executive in the Town (Town Supervisor) and Village (Mayor), but he has a wide berth in running the department. Each party purchases and maintains their own vehicles, although there have been joint purchases for vehicles or equipment that are needed in both the Town and Village.

The benefits and disadvantages of joint services are similar to those of shared services, but there are some important differences. In joint service agreements, both towns make provision and production decisions, the former through the governing bodies and the latter through the staff, which may be jointly appointed or may be employees of either partner with a reporting relationship to each partner or to the joint oversight body. This limits the sense of loss of control, both on the part of the governing body and the public. Depending on the situation, the logo of an individual town may even appear on the vehicles most often used to provide the service in that town, but when needed, the department head may allocate the other town's vehicle to provide the service. Therefore, although there is a lessened loss of identity, the ability to use a wider resource pool to get the job done means a reduction in service delays and a reduction in costs to maintain adequate backup resources.

The jointly appointed department head (in Cobleskill, the Superintendent) must be adept at serving two masters and making allocation decisions that satisfy both. The partners and their elected officials must be willing to make it work and not resort to too careful accounting that may scuttle the flexibility necessary in order to save money for the total enterprise. The joint services agreement has been successful for eighteen years, saving hundreds of thousands of dollars. However, it was slated to be dissolved. The Village will dissolve their Highway Department and remove its cost from its budget but continue to receive highway services from the Town.[51] There will not be an immediate reduction in costs, but the Highway Committee expects an increase in administrative efficiency. The need to separate out the costs and to account for the use of personnel in each town will disappear, freeing the Assistant Superintendent to do other tasks in this small, combined department of twelve.

New York State, like many other states, has felt increased pressure to increase local government efficiency. The joint service agreement in the Cobleskill's, successful for eighteen years, may have paved the way for the more drastic step of dissolving the department in the Village, a municipality that watches its services carefully to make sure it gets its fair share of services in its role as a commercial center for the county. In better financial times, the balance was tilted in the direction of the Village incurring extra costs to make sure the service levels were adequate. Priorities everywhere are changing.

Contracting

Contracting, often termed privatization, is very similar to shared services from a legal point of view, but removes government from the production of the service. The municipality awards a contract to produce the service (that is, prepare and distribute the service) to another entity. If that entity is another government, it is a shared service agreement. The discussion above of shared services compared them to contracts with for-profit and not-for-profit organizations to provide the service. Some studies have shown that privatizing can result in lower costs than direct delivery, but the amount of outsourcing that municipalities initiate is closely matched by the amount of times the municipality brings the service delivery back for direct delivery (Feiock, et al, 2004). The literature assumes this is because the municipality finds the service quality is less than expected.

One situation that sometimes occurs is that the municipality never fully realizes the expected reduction in the budget when a service is outsourced, but it now has a new cost of the contract. The most common reason for this is not reducing the staffing by the total amount that was budgeted prior to the service contract. The employees that were budgeted for the now outsourced service may have also been performing other tasks. If the municipality retains the employees to continue to perform these other tasks, the budget will not be fully reduced, so overall costs increase even if these employees are now assigned to other tasks. This impact holds with equipment, also, because a municipality commonly uses equipment resources for more than one service.

---

[51] This is not as unusual as it appears, given the taxing structure in New York. Village residents pay a village tax in addition to the town & county tax, which Town residents pay. Therefore, they are still paying for the service through the town & county portion of their tax bill. When the dissolution of the Village Highway Department occurs, Village taxes will decrease, but Town taxes will increase slightly.

An example is the outsourcing of solid waste. One community is considering returning to direct delivery of the solid waste collection service, although it has not had quality issues with the contractor. The reason to take back the responsibility is to reduce costs, which, oddly, is the same reason the municipality outsourced solid waste about five years prior. The outsourcing avoided capital costs at the time, because the municipality needed new trucks both to replace those that it had not maintained properly since the municipality began using one-man trucks and to respond to population growth. When the contract began, the municipality retained most of the employees formerly involved in garbage collection to do buildings and grounds maintenance, which was underserved for many years. Although the budgeted costs for solid waste did not increase, the cost for all public works activities did. If they bring the service back in-house, it is not certain they will recognize the need to increase budgeted costs for buildings and grounds maintenance.

The lesson here is to be realistic in the evaluation of projected costs for any new initiative, whether it is total municipal consolidation or the outsourcing of a single service. It is important to understand what the reaction of the public, the employees, and bargaining units will be, so that the new initiative does not produce greater costs when some intended changes cannot practically be realized. To fully understand the implications of any initiative, it may be necessary to dig deeper than the budget and expenditure categories to determine how resources are really used. Unfortunately, the tendency of municipalities to be imprecise in the allocation of costs to sub-categories of expense can be misleading.

One of the disadvantages of privatization is that the municipality loses the capacity to produce the service. If the contract goes awry, the municipality may not be prepared to begin again to produce the service. If it reduced its costs by contracting out, it must have lost its employees skilled in this area and may have sold its equipment necessary to prepare and distribute the service. Joint production or joint contracting mitigates this disadvantage of privatizing while taking advantage of reduced costs through privatizing. Essentially, the municipality retains some of the responsibility to produce the service, thereby retaining the capacity, at least partially, to bring the service back in house. It contracts only for a specified portion of the service delivery and keeps its hands in the remaining portion.

Competitive Contracting

Finding the means to deliver a service most efficiently can also involve inter-governmental competition. Competitive contracting is the term for the mechanism to allow the municipal department to propose a service solution and cost, as an option to proposals of other governments or private organizations. The municipality solicits proposals for the service but allows its own department to compete for the work. Competitive contracting is well established in some municipalities and has been increasing in popularity nationwide. Some of the benefits of the municipal department competing for and being awarded the service delivery contract are the retention of the knowledge of the service within the municipality, the boost in employee morale, and the potential to use the resources for other purposes when the service need wanes.

> Competitive contracting can be achieved informally. One manager has eliminated several private contracts by re-organizing the work force. For example, by combining all maintenance activities in one department that were previously provided by several departments, the excess capacity was used to provide services that were previously contracted, reducing the overall cost of maintenance activities.

The municipality that chooses to outsource the service production to another entity may include other governments in its solicitation of vendors to bid on the contract. If a government is successful in winning the contract, essentially the municipality has introduced competition into the development of a shared service agreement. When we compared shared services to privatization, we recognized that municipalities would rather contract with another government because it is easier to monitor the contract or to terminate it. This is because of the perceived collegiality between the parties, both of whom are in the business of providing government services. This bond is the basis of the perceived ease of monitoring the contract. It is not actually easier to monitor; rather there just does not seem to be the need to do it as comprehensively as when a for-profit firm is the contractor. The contractor's need to make a profit is also missing if the contractor is a government, so there may be greater "slack" in providing better quality even if costs of delivery of the service begin to approach the contract compensation. Another government may also be less likely to know precisely, or to care, when the point of losing money on the contract is approaching.

> In comparing costs for a private contractor and a government contractor, it is important to look at all costs, even indirect, of the mechanism to produce the service. Woodbridge Township, New Jersey recently took over the custodial services for its School District (Hutchins, 2010). The district had originally gone out for private bids, but the Township offered a competitive price through a shared services contract. The analysis of the costs of the two alternatives included other items of total cost such as unemployment insurance and other services, which were already provided by the Township. The Township rehired many of the school employees, avoiding unemployment payments, and included snow plowing, which they had been doing. Woodbridge Township has bid on other contracts as a way to increase its revenues and utilize excess capacities.

In the real world, all of the things that purport it is easier to cooperate with another government can be true. However, they are not guaranteed. In tougher financial times, the contractor municipality will have more pressure to deliver the service at less cost than the contract compensation. If they have expanded resources based on the revenue expected from the contract, they may be less friendly about terminating the contract. However, there also is an inherent reason a government bidding on the service production has lower costs. A contracting municipality does not have the same marketing and contract administration costs. The private firm is built to compete, and willing to spend money to do so.

Governmental entrepreneurship takes competition another step further and puts the municipality soliciting contracts on more equal footing with for-profit organizations. The municipal department bids on contracts to produce services for other governments. This is akin to what the lead agency is doing in a shared service or inter-governmental agreement. However, some municipalities have developed the competitive capability to solicit additional work and respond to requests for proposals from other municipalities. This provides a source of revenue to offset the costs of delivering the service to their own municipality, utilizes excess capacity, and takes advantages of economies of scale, such as fostering the development of specialized expertise in their staff and the acquisition of resources or equipment allocated to the service. These entrepreneurial governments have an advantage over non-government competitors in winning a contract because they are perceived as requiring less capacity for contract monitoring by the municipality seeking a service producer. It is assumed they know the needs of governments and will meet those needs without prodding or significant oversight.

When a municipality engages in governmental entrepreneurship, there may be a line, on one side of which the competing government is able to propose and produce the service at less cost than a for-profit organization can. On the other side, the competing government may get good enough at competing that they are willing to spend money and resources on the act of competing. This new capacity may drive their costs up as they devote resources to the administrative tasks of bidding and competing. No matter what the situation, it is wise for the government seeking a contractor to evaluate all of the proposals completely, even from other governments, but without driving up the total costs of the service delivery inappropriately through a lengthy bidding process.

Franchises

This is a form of service delivery, which governments only consider narrowly. The SouthEast Michigan Council Of Governments (SEMCOG, 2003) lists it, appropriately, as a service delivery mechanism. The government only has responsibility for provision of the service, and only for the planning portion, at that, since the funding for the service is part of a direct agreement between the franchisee and the citizen. Examples are cable TV and garbage collection. The advantage of this mechanism is that the government negotiates the contract with the private provider and licenses the provider as a supplier. By negotiating for the entire municipality, the government obtains a less expensive price than the citizen would individually. The study in New York State (Community Benchmarks Program, 1999) of comparative costs of different methods of garbage collection showed the government-controlled negotiation does reduce the cost to the citizen.

> One advantage of the franchise is the reduction of costs for the vendor, which the vendor can pass to the citizen. Towns that determine not to provide the service and allow the market to determine which vendors will provide the solid waste collection and at what cost to each citizen, individually, are creating a scenario in which each vendor covers the same routes as every other vendor, stopping only for their customers. The franchise agreement brings efficiency to the system by designating a single vendor for the area. Franchises can combine the advantages of privatization, such as cost reduction and regulation of the service delivery, with the advantage of limited government involvement and very limited costs. The government abandons the delivery of the service, but represents the interest of the public through regulation.

Perhaps this mode of service delivery deserves more attention and creative application. It uses government as the regulator, but that is the limit of the government involvement. Tax-based cost will be very low, because the only resources that the government will expend will be for administration of the franchise agreement. Both sides of the municipality's budget, revenue and appropriations, should decrease accordingly. Franchising requires that the service is one that has a competitive market of providers, although even with near monopolies, government's involvement seems to pay off for the public.

Vouchering

Vouchering is similar to abandonment of service production, except the local government retains the responsibility for funding the service and, depending on the circumstances, defining the service. This mechanism allows the citizen to choose the producer of the service, but provides a voucher for payment. (Dollery, et al, 2009) As a variation on vouchering, if the government identified a service producer, it could create efficiencies for the vendor, which could be passed on to the citizen, and it could negotiate the contract. Otherwise, unless the service represents a social good that the government requires its citizens to obtain, there seems little reason that the government chooses to pay for a service from general taxes without retaining responsibility for defining the service. Education fits this description and there is a great deal of interest in vouchering among some officials. This interest stems from a concern over quality of education, particularly as it is delivered to some segments of the population.

Co-production

Co-production is another mode of service delivery that limits government involvement and reduces tax-based cost. In this case, the client or citizen is part of preparing and distributing the service (Advisory Committee on Intergovernmental Relations, 1987). Volunteerism is an informal version of this, although the municipality may structure the volunteerism in order to improve its benefits and reduce the potential for other disadvantages. Neighborhood watches to augment public safety services offered by the municipality are examples of co-production.

Volunteerism is used frequently in smaller municipalities as a way to deliver services without additional costs. For example, members of the governing body may handle administrative responsibilities, which would fall to the office of the administrator or manager in larger communities. These responsibilities could include human resource functions and detailed budget preparation. Events in small towns are often organized by volunteers, both from the governing body and from the involved citizenry. Volunteerism can save tax costs and provide the small town America community, which many people desire. The downsides are reduced professional expertise in the operations and the difficulty of retaining the volunteer base.

Co-production may also be accomplished with a non-government organization that is the beneficiary of the services. Private homeowner associations reduce the need for municipal services because the association chooses to provide the service according to its own specifications. If state law or local practice requires a refund of the tax-based cost savings to the association, there may be no real reduction in governmental costs, depending on the amount of the refund.

The potential for efficiency gains through co-production is very dependent on the specific circumstances. If the co-producer is motivated or has specific needs not easily met by the municipality, and makes the service delivery easy to administer, benefits could accrue. Because the producer is also the client, much of the benefit may be less tangible than cost reductions, such as increased civic engagement and resulting identification with the community.

Special Districts

Special districts are created by the municipality to deliver a specific service or services. They are an additional government and may have taxing or rate-setting authority and ability to incur debt, often with voter approval. Some have an elected governing body, but others have an appointed board. The advantage of these added governments is the focus on a single service, or a few related services. Water and sewer utilities and fire districts are examples. The municipality transfers all responsibility for both providing and producing the service to the special district. It represents a service transfer, but creates a new government rather than utilizing an existing one.

Proponents of special districts feel the nature of the service requires specific expertise, but this is questionable because most of these services are provided in other areas through municipal government, acquiring the expertise that is needed by hiring, training, or contracting. One service, education, is accomplished in most states through special districts, although these districts are often creatures of the state, rather than being created by municipalities. Because of the size of the education enterprise and the public perception of its importance, education is uniformly believed to benefit from a different administration than municipal government, so its status as an additional government is not questioned.

> There are other indications of how differently governments perceive the administration of schools. A different set of laws often exists for the same administrative functions in municipalities and schools. New Jersey, for example, has two sets of laws for public purchasing, and two different state government departments monitor adherence to these rules. There is no apparent need for the differences, yet the purchasing practices are different.

For other special districts, there have been periods when they are in vogue and others in which states or municipalities have curtailed their use. In order to provide better monitoring of performance and cost, districts have been dissolved to bring the service back under the auspices of municipal government. Because of their arms-length distance from public scrutiny and the restricted focus on a single service, in many states and in specific situations, management abuses have occurred in special districts. If the board is appointed, the only mechanism for monitoring and correcting the service delivery is through the appointment process, but that is an infrequent event. If the board is elected, usually the voter turnout is very small and disinterested because of the lack of interest for just one service. Often the light turnout is exacerbated by elections that are not held at the same time as the November elections for most government positions.

The offsetting point to the perceived benefit of a focus on a specific service is the need to replicate the administrative functions and resources available in the municipal government. If the special district serves an area totally within the municipal boundaries (some serve only part of the municipality), there are no economies of scale to offset the loss in economies of scope that would be gained if the municipality provided the administrative functions to support the service. Regional districts can change the balance if increase in scale produces benefits.

Regional Districts

A regional district is a special district formed by multiple municipalities to provide a service or several related services. As with a special district, creating a regional district results in an additional government, but if the services around which the regional district is formed benefit from economies of scale, the scale of the regional district may offset the disadvantages of duplicating administrative functions. Without any correcting mechanism, a regional district, due to its multiple municipal masters, intensifies the issue of distance from municipal or public scrutiny that exists in a special district, which operates within the confines of a single municipality.

Municipalities often form regional districts for services that are capital-based, which takes advantage of economies of scale. Water and sewer infrastructure provides a good example. Fire response is another example because of the expensive equipment, the costs of which spread over a larger area become a much more efficient use of resources than having the same piece of equipment owned by every municipality in order to provide appropriate public protection.

Joint Meeting

Multiple municipalities may form a joint meeting, usually for one, or several related services. Representatives of the founding municipalities manage it and set its policies on service delivery (provision). A joint meeting is a separate corporation, but it has no taxing or rate setting authority and cannot incur debt. The constituent municipalities provide its funding. The board of representatives hires the staff as part of their policy-making responsibilities.

A joint meeting is a regional district with mechanisms to provide much improved oversight. The board consists of municipal representatives, fostering the involvement of each municipality in the performance of the joint meeting. Further, the approval of the funding for the joint meeting brings public transparency at each constituent municipality. The other edge of this enhanced cooperation can be increased difficulty in reaching policy decisions if there is inter-municipal controversy.

Joint Board[52]

A joint board is primarily a mechanism used in other countries to promote cooperation without losing the autonomy of the constituent municipalities. Like a regional district, typically it is formed for only one or a few related services. The board members are elected at large from the constituent municipalities, but policy decisions about provision remain the responsibility of the constituent municipalities, acting individually. The joint board is responsible for overseeing the administrative structure resulting from the merger of the administrative staff and resources from the constituent municipalities. Although public assets remain the property of the constituent municipalities, the municipalities transfer ownership of the furniture, equipment, and vehicles to the joint board. If the municipality leaves the joint board, the transfer of these operating assets will be reversed.

The constituent municipalities retain responsibility for providing the services produced by the joint board. The constituent municipalities make the decision of the quality and amount of the service and fund the production, but the joint board, through its staff, prepares the service and distributes it. The constituent municipalities are responsible for policy and the joint board is responsible for operational execution of those policies.

The advantages are the economies of scale in the operations while keeping the policy decisions local and maintaining the autonomy of the constituent municipalities. Citizen involvement and public scrutiny are maintained, as well as the access to elected officials on a local level. This mechanism may produce or even intensify the same difficulties found in most regional models: ambiguity about whether the decision is the province of the joint board or

---

[52] This conception of the joint board model is from Dollery and Johnson (2005). It was the most comprehensive we found despite some gaps. It may vary from some actual implementations and may be defined differently in countries that use the model. Dollery and Johnson also describe the terms virtual government and agency model. Our use of the term regional policy group is based on their description of regional operating council.

the municipalities and controversy and conflict between municipalities with different demands for service.

Virtual Government

A virtual government (Dollery and Johnson, 2005) is a policy making body only. It transfers all responsibility for producing all municipal services to an administrative service center that is formed with other municipalities. The service center may directly deliver the services or contract out for the delivery. The municipalities each have a council and a small administrative staff to monitor service delivery and carry out policy decisions of the council. They retain no operating capabilities, since they are totally moved to the administrative service center.

A virtual government essentially relinquishes all service production to the administrative service center or its contractors, making it a joint board for all municipal services. It retains the responsibility for policy decisions about service provision in each municipality. Hence, it retains complete local control over service provision and maintains the policy independence of its council. It makes a complete bow to economies of scale and scope, so it will receive these benefits in full for all services for which they exist. Compared to a joint board, it has reduced potential for controversy because it includes no additional centralized board. Returning to direct service delivery, if something should falter, is extremely difficult, because the municipality must rebuild its entire capacity to produce and administer all services.

Regional Policy Group

Member municipalities form a regional policy group (also a council of governments or regional council) to provide local representation in regional or collaborative efforts in service delivery. Each constituent municipality has representation in the policy group. The group is policy making, but has no operational capacity. It provides input from the group either to a regional operating organization producing services for the member municipalities or to member municipalities that may be providing services directly. The group often has a small administrative staff, which is supported by a small fee charged to each municipality for membership.

Many regard these groups as promoting enhanced collaboration. Since they usually result in response to a perceived need to achieve cooperative local involvement, the environment in which they are formed is often ripe for their positive impact on collaborative efforts. They promote exchange of ideas and a mechanism to bring up concerns and share best practices. They cannot exist without another service delivery mechanism or mechanisms to produce the service, so they are, by definition, part of a hybrid service delivery arrangement. Often, they have little formal authority and must achieve their recommendations through persuasion, but they are viewed as effective.

Centralization

A higher level of government taking the responsibility for both the provision and production of a service to all constituent municipalities is centralization. The municipality has no responsibility for the service delivery and no formal control over it, even when the delivery is to the citizens of the municipality. Both increased scale and scope will result. If a municipal service is centralized, the funding (and, in theory, supporting tax component) is removed from the municipal budget and transferred to the county (or other appropriate level) budget.

Centralization uses an existing government, such as a state or county, to deliver the services, rather than forming a regional district or other form of new government. Because there is no agreement between the parties, centralization does not provide the same control a shared service does because of the contract that the parties negotiate. If this lack of control for the municipalities is a problem, municipalities may institute mechanisms such as a regional policy group or agency model to provide local influence while capturing economies of scale.

Typically, centralization occurs at a county or state level. The issue with loss of local control is related to a concern that county governments, somewhat like special districts, are more distant from the public and their operations are less transparent. Both counties and special districts are popular locations for patronage appointments in those states that are saddled with this political phenomenon. Although there is little evidence of a trend towards decentralization, there is evidence of an emerging push (or perhaps just a posture) to dissolve counties as well as special districts. In New York State, as pressure grows to pass legislation to make local government consolidation more practical to achieve, the push back from local politicians is to put dissolution of county governments on the table.

States vary widely in which services are centralized. As was seen in the literature, this provides an opportunity to analyze the relative cost of county and municipal service delivery for the same services, but this has only been done in a few specific instances. If economies of scale are appropriate to the particular service type, the potential gains should be substantial, unless mismanagement is more prevalent at the larger levels of government in particular states, perhaps because of a tradition of county patronage positions.

Agency Model

In this model, a larger government, such as a state or county, produces all services, with the quantity and quality determined by each municipality (Dollery and Johnson, 2005). Most implementations of the agency model establish a global budget for each municipality, allowing increases in one service only if there is a concomitant decrease in another service, so the service mix maintains the global budget for the municipality after it reconfigures its service levels.

This mechanism attempts to capture economies of scale while allowing local control of the mix of services. However, the larger government controls the total cost of services for a municipality, usually based on a formula.

Local Unit Production

Another variant on centralized or regional models permits the production of the service to be accomplished at the local level. This is often done through a contract between a county and a municipality. An example is the plowing of county roads within the municipality by the municipal public works department for a contracted level of compensation or in trade for another county produced service or product. Opportunities to contract back to the local unit are more likely to be seen when the provision of a service is first being transferred to the county and the capacity to produce the service is still available in the municipality. It is an interesting idea for services, such as emergency services, which are delivered largely by volunteers in some areas. It allows for a regional perspective on the mix and citing of specialized and expensive equipment, but retains a local presence and involvement in the distribution of the service.

> **Local unit production may be appropriate for customer service. A recent study on producing countywide services in Somerset County, New Jersey, proposes a model that, if implemented, would satisfy the local citizens who find it comfortable and convenient to inquire at the municipality in which they reside. It would also provide better expertise for the difficult issues, because of the development of a knowledge network at the county level. This is reminiscent of the expert systems popular in the 70's and 80's in industries, such as insurance, in which the same inquiries are made countless times, but some occasionally involve more complex circumstances. Expert systems in that era were one of the applications of the field of artificial intelligence in computer science, but a well-constructed human and computer interface can provide the expert solution. The highest level of expertise would exist at the county accompanied by computer-aided systems, and would be virtually available to all constituent municipalities, making it unnecessary for the same high level of expertise to be physically available at each constituent municipality.**

In Monroe County, New York , the county has constructed an All Seasons Agreement (New York State Commission on Local Government Efficiency & Competitiveness, 2008) to allow local governments to perform mowing, animal carcass removal, and highway resurfacing, in addition to snow and ice control. The agreements fostered good working relationships between the municipalities, as well as being particularly helpful in emergencies.

Features of Service Delivery Arrangements

The table below contains all the service delivery arrangements defined above. The table identifies the features potentially associated with each mode of delivery, but continues to remain consistent with the descriptions used above, which attempted to use terms that are not value laden. Associating value with the features is the decision of governing bodies and is the final result of this book, following the identification of service delivery alternatives, their potentials, and the comparative benefits when the values are determined and aligned with those features by a governing body engaging in a rational evaluation of its service delivery.

Characteristics Associated with Service Delivery Alternatives

Service Delivery Arrangement	Other Terms	Features
TRADITIONAL MUNICIPAL SERVICE PROVISION AND PRODUCTION		
Direct Delivery		• Responsibility for service definition • Responsibility for funding • Responsibility for service preparation • Responsibility for distribution • Community identity • Full scope
INTER-GOVERNMENTAL		
Shared Services	• Inter-local services • Intergovernmental service agreement • Contracting with another government • Vertical integration	• Responsibility for service definition • Responsibility for funding • Increase in scale
Joint Services	• Inter-local cooperation • Mutual aid	• Responsibility for service definition • Responsibility for funding • Shared responsibility for service preparation • Shared responsibility for distribution • Community identity (depends on arrangements) • Increase in scale • Resource flexibility • Retain service knowledge and capacity
Competitive Contracting	• Governmental entrepreneurship	• Responsibility for service definition • Responsibility for funding • Responsibility for service preparation • Responsibility for distribution • Community identity • Full scope • Increased scale (contractor for other towns) • Increased competition • Increased administration/marketing
Local Unit Production—as part of regional or central provision		• Responsibility for service preparation • Responsibility for distribution • No responsibility for administration or management • Increase in scale • Resource flexibility • Retain service knowledge and capacity • Revenue (depends on arrangements) • Tax base broadened • Regional perspective

(continued on next page)

(continued from previous page)

Service Delivery Arrangement	Other Terms	Features
NON-GOVERNMENTAL		
Contracting	• Privatization • Joint contracting • Joint production	• Responsibility for service definition • Responsibility for funding • Increase in scale • Decrease in scope • Increased competition (if there are multiple vendors) • Retain service knowledge and capacity (joint modes only)
Franchises		• Responsibility for service definition • Responsibility for pricing, but not funding • Increase in scale (depends on supplier) • Decrease in scope • Increased competition • Tiered service levels • Limits monitoring, but still possible
Vouchering		• Responsibility for service definition • Increase in scale (depends on supplier) • Decrease in scope • Increased competition • Tiered service levels • Limits monitoring, but still possible
Co-production	• Volunteerism • Private government (homeowner associations)	• Responsibility for service definition • Responsibility for funding • Responsibility for service preparation (depending on arrangements) • Responsibility for distribution (depending on arrangements) • Community identity • Full scope • Possible increase in administration • Assuring service quality is difficult
ADDITIONAL ENTITY		
Special District	• Service district • Fire (or other service type) district • Authority • Commission	• Transfer all responsibility, including funding • Creates additional government • Singular focus on a particular service • Decrease in scope • Community identity retained • Monitoring and termination not part of the transfer

Service Delivery Arrangement	Other Terms	Features
Regional District	• Regionalization	• Transfer all responsibility, including funding • Creates additional government • Singular focus on a particular service • Increase in scale • Decrease in scope • Homogeneity of service • Community identity lost • Regional perspective • Monitoring and termination not part of the transfer and more at a distance
Joint Meeting		• Transfer all responsibility, other than funding and is represented on board • Creates additional government, but without revenue generating authority • Singular focus on a particular service • Increase in scale • Decrease in scope • Homogeneity of service • Community identity lost • Regional perspective • Monitoring and termination not part of the transfer and more at a distance
Joint Board	• Area integration model	• Responsibility for service definition • Responsibility for funding • Increase in scale • Retain scope if all or most services are transferred • Community identity lost • Regional perspective • Monitoring encouraged by provision responsibility • Difficult to terminate
Virtual Government		• Responsibility for service definition • Responsibility for funding • Increase in scale • Retain scope • Community identity lost • Monitoring encouraged by provision responsibility • Difficult to terminate

(continued on next page)

Service Delivery Arrangement	Other Terms	Features
Regional Policy Groups	• Regional council • Council of Governments (COG)	• Features vary depending on the service arrangements the group oversees • Provides mechanism for oversight of transferred services • Provides mechanism for identifying other opportunities for collaboration • Regional perspective • Part of a hybrid service delivery arrangement
SERVICE TRANSFERS TO EXISTING GOVERNMENT		
Centralization	• County (or equivalent term) services • Regionalization (to existing entity) • State services	• Transfer all responsibility • Increase in scale • Increase in scope • Homogeneity of service • Regional perspective • Shifts revenue support (e.g., county tax) • Tax base broadening • Community identity lost • Monitoring and termination not part of the transfer and more at a distance
Agency Model		• Responsibility for service definition (within producer constraints) • Responsibility for funding (within global budget constraints), although revenue is not provided through a municipal tax • Increase in scale • Increase in scope • Community identity lost • Monitoring encouraged by provision responsibility • Difficult to terminate

CHAPTER 9

Recommendations to Align Service Delivery Arrangements with Service Types

The first six chapters reviewed what was available in the literature. They used the literature to determine what we knew and what we still needed to understand more fully. Chapter 7 departed from the writings in the literature and provided a detailed inventory of municipal services in light of the general characteristics of those services. Chapter 8 went back to our knowledge of service delivery arrangements, investigated in more detail some that are uncommon in the United States, provided a standard description of each of these arrangements and produced a list of comparative features of each. Now, this final chapter begins to match what we have learned about service types with what we have learned about delivery arrangements. Only this perspective will put local government in the position to rationally evaluate the specifics of each situation and choose the best mechanisms to deliver local government services.

This alignment will provide a template for practitioner-based decisions in any local government. The template will take the form of the set of best alternatives for service delivery for each service type with specific examination of sub-tasks within the service area that have different requirements than the service type, in general. In a local government, the governing body or manager can look at each service type within the context of the specific situation of the municipality and evaluate the alternatives against the specific goals and conditions of the government. From the perspective of a state or county government, one can begin to think of different structures that could alleviate the service burden on the constituent municipalities.

Grouping the Service Delivery Alternatives

The presentation in the last chapter of alternatives for delivering services grouped the arrangements into categories of inter-governmental, non-governmental, additional entity, and transfers to existing government, comparing these alternatives to direct delivery of service by the municipality. That scheme served us well to describe the nature of the entity involved in the relationship. At this point, it is better to investigate the alternatives in a framework based on the nature of the reason for forming the relationship. Some delivery arrangements provide more than one reason to utilize them, so they may appear in more than one group below. The prior chapter contains more details about each of the individual arrangements categorized in such groups. We will use the following terms in the subsequent analysis of potential solutions:

▶ **Cooperation**—This term will include shared services and joint services, both of which determine who is responsible for production of services. The primary difference over direct delivery is the increase in scale. Cooperation represents a collaboration with another existing government, usually described in an agreement or contract. There may be compensation, in the form of monetary payment or an exchange of services. Mutual aid and informal arrangements may also be effective ways in which to achieve the benefits of cooperation arrangements.

Shared services are more of a one sided contract with a producer than joint services, since one government becomes the lead agency, with full responsibility for both preparing and distributing the service. If a joint service is practical, it may have additional benefits. It allows all parties to retain the capacity to deliver the service and is more likely to retain community identity of all partners. There is a better ability to monitor the performance of the service because there will be personnel from all of the partners involved.

For a joint service to be successful, reporting relationships must be clarified, because the joint service has at least two masters. The partners must be committed to the success of the joint service, seeing the whole benefit as being greater than the details in the parts. That is, they must not get bogged down in accounting for minutiae.

▶ **Contracting**—This term will include shared services, competitive contracting, privatization, co-production, contracting with a not-for profit, and franchising. (Note that we classified shared services in two groups, which is appropriate, depending on the motivation behind the arrangement.) Similar to some cooperation alternatives, contracting transfers responsibility for production, but always in exchange for compensation. When evaluating these alternatives, the municipality should account for the full reduction in costs associated with the reduction in personnel, as well as capital purchases, if they are part of the transferred service. If the intention is to cut overall costs, the municipality must be willing to reduce the personnel costs rather than just transferring the personnel to another function and increasing the costs of that other service. The specifics of any contract and the contractor chosen will determine if costs are reduced, if scale is increased, or if scope is decreased.

Competitive contracting and shared services are the easiest to monitor and terminate. Joint contracting or joint production emphasizes the capability to return to direct service delivery, maintaining some capacity for production, so the municipality can more easily evaluate performance and more easily assume production after termination, because it can build on the capacity that was retained. Franchising is different from the other contracting alternatives because the municipality removes the need to fund the service, thereby decreasing its budget, by allowing citizens to pay for the service directly, but at a price negotiated in a bulk agreement by the municipality. Service heterogeneity is easy to achieve with tiered pricing agreements, allowing citizens to choose their level of service. Co-production is useful in specific situations, usually when there is an interested partner who initiates the agreement, but the municipality can be successful in creating this interest, such as with the Neighborhood Watch program. Assuring quality of service is difficult in any contract for service production, but franchising and co-production present the greatest challenges, although for different reasons.

▶ **Service Transfer**—Service transfers include special districts, regional districts, and centralization. This group of alternatives transfers all responsibility for the service, including determining what the service levels should be and funding the service. Therefore, one of the most important potential problems is the lack of local control or input into the service delivery. Community identity with the service is lost. In addition, each of these options makes the governance of the service less transparent to the public. Monitoring and termination is difficult. With the exception of a special district that serves only one municipality, or only a portion of the municipality, these options increase scale.

Special and regional districts decrease scope. Regional districts and centralization tend to increase the homogeneity of service and broaden the tax base, providing a regional perspective. Depending on the goals of the municipality, these features may be positive or negative.

▶ **Centralized Service Administration**—This term includes joint boards, joint meetings, virtual governments, and agency models. These alternatives retain the responsibility for service provision, which increases the capability to monitor performance of the service delivery. All of these alternatives use another entity to produce the service, resulting in an increase in scale, but a loss of community identity with the service delivery. However, there is still local control through funding and decisions on the nature and level of the service, although the extent of these varies with the particular delivery arrangement. Note that regional districts and centralization have many of the same features, but because the municipality relinquishes responsibility for provision, disadvantages may accompany regional districts and centralization for services for which the municipality wants to determine the parameters of the service for its citizens.

With the exception of joint meetings, which are often formed to deliver one service, all of the other arrangements maintain some level of scope, because several or all services are administered and produced through the created entity. A joint meeting creates redundancy in administrative support services, because both the joint meeting and the municipality provide identical forms of support for their different services. Joint meetings are very similar to regional districts, but there are differences. Funding responsibility remains with the constituent municipalities, as is the case with joint boards. It appears the municipalities retain more responsibility for defining service levels in a joint board than in a joint meeting, which increases the transparency of the joint board and the monitoring of the service.

Joint boards and joint meetings have local representation through the board that oversees the production of the service. There is no such representation in virtual governments and agency models. The responsibility for service provision keeps the municipality involved, but only in policy decisions, not administrative production decisions.

Virtual governments and agency models cannot be created by a municipality or a few cooperating municipalities. To be effective, they require broad regional or state initiatives.

▶ **Correcting Arrangements**—We do not use this term in the ensuing analysis of service types, but it is useful to include such miscellaneous arrangements in our discussions. We identified two arrangements that are added to another arrangement to improve the results. Regional policy groups, also known as councils of government, provide local input and control, depending on the authority of the group. These groups are often created to offset the loss of local control for arrangements, such as centralization, that transfer the total responsibility for service delivery. Although this is not always the reason for establishing the group, it does add local input to any arrangement of full service transfer. In general, regional policy groups are effective in promoting collaboration and providing a regional perspective. A regional policy group is often part of an overall hybrid arrangement for service delivery, such as a two-tiered service delivery structure.

Local unit production can be added to a full service transfer. By having municipal personnel involved in the distribution of the service in the municipality, the sense of community identity is recaptured. It may be more cost-efficient to distribute the service locally, but administer it centrally. This would constitute a shared service or inter-governmental contract -- contracted from the larger entity to the smaller entity in order to take advantage of local responsiveness while also taking advantage of scale for tasks requiring special expertise or capital funding.

Some of the alternatives we have outlined would be difficult for an individual municipality to utilize, if a basic structure did not exist. While joint boards, virtual governments, and agency models may be among the best of solutions for a specific service type from an analytic point of view, if the central structure does not already exist, it may be difficult to establish. They may also require as long a timeline for implementation as a full consolidation, so they may not be practical without considerable resolve or a regional interest that will maintain focus for the long term.

On the other hand, centralization implies there is an existing structure, such as a county government. This may be more practical, particularly for the individual municipality pursuing a first step of contracting with the county until general interest evolves into full centralization of the service or developing a centralized administrative service function. Centralization forfeits local control, which may be a significant disadvantage depending on the service type.

A council of governments or regional policy group can be instrumental in the evolution to regional and central service organizations, while maintaining constituent government input. Forming such an organization is a reasonable step that encourages looking at a broader range of service delivery models, such as we have described.

Solutions by Service Type

Public Works

Public works functions divide into major tasks groups of labor-intensive maintenance activities (with and without high equipment costs) and specialized skills (with and without high infrastructure costs). Public works is a service type that municipalities commonly share in formal and informal agreements. Because of centralized maintenance of some assets, such as county parks and roads, there is an existing basis for greater centralization than what currently occurs in many regions of the country. A community identification issue arises because of municipal logos on trucks. Related to that, a desire of elected officials to be able to control response to a citizen's request for targeted maintenance may be another barrier to transferring service production.

The maintenance activities utilizing labor and somewhat costly equipment include solid waste collection and recycling, road maintenance and sweeping, and removal of snow and leaves. The specialized equipment used for solid waste and road maintenance provides the potential for achieving economies of scale in the acquisition and maintenance costs for that equipment, assuming the economies are not offset by diseconomies involved in managing a larger labor force. Contracting allows full utilization of the expensive equipment over a larger area. Regional districts and joint meetings can achieve the same scale economies, but they will create duplicative administrative functions that offset their advantages. Joint boards, virtual governments, agency models, and centralization do the same, but if they provide a multiplicity of services, spreading those functions over all of the multiple services avoids the redundancy of administrative functions created by joint meetings and regional districts. The loss of local control under shared services, centralization and regional districts may not be a factor in solid waste and road maintenance, as long as good mechanisms exist to respond to complaints of the public.

Franchising is a promising alternative that has been cost-effective for solid waste compared to the common options of direct delivery and privatization, but does not apply to road maintenance or sweeping because they are not property-based services. Franchising permits the municipality to negotiate the cost of service as a bulk purchase, but the municipality can remove the funding from the municipal budget because the contractor directly invoices the property owner. A franchise agreement can provide varied service levels, meeting heterogeneous needs through a tiered pricing agreement. A collaboration of municipalities negotiating the franchise agreement might provide incentive to bidders because of the increased size of the contract, while allowing properties with rural, suburban, multi-family, and commercial land uses to choose an appropriate level of service at an appropriate price. It could allow co-production (residents taking their own trash to the dump) in the most rural areas.

The analysis suggests a municipality should evaluate franchise agreements for solid waste and examine contracting (including inter-governmental) for road maintenance. A centralized service administration solution, such as a joint board, would be a goal toward which to evolve. The formation of a regional policy group might facilitate this thinking beyond municipal boundaries and, over a period of years, lead to a solution with benefits similar to those of a joint board for solid waste and road maintenance. Tradition may make it difficult to implement any of the uncommon centralized solutions. If that is the case, joint services are a good improvement over direct delivery and maintain more community identity and resource flexibility than shared services, although shared services also are an improvement over direct delivery in most conditions.

As snow and leaf removal are widely required at the same time (concurrent demand) by all municipalities in a given region, sharing expensive removal equipment is difficult, so mechanisms that increase scale are not particularly effective. The only useful structured response to the service needs of snow plowing and leaf removal is contracting out, not because of scale, but because of competition, bolstered by a potentially lower wage and benefit structure or more flexible work rules for a competing contractor. Only bidding will determine if there is a market of bidders and an advantage in contracting over direct delivery of the service.

However, depending on the configuration of the roads, the responsibility for their maintenance may benefit from some collaboration because more than one government has responsibility for the roads in a municipality. Snow removal on county secondary roads is a good example. Although there is no economy of scale (assuming there is no need for specialized equipment), the municipality may be in a better position to give priority to plowing the county secondary roads, which are an important part of the municipal road network, even though they are county owned. It may be beneficial to institute local unit production or some other form of agreement to have the municipality take the responsibility for producing the snow plowing service, which is a greater priority for the municipality on county roads providing major routes through its area, but not considered as major arteries by the county. It clearly depends on specifics, whether this type of arrangement works.

Activities such as building and grounds maintenance, which includes parks and playgrounds maintenance, are labor-intensive, but do not require expensive equipment in most situations. If the municipality fully utilizes the labor resource devoted to theses services for this or other tasks, there should be no benefit to arrangements fostering economies of scale. As above, bidding the service may reduce costs, but only because of competition uncovering a contractor with a lower wage and benefit package. Our analysis suggests a municipality should directly deliver building and grounds maintenance, unless there is under-utilized excess capacity or likely cost reductions from private contracting. Specific conditions may change this recommendation. Locally sharing more costly landscaping equipment that is not fully utilized may pay off, at least in small measure. Excess capacity of labor or equipment resources often goes unnoticed[53] until there is pres-

---

[53] Conducting an inventory of equipment utilization may show potentials for sharing. This does not work well with labor resources, which are always allocated to some task, even if productivity is not forced to a high level by the workload.

sure from contracting or a reduction in total resources from a merged maintenance function, such as the school and municipality agreeing to combine efforts.

Areas of public works requiring specialized skills include waste water systems, storm water systems, water supply, forestry, and engineering. The first four involve a majority of tasks that do not require special expertise, but engineering is almost completely the province of credentialed professionals. Larger towns can afford engineers as full-time employees, because they fully utilize their time. Smaller towns resort to private contracting primarily, but there are some shared services. The comparative costs will be specific to each situation. The profession of municipal engineering is highly competitive because of the large sums of money expended, so a town wanting the most cost-effective arrangement should be able to achieve it. A municipality should evaluate full-time staff, shared or joint services, or contracting, as is appropriate to the engineering needs of the municipality.

For those tasks in wastewater, storm water, water supply, and forestry that require special expertise, the issues are the same as for civil engineering. A municipality should evaluate full-time staff, shared or joint services, or contracting, as is appropriate to the sanitary sewer engineering, water systems engineering, and arborist needs of the municipality.

The routine labor component of each of the water systems and forestry should be evaluated as would any other public works function. Sewer, storm water drain, and water line maintenance, like tree pruning and cutting, are labor-intensive, but they can have a component of on-demand service needs. This can be reduced by good maintenance programs, which can be scheduled and, in particular, scheduled to fit around other tasks performed by the same employees so these tasks fully utilize labor resources. Despite good maintenance programs, the on-demand component will always be there. Since the service need is often an emergency (fallen tree or sewer/water line break), quick response, even after normal business hours, is essential. This need will encourage direct delivery, which can be controlled by the elected officials, but a proper agreement or arrangement that utilizes increased scale may be a better solution in the end, if the agreement guarantees emergency response. Scale is important because of the somewhat expensive equipment (and operators) needed, which includes storm drain jetters, sewer line cameras, bucket trucks, and stump grinders.

If it were not for the on-demand service component, this analysis would be the same as for road maintenance. All of the services are labor-intensive, which means they will not benefit from increases in scale, and have high equipment costs, which should allow them to benefit from increases in scale. Because of the increased concern with emergency response, most municipalities will want to have some capacity for this response, but this does not rule out contracting, particularly to another government or by a joint service with shared responsibility for producing the service. Direct delivery of services can perform the day-to-day maintenance services when they do not require the use of expensive equipment. A municipality should evaluate contracting, including shared or joint services, for maintenance of sewer, water, storm water and trees. It should assure adequate emergency response through the agreement made or through municipal employees that are the first response to the situation, but have the authority to call in the contractor. Because of the flexibility required both to use municipal employees for day-to-day maintenance, yet call on the contractor when equipment is needed, the agreement may be easier to construct with another government, or, if with a private firm, under a joint contract that specifies when the contractor is used and when the municipal employees are used.

Infrastructure replacement or development is a service associated with many of the public works functions we have reviewed. Although the need is infrequent, municipalities will need to replace or construct roads; lines for sewer, water, and storm water; street lights; and buildings and other facilities. Municipalities usually contract with private firms that have the equipment, staffing, and expertise to complete capital projects. The use of professionals for financing, bond counsel, development of bid specifications, and project oversight all require specialized expertise. These skills can be contracted for, almost always with for-profit firms. However, there is a possible benefit in the use of a larger governmental organization to control and coordinate these professionals and the functions they perform. County governments or other organizations, such as county improvement authorities, will have much greater expertise in financing and implementing large projects. A municipality should solicit the assistance of county government or county or regional authorities that specialize in implementing large capital projects. Evaluation of the potential benefit of using the larger government is recommended because of the political vagaries often associated with large capital contracts, some of which may increase, rather than reduce, costs.

Public Safety

In most states, the cost of public safety services is usually far higher than any other service, with the exception of education. The components of public safety are police, fire, and emergency medical services. There is a great deal of diversity in who delivers public safety services throughout the United States. In many states, it is a county function, but in others, there is staunch resistance to any initiatives that threaten local control of public safety. That resistance comes from the public, elected officials, and a well organized and represented labor force. Yet, as the biggest cost-driver for municipalities in many states, there is increasing interest in looking at cost saving mechanisms that, only ten years ago, would not have been considered.

Personnel costs and the equipment necessary to support the patrol officers – guns, vehicles, and communications equipment – dominate the cost of police services. Police patrol is the main service, including traffic enforcement and the non-criminal enforcement of local ordinances. As a labor-intensive service, there is no benefit from economies of scale and there is evidence of actual diseconomies in larger governments. Since the officer fully utilizes the equipment assigned to him or her (we are not addressing the number of vehicles that should be required for patrol, which is an internal management issue), it is not beneficial to have that equipment controlled by a larger organization. It is needed everywhere at the same time, so it cannot be shared over a broader service region. Since there is public interaction, for both patrol and enforcement of local ordinances, there is an advantage to have the same municipally-identified officers.

We have identified an inconsistency in the literature that involves police services. The diseconomies of scale that are reported for police services by some authors are inconsistent with allegedly successful initiatives in some states to merge departments or provide centralized police services to small towns. Given this inconsistency, we will temper our statements with the always wise admonition to realistically analyze the cost and service impacts of an alternative delivery mechanism.

In very small towns, it is difficult to financially support a full 24/7 police patrol. Patrol is a scheduled activity, but call response or even response to a situation encountered on patrol is not. Patrol and call response are inextricably linked in every jurisdiction. With proper backup for safety, which demands a minimum of two officers on a shift, and the need for supervision, the minimum staffing is about twelve employees and the supporting equipment they require. That results in a costly sum for a small municipality.

> We have observed situations in which the financial costs were not the main driver for the public in police services. There is often intense public reaction to potential loss of local officers. Public reaction thwarted several attempts at collaboration in police patrol. Some taxpayers have been quoted as stating they wanted an officer they knew bringing their teenager home, when an encounter with the police occurs. While this is often ascribed to affluent communities, where the public is willing to pay high taxes, there is evidence it occurs in other communities, also.

If conditions otherwise permit, there are alternative means to provide adequate 24/7 coverage. None of them will reduce costs if they result in the same number of officers assigned to the same municipal patrol area. Any cost saving solution must expand the coverage area to include other jurisdictions or reduce the personnel allocated to patrol while providing an on-call resource that can respond to a situation. Any agreement that reduces the total personnel on shift per capita (or, perhaps more appropriately, per crime incident) while maintaining adequate levels for public safety in a given geographic service area should be evaluated.

Centralized services (or a virtual government or agency model) do that by spreading the coverage area, while maintaining an adequate capacity for backup because of the flexibility of a supervisor or dispatcher to discharge any of the shift personnel from the broader area to assist in a situation. In some rural areas, the state provides the only coverage, which includes limited patrol in low crime rate areas, but a responsive reaction to a call for service.

> Responsiveness of police provided by a centralized service is not always prompt. Because of the geography of patrol in rural areas, there are examples of slow response when no officer is near the location of the call for service.

Shared or joint services can maintain adequate levels for public safety using the number of patrol and call response officers that the partnering municipalities determine is appropriate. Joint boards or joint meetings can accomplish the same full utilization of shift officers, while establishing an oversight board. With the professionalism of police services, this may not be required in well-managed organizations. In sum, our analysis indicates a municipality should evaluate centralized, shared, or joint services to achieve the desired patrol presence and the capability for adequate backup and call response when needed.

Traffic control, as opposed to traffic enforcement, is not needed in many municipalities other than for specific situations, some of which are funded by private organizations or other entities. In some states this is contracted for with officers being paid outside of their normal municipal shift, through the municipality, but not requiring the municipality to retain extra resources to meet the need. That is, there is no problem. Even under these conditions, two situations may create extra costs. If a police vehicle is required for traffic control, it may create the need to acquire more vehicles than are necessary for the municipal police function. If traffic control does not fully utilize and fund the vehicles required, it becomes an unnecessary portion of the municipal tax. School crossing is another traffic control need that can cause unnecessary expenditures because of the concurrent demand for the service at the same time—the beginning and end of the school day. Since municipalities widely use school crossing guards and pay them on a per hour basis, there should be no need for patrol officers to perform or supplement this task.

Police investigation and laboratory analysis have different service needs than police patrol. Neither is labor-intensive, but they require special expertise that would not be used to full capacity in a small municipality. In addition, lab analysis also requires special, and somewhat costly, equipment. Investigation requires some public interaction where the municipality is located and the skills needed to deal with the public, but a familiar face is not necessary, so a larger government can provide the service. Both of these services are infrequently needed, particularly the laboratory analysis. Local control should not be an issue because of expected professionalism of both these services. Centralized services or other centralized service administration models such as a virtual government, agency model, or joint board could provide the lab analysis cost effectively. The somewhat greater frequency of the need for detective work and the working relationship with the local force may indicate that an increase in scale, but of a lesser amount, will still be cost effective but maintain a better relationship with the municipal police force. In addition to centralized service administration models and centralization, shared and joint services should be evaluated for police investigation services.

The police tasks involving administration and record keeping consume a lot of personnel time and detract from the time spent on patrol, responding to calls, or supervising those who do. State and federal requirements for reporting are part of this demand, as well as providing sufficient documentation for court cases and to demonstrate effective performance. Even with increasing technology, these tasks are time consuming. Some are unavoidable, such as the patrol or responding officer completing incident reports, but others could be transferred to a larger organization, with less well-paid purely administrative staff. However, if a larger organization provides no reduction in total staff time or pay rates and, therefore, total staff cost to complete administrative tasks, there is no apparent reason to do so.

Good technology and a larger reporting base may reduce administration for the preparation of summary reports. Transferring this function to a larger government may achieve this result. Supervision, after a point, seems to get more unwieldy with more officers and additional layers of management. Without better information about the cost effectiveness of pushing more administrative tasks to a larger government or the ability to separate administrative from supervisory tasks, it is inappropriate to make a recommendation for change without appropriate evaluation of the specifics of the administrative burden. Municipalities should directly deliver administrative police services in the absence of information that shows efficiency gains from transferring these functions to a larger government.

Dispatch is used for all public safety components: police, fire, and EMS. Governments have been centralizing this service with considerable success, resulting in reduced costs and appropriate response to 9-1-1 calls. There are still local governments doing dispatch directly, and, worse yet, doing it with highly paid police officers. These situations are an opportunity for savings in a service that involves some moderately costly equipment and facilities. Public interaction skills are essential, as well as knowledge of the area served, but centralized implementations have been successful in achieving these requirements, particularly with technology. Although this could be termed a labor-intensive service, the need to have sufficient capacity to handle all callers in an on-demand environment puts strain on a small town to have more dispatchers than necessary for non-peak times, in order that the peak is adequately covered. Moving to a larger organization levels out the peaks and reduces the need for capacity that is excess and under-utilized in non-peak demand circumstances. If it is not already implemented, a municipality should move to a centralized administration model (centralization, joint board, virtual government, or agency model) or a large-scale collaborative model (shared or joint service, joint meeting).

Fire prevention and response are costly services that receive diverse treatment throughout the United States. Many small communities provide these services with a volunteer force, restricting the source of cost to general administration, facilities, and equipment. These communities, in many states, are beginning to feel the pinch of the increasing difficulty in recruiting volunteers. Most of the larger communities have a paid force, adding another large annual cost to the already costly capital facilities and equipment. Fire companies are often formed into special districts, creating another level of government, usually with taxing authority, operating separately from the more transparent municipal government. Many states provide county firefighting services.

Fire prevention tasks are not the problem in cost effectiveness. The culprit is firefighting response, a service supported strongly by the public. It is an on-demand service that necessitates adequate response when required. The result is personnel and equipment that is not used to full capacity between incidents. Broadening the service base always reduces the amount of resources per unit needed in order to adequately cover the peaks for the total coverage area. Mutual aid is commonly in place for fire services to accomplish this broadening. It works because Town A agrees to provide coverage when Town B's resources are inadequate, that is, when multiple calls occur at the same time. This is usually done without compensation because it is a mutual agreement. This is particularly helpful with volunteer firefighters because availability of those firefighters is unpredictable.

Although fire fighting is labor intensive, the on-demand nature of the service need means that a larger geographic area of coverage can provide benefits because per capita resource needs will be reduced by leveling the demand peaks. Further, firefighting uses relatively expensive vehicles and equipment and facilities to house those vehicles. In areas that have many distinct fire departments or fire districts, there are usually more vehicles than are needed, if they were pooled to serve the broader area. Specialized equipment may be particularly redundant. A municipality should evaluate more centralized service administration models, centralization, or collaborative models. If the municipality is currently served by volunteers, one must be cognizant that a centralization of the service may lessen the interest of volunteers, particularly if vehicles or facilities are relocated to a common service center. The reduction of redundant vehicles will be a source of savings, but it may also reduce interest of volunteers. The response areas of each fire station under a larger area service model may also yield benefits in response time compared to the irrational coverage that often occurs because of the boundaries of smaller areas.

Investigation activities to determine the cause of a fire are infrequent and require special expertise. Much of the activity will occur in the municipality where the fire occurred, but analysis can occur at other sites with equipment and facilities such as that required for police laboratory analysis. The evaluation of the most cost effective means to provide these activities should be similar to the analysis of police investigation and laboratory analysis. However, unlike with police investigations, there is no need to be concerned about the working relationships with the municipal firefighters, since they have no involvement with investigation. Centralized services or other centralized service administration models could provide both the investigation services and the lab analysis cost effectively.

Inspections and the enforcement of regulations require a moderate amount of special expertise in the fire code and prevention practices. These services also require the ability and availability to interact with the public as a representative of the municipality and may benefit from consistent enforcement from the same individual or team. This activity will require record keeping and administration, as well as someone who can pursue severe cases in court. Many small municipalities use a part-paid department, so there is someone designated to follow up on non-firefighting tasks who is not a volunteer. Most volunteers will not want to be as persistent or detailed as required for such tasks. Shared services may be more cost-efficient in small towns with limited needs for inspection.

Emergency medical services (EMS) is very similar to fire services. EMS is often part of the fire service, which the municipality provides. It is an on-demand service that requires quick response when it is needed, but, otherwise, creates under-utilized resources when demand is not there. The equipment is a little less expensive, but an outfitted rig constitutes a large purchase for a small town. When EMS is separate from fire, more responders are needed because the peaks need to be covered adequately by each service. A combined service offers cost efficiency. If the fire and EMS responders are paid, there is little good reason to allow them to be separate, but volunteer organizations sometimes create stumbling blocks for a municipality that wants to achieve the efficiency of a combined department.

The difficulty of recruiting and retaining volunteers seems to be more of a problem for EMS than for fire. A market of EMS organizations, both for-profit or non-profit, has emerged that is responding to requests for privatization proposals. More often than not, municipalities are soliciting bids from this market because of response problems during the business day, if they use a volunteer squad. If possible, a municipality should combine fire and EMS, and follow the recommendations for fire service. If EMS and fire must remain separate, one should evaluate contracting or the centralized administrative or collaborative models mentioned for fire. Response time is a necessary part of this evaluation.

Public Health

Public health is a service that is inherently more of a state or federal service than it is a municipal service. However, in many states, public health is the responsibility of the municipality. Public health includes immunizations and clinic care, multi-unit residential inspections, commercial inspections, enforcement of regulations for environmental and sanitation concerns, and animal control. Standards that are generally set at higher levels of government determine the nature of these services, but the municipality determines in what manner and how much of these services to provide. These services often are delivered infrequently and require special expertise. Economies of scale should serve this service type well, and the existing use of centralized, regionalized, or contracted services is testimony to the fact that many municipalities have looked for a larger and more cost-effective solution. Contracting and centralized service administration will usually be most cost-effective for the full range of health services (animal control may have a different service producer). Regional arrangements are good solutions, such as county provided full health services, a joint meeting, or as part of the range of services produced by a joint board, virtual government, or agency model.

Immunizations and clinics require medical practitioners, as well as a facility to deliver the service. This would be cost prohibitive in a small municipality. To spread these costs and utilize the resources near their capacity, the municipality needs to make arrangements that can fully use the expertise and facility or pay for it only when it is used. The services need to be available where the public can access them. When increasing the scale of the service delivery, it is beneficial to put the facilities at centers of transportation or provide visiting or mobile services. Contracting or centralized service administration arrangements are best for this service. The municipality should contract with a large municipality, a not-for profit, or a for-profit practitioner with an agreement that pays for the service when the producer is fully utilizing its resources (such as payment per transaction, or limited clinic hours). Alternatively, evaluate centralized and centralized service administration models or fund a regional solution, such as a joint meeting, through the municipal members without creating an additional government.

Both commercial and residential health inspections require some, but limited, special expertise and the availability to deliver the service in the municipality. Inspections require public interaction. Environmental and sanitation inspections are similar. The municipality or its service producer can schedule these tasks. A small municipality will only need a part-time employee to perform these tasks, or with proper expertise, it can be a task performed by an employee with other duties. These are not ideal solutions in most cases, because of the high cost of a part-time skilled employee or because of the limited priority given to the task by someone who has other duties to perform. Contracting to another government or centralized service administration arrangements are the best solutions for inspection services. These best solutions will often include performing these tasks as part of the overall health services required.

Animal control and the related animal sheltering require some specialized expertise. Animal control services are delivered on-site in the municipality and require some public interaction. It is an on-demand service, but many situations are not emergencies. It is more labor-intensive than capital intensive. The shelter must be at a reasonably convenient location and requires a facility, which makes it capital-intensive. Although contracting is a good solution, there may be a limited market of competitors because profit is depressed by non-profit providers interested in animal welfare. Not-for-profit contractors may provide a cost effective solution, but their goals may not align with those of the municipality contracting for the service. Regional and centralized public health service organizations sometimes provide animal health services, but not always, so it may be necessary to find more than one producer of public health services. In addition, animal control officers are not commonly shelter operators. Financially supporting a shelter through shared or joint services may be costly unless there are a large number of municipalities involved or the municipalities involved are large. Private contracting may be less expensive than shared or joint services for animal control because the service is on a fee per transaction basis. This will avoid excess capacity that would result if the municipality hires full-time personnel. Centralization to a county level is a good option, but efficient animal transport and convenience of the public may require more than one shelter location. Private contracting will normally be the most cost effective means to provide animal control. Not-for-profit contracting should be evaluated for both control and the shelter, because it may be the least expensive alternative if a producer is available. Centralized service administration is a good solution if a service district is established.

Recreation and Cultural Programs

The diversity of recreation and cultural programs and the variety of ways municipalities organize them makes it difficult to discuss the service type in the abstract, but a few points bear mention. Recreation and cultural programs consist of sports and general youth activities, social events and celebrations, music and arts entertainment, and cultural and tourism sites.

The normal youth activities and similar programs for adults are considered a local concern and a reflection of the desires of the local public. These programs provide recreation for the residents rather than bring in visitors. This is the primary focus of most recreation programs, other than in very large municipalities. The personnel costs to administer these programs are not usually a major budget item and, in many areas, user fees that offset the costs of materials and personnel support recreation programs. The real issue may be the facilities costs. Again, there are many different ways that towns go about this, including sharing facilities with the schools, creating public/private partnerships (essentially co-production with, for example, a Little League that needs more fields), getting aid from higher levels of government, or paying for it, which makes recreation a capital-intensive service. Direct service delivery serves routine activity programs well, augmented with co-production by parent groups and senior associations. Good collaboration with county parks departments or the development of an interest in recreation by a regional policy group might help with capital-intensive facility needs.

A regional outlook is beneficial because of the growing tendency for different governments to compete, particularly in the hosting of events such as music and arts entertainment. Celebrations and visitor sites, to the extent they bring potential shoppers to a commercial area, also need a regional perspective. Hence, many counties or specialized regional organizations (often public/private) are involved in tourism and cultural activities, but they may have little control over the towns and the individual programs they run. A regional policy group is a good mechanism to bring out new ideas and collaborative efforts, as well as to avoid event scheduling conflicts between towns.

Administration

This is a diverse service type, including both services with a high amount of public interaction to respond to the public need for information, and services that provide internal support functions for other departments. We will also include the distribution of consumables in this discussion, such as energy for support of other services. A municipality should evaluate cost-savings arrangements for distributing consumables, even though they are not a service that the municipality provides to an end-user. We will start with the administrative services that are more public.

Land use planning decisions and economic development benefit from a high level of expertise and a regional perspective. A municipality often contracts with consultants for expertise in planning and economic development. Typically, these projects develop new and amended planning ordinances and regulations and determine what strategies and plans are necessary to reach the future goals of the town. More centralized levels of government may also have oversight for these plans to instill a regional perspective, but the effectiveness of this varies widely. Regional policy groups have been effective in many areas by providing a coordinated approach for a region.

In small towns, local officials with expertise gained on the job implement and interpret these laws, regulations, and strategies on a case-by-case basis. Planning decisions on specific projects and zoning rulings are the first level of interpretation, and code enforcement is the on-the-street manifestation of these interpretations. The only direct costs involved are for personnel for enforcing zoning regulations, the municipal code, and the construction code. All are labor-intensive and can be scheduled, so there are no benefits from economies of scale. However, because the needs of small towns may not be sufficient to fully utilize full-time employees for these functions without creating under-utilized excess capacity, contracting arrangements may be more cost effective. Centralized solutions are awkward for all except construction code because of the differences in local zoning regulations and municipal codes. There is also a need to have a local presence because of the enforcement aspect of these functions. A municipality should evaluate contracting arrangements as an alternative that will avoid excess capacity in staff functions. Contracting is also appropriate for acquiring planning and economic development expertise, but centralized service administration and regional policy groups will provide a regional perspective, while retaining local input and control. Centralized service administration may also be an effective mechanism to provide planning expertise, the costs of which are shared throughout the region.

Municipal courts and the local administration of justice are outside the jurisdiction of local control in terms of the rulings of the court and the mechanisms to ensure compliance. The municipality can control behavior through the ordinances it enacts and local traffic laws, but the interpretation of these local regulations is supposed to be unchanging. For the most part, this is the reality, and the court, while perhaps producing significant revenue for the municipal fund, does not need local input to operate effectively. Expertise is required in the functions of judge, prosecutor, public defender, and, to a lesser extent, the court administrator, recorder, interpreter, and other supporting roles. Other than the actual court proceedings, the tasks are essentially collection of fines and recording, requiring some costs for equipment. Facility costs and the related issue of security can be large capital-intensive costs, particularly with increasing concerns that require security to be part of the facility's physical configuration.

The municipality usually contracts for expert personnel, so cost should be proportional to the limited time needed to complete the function. Rates for part-time contracted professionals are often at a premium, however. The administrative tasks are primarily labor-intensive so there are no benefits to increasing scale unless the municipality is paying for excess capacity through their current staffing. There is little need to provide a convenient court location, since many of the "clients" are not local residents (traffic court, in particular). The savings achieved through collaborative services are not going to be large for personnel costs, but the capital-intensive costs may be significant. The municipality must assure that the collaborative agreement maintains their revenue from fines and court costs. A municipality should evaluate collaborative agreements, particularly joint services that establish one facility for all the partners and jointly appointed professionals.

> **Excess capacity in staffing for court administration is common in New Jersey where there are restrictions on which personnel have access to the records of the court. This creates obstacles to sharing personnel between several functions that need adequate backup or might not require full-time staff in a small town.**

Public service functions provide information to citizens and provide the opportunity for the citizens to complete tasks required by the municipality. These include information requests and filing of forms regarding municipal records, property taxes, election laws, and licensing and permitting. These functions are labor-intensive and require public interaction, although improved technology is providing increased convenience and lessening service demand, as municipalities provide more information and application filing services through their websites. Many citizens prefer personnel interaction at their municipal building, showing the importance of community identity, but with accompanying costs. These routine services are on-demand, although many of them that occur less frequently or require more expertise to provide the service can be scheduled. Tax assessment is unique in that it requires field work in the municipality, but that is a scheduled task that could be provided from another organization.

There is some cost for equipment for record keeping and providing information. Equipment costs can increase with improved technology, particularly good records archiving, retention, and retrieval software and hardware. Increases in scale could reduce those collective costs for constituent municipalities in a collaborative arrangement. Increases in scale will not reduce the personnel costs, if there is not an existing level of excess capacity. Small towns that are well run limit excess capacity by having staff wear many hats. Although this is very cost-effective for routine tasks, it leaves gaps in expertise for less common tasks. Municipalities use part-time employees, contracted consultants, and shared personnel to address the need for expertise, but the costs may be high for the quantity of work provided. The other alternative is to use the normal employees to provide the expert services as best they can, but this can lead to problems and create the potential of large costs to resolve the problems. Examples include legal issues such as tax liens or bankruptcies and property assessment appeals.

The two real potentials for cost savings are in equipment and special expertise. Municipalities that wish to be more proactive may see value in reconfiguring how information is delivered, relying more on technology for the routine information, supplemented with a local presence to maintain community identity, but relying on a more centralized organization for anything beyond the mundane. A municipality should evaluate centralization or central services administration to provide a higher level of expertise and better equipment and technology at lower per capita costs. In the long run, and with appropriate central agency services (personnel and technology), it is possible to reduce significantly the quantity of personnel with special expertise in specific functions. The optimal model proposed for administrative services would be a centrally provided set of expert systems, consisting of technology and staff with specialized expertise at the central agency. Municipal customer service personnel at municipal locations would have access to the centralized systems and personnel with specialized expertise.

Some administrative services are support services to other functions in the municipality. These include finance and purchasing, general management, technology, and legal services. Purchasing does have some public interaction with vendors providing products and services to the municipality. The other support services entail no public interaction. Tasks can be scheduled, but exceptions include management crises and technology outages or problems that affect the functioning of the municipality. Technology is the only service that has large equipment or capital-intensive costs. Finance and purchasing and general management require some level of special expertise. Technology and legal services can require substantial expertise. Legal services have infrequent demand.

Neither finance and purchasing nor general management will benefit from increased scale, but there is potential for excess capacity for the higher level of expertise for some tasks such as grant writing, negotiation, investment, borrowing, higher level accounting, and bid solicitation. Often the same person possessing expertise is doing the mundane tasks, too, at a high rate of pay. In small towns, this need for expertise is met by part-time, shared, or contracted personnel. Sharing is more likely to reduce the cost, compared to part-time and contracted experts who may charge a premium for small quantities of work. A municipality should evaluate options for shared or joint services for the expert tasks in finance and purchasing and, if appropriate, general management.

Legal work is usually contracted in smaller municipalities, often at preferential rates for government. Sometimes these preferential rates are offered because government provides some other personnel benefits to the municipal attorney or because the attorney's agreement contains base services under an inexpensive retainer, but additional charges for other services. The total bill for municipal attorneys can get high and it is impossible to monitor that the work billed is being charged to only one municipality. Larger municipalities have full-time staff attorneys that avoid these billing issues. A municipality should evaluate shared service arrangements for attorney services with larger towns having in-house legal staff, which may reduce overall costs for total legal services.

Technology is an ever-increasing cost but has tremendous potential for reducing other costs, if municipalities make good investments in technology infrastructure. The costs of technology infrastructure development are cost-prohibitive to all but the largest municipalities. Increasing scale changes the equation and may permit the development of capabilities that transform the nature of municipal operations. For example, records retention and archiving can reduce dependence on paper records and provide much improved search capabilities compared to file drawers and boxes in the basement. The costs involve expensive high-capability software, efficient scanning equipment, and a sophisticated network that gives access to all users with appropriate security based on user and content. The savings can be in considerably reduced staff time for records retrieval and an automated capability that provides appropriate documents to the public with limited or no personnel involvement. A small town cannot afford this investment, but a consortium of towns or a centralized agency can.

Publicly visible technology, such as websites, can provide more transparency in government and increase citizen participation, as well as make dealing with government more convenient. Marketing the community may be very effective with good web technology. Because of the public aspect, municipalities will want more control over the product than with an internal administrative support product. It may be more difficult to develop a single website framework to serve multiple municipalities (with individualized content updated locally), but it is possible to have shared technical expertise for these functions at a cost much less than contracted costs from private vendors. A municipality should evaluate cooperative services, but if central service administration is practical, investigate that potential to provide a technical capacity at the largest scale possible in order to spread the cost of technical infrastructure development and technical expertise.

The final administrative service we will consider is not an activity, but a commodity. Bulk purchasing to achieve a better price is well established. Another variation is the distribution of commodities at a central location serving several municipalities. This mechanism insures the bulk purchase price but eliminates multiple facilities for storage and dispensing. The trade-off can be in travel time and travel costs. Examples include diesel and gasoline fueling and sand and salt storage. A municipality should evaluate cooperative services, central service administration, or centralization, if practical.

Specialized Services

Individual municipalities may provide structured parking, airports, electric power, or other services that are not common. These services may not only provide a service, but also be a revenue generator for the municipality. Often these are established with separate governments overseeing them, resulting in redundant administrative services, as is found in most non-regional special districts. They also have a tendency to become independent bodies, drawing power from the revenue they generate, and sometimes not protecting public monies with the same level of concern found in most municipal governments. If there are no advantages in terms of borrowing capacity or other operational flexibilities, avoid establishing an additional government for a single service that is delivered completely within one municipality. A municipality should evaluate delivering the service from the municipality, which already has an administrative organization in place to support other services.

Using the Service Alignment Framework

There is no substitute for knowledge of the specific conditions affecting your municipality, if you are a local government practitioner. This chapter presented considerations about specific service types and examined how they fit best with specific service delivery alternatives. The best way to use the information presented is to let it guide your considerations and evaluations. The specifics can change the picture completely. It is incumbent upon the practitioner to assess the current service delivery alternative and compare it to potential improvements. It is important to be realistic, not assuming that one can remove all management inefficiencies or productivity problems when making the proposed change. Assume the same level of efficiency and productivity will accompany the change, unless the change specifically will affect the source of inefficiency.

Identify all the costs in the current solution and in the proposed solution. If resources are being removed to save money, consider what other functions those resources are currently used for and how those functions will be accomplished with the reduction in resources for the targeted service.

An individual municipality cannot implement some alternatives discussed. They require an existing mechanism at another level, willingness on the part of a higher level of government, or a regional organization or consortium to initiate action to form an organization to provide mechanisms that are the core of the alternative. Virtual governments and joint boards are examples. While they hold great potential for economies of scale in preparing and distributing a service, they require an organization to do so.

APPENDIX

Annotated Bibliography

Accenture (2005). "The Government Executive Series—Driving High Performance in Government: Maximizing the Value of Public-Sector Shared Services." 1 - 40.

> This report was prepared by Accenture and describes key findings when a study was commissioned to see how well shared services had worked. With the new study, Accenture sought to identify the drivers, challenges, benefits and critical success factors for shared services initiatives in government. This study, managed by Accenture's in-house research arm, Accenture Research, surveyed 143 senior executives at all levels of government in a selection of agencies across 13 countries.

Advisory Commission on Intergovernmental Relations (1987). The Organization of Local Public Economies: 1 - 56.

> This commission report reviews the optimal structure of local government. The report declares that a multiplicity of general and special purpose governments contributes to democratic values and a coherent local public economy. The report distinguishes between the provision (that is, the determination of what) and the production (that is, the determination of how) of public goods and services.

Alesch, D. J., and L. A. Dougharty (1971). Economies of Scale in State and Local Government.

> This report was referenced by another author as showing mixed results for economies of scale.

Allen, S. (2008). Suburbs Split on Shared Services; City as Hired Help Gets Mixed Reviews. *Pittsburgh Post-Gazette*. Pittsburgh: 1.

> Pittsburgh Mayor offered the city's services at bargain rates to its neighbors in the suburbs. While some municipalities place an absolute priority on autonomy and have no desire to deal with Pittsburgh, others are eager to negotiate shared services with the city in any cost-effective agreement. Services offered included trash-hauling, animal control, building inspection, computer, ambulance, firefighting, personnel, police and public works. Bulk purchasing on goods and supplies and even electricity, and the sale of city water were offered.

Amirkhanyan, A. A., H. J. Kim, and K. T. Lambright (2008). "Does the Public Sector Outperform the Nonprofit and For-Profit Sectors? Evidence from a National Panel Study on Nursing Home Quality and Access." *Journal of Policy Analysis and Management* 27(2): 326-353.

> This study explores the impact of organizational ownership on two complementary aspects of performance: service quality and access to services for impoverished clients.

Derived from public management research on performance determinants and nursing home care literature, the hypotheses stipulate that public, nonprofit, and for-profit nursing homes use different approaches to balance the strategic tradeoff between two aspects of performance. Panel data on 14,423 facilities were analyzed to compare measures of quality and access across three sectors using different estimation methods. Findings indicate that ownership status is associated with critical differences in both quality and access. Public and nonprofit organizations are similar in terms of quality, and both perform significantly better than their for-profit counterparts. When compared to nonprofit and, in some cases, for-profit facilities, public nursing homes have a significantly higher share of Medicaid recipients.

Ammons, D. N. (1997). "Raising the Performance Bar...Locally." *Public Management Magazine* 79(9): 10-16.

The article elaborates on the belief that citizens care about government services and discusses how performance measurement can help provide appropriate information to citizens. Efficiency measurement as opposed to resource input measurement can benefit local governments. The potential uses and benefits of efficiency measurement are discussed. The article emphasizes the use of inter-jurisdictional comparisons.

Ammons, D. N. (2000). "Benchmarking as a Performance Management Tool: Experiences Among Municipalities in North Carolina." *Journal of Public Budgeting, Accounting & Financial Management* 12(1): 106-124.

The article defines benchmarking. Benchmarking takes 3 distinct forms in the public sector, each serving a different purpose. The first form is corporate benchmarking, which is tied to best practice processes. The second form uses targets as goals. The article investigates the third form of statistical comparisons and concludes that when applied properly and with care, benchmarking is a performance improvement technique that can yield tangible results, as demonstrated by the North Carolina cities of Greensboro, Wilmington, and Winston-Salem.

Ammons, D. N., Charles K. Coe, and Michael Lombardo (2001). "Performance-Comparison Projects in Local Government: Participants' Perspective." *Public Administration Review* 61(1): 100-110.

This article examines three prominent projects designed to measure and compare the performance of local governments. All three projects are assessed from the perspective of the local government participants in these projects, revealing gaps between high expectations and subsequent results, but, never the less, suggesting an array of benefits for participants.

Ammons, D. N., and William C. Rivenbark (2008). "Factors Influencing the Use of Performance Data to Improve Municipal Services: Evidence from the North Carolina Benchmarking Project." *Public Administration Review* 68(2): 304-318.

> Many local governments measure and report their performance, but the record of these governments in actually using performance measures to improve services is more modest. The authors of this study examine patterns of performance measurement use among a set of North Carolina cities and conclude that the types of measures on which officials rely, the willingness of officials to embrace comparison, and the degree to which measures are incorporated into key management systems distinguish cities that are more likely to use performance measures for service improvement from those less likely to do so.

Appleton, J. (2008). 3 Towns Consider Plan to Unite Police Forces. The Republican. Springfield, Massachusetts: 1 - 2.

> A newspaper article discusses the effort of three small towns around Brimfield, Massachusetts to provide police services in a shared arrangement. The elected officials, after a preliminary meeting with the three chiefs, requested a detailed analysis of the feasibility of replacing the current part-time service augmented by the state police. One chief felt there might be long-term savings, but an immediate improvement in service quality was possible.

Askim, J., Åge Johnsen , and Knut-Andreas Christophersen (2008). "Factors Behind Organizational Learning from Benchmarking: Experiences from Norwegian Municipal Benchmarking Networks." Journal of Public Administration Research and Theory 18(2): 297–320.

> Benchmarking rests on the assumption that it supports organizational learning and innovation, but the empirical knowledge that underpins this perceived means-end relationship is limited. This article draws on existing research to develop a framework for analyzing organizational learning outcomes from municipal benchmarking. The framework incorporates explanatory factors at different levels (network and municipality), and with different time perspectives (past and present). The study uses empirical results from a nationwide Norwegian benchmarking project.

Barretta, A. D. (2008). "The Exclusion of Indirect Costs from Efficiency Benchmarking." Benchmarking 15(4): 345-365.

> This study aims to evaluate the effects produced by a strategy aimed at neutralizing one of the "disturbance factors" that may impede the focus on "real (in)efficiency" in relative efficiency assessments within the health-care sector: the exclusion of indirect costs from these comparative analyses. The empirical analysis is based on the statistical elaboration of data from a sample group of hospital sub-units within Italian health care trusts.

Barros, C. P. (2007). "The City and the Police Force: Analysing Relative Efficiency in City Police Precincts with Data Envelopment Analysis." *International Journal of Police Science and Management* 9(2): 164-182.

> This paper analyses the efficiency of the Lisbon police force precincts with a 2-stage data envelopment analysis (DEA). In the first stage, the study estimates the DEA efficiency scores and compares the precincts with each other. The aim of this procedure is to seek out those best practices that will lead to the improved performance of all of the precincts. The author ranks the precincts according to their efficiency for the period 2000-2002. In the second stage, he estimates a Tobit model in which the efficiency scores are regressed on socio-economic issues, identifying social causes which vary across the city and that affect deterrence policy. The study considers economic implications of the work.

Behn, R. (2008). "The Performance Target Ethic." *Bob Behn's Public Management Report* November, 2008; Vol. 6, No. 3 Retrieved February 5, 2009, from http://www.hks.harvard.edu/thebehnreport/November2008.pdf.

> Part of Bob Behn's monthly public management series, this edition discusses performance targets. The author takes the position that managerial target setting is not only important, but is a responsibility of elected officials. This position is different than, but not totally incompatible with, benchmark targets based on inter-jurisdictional comparisons.

Behn, R. D. (2007). What All Mayors Would Like to Know About Baltimore's CitiStat Performance Strategy. *Managing for Performance and Results Series.* Washington, DC, IBM Center for The Business of Government: 1 - 59.

> This report summarizes and presents the questions most frequently posed to CitiStat staff and to Mayor Martin O'Malley by visiting mayors who want to investigate the success of CitiStat. When CitiStat is viewed as a leadership strategy rather than a management system, Behn argues, the program can be replicated and customized to each mayor's individual needs and priorities. A key insight from this report is that there is no single, right approach as to how to develop a successful management performance and accountability structure. Success depends heavily on clear goals, committed leadership, and persistent follow-up.

Benton, J. E., and Darwin Gamble (1984). "City/County Consolidation and Economies of Scale: Evidence from a Time-Series Analysis in Jacksonville, Florida." *Social Science Quarterly* 65(1): 190 - 198.

> Although much of the reform literature and consolidation rhetoric suggests that consolidation is likely to save money or reduce taxes, the actual relationship between city/county consolidation and "efficiency" is an empirical question. The results of this case study show that city/county consolidation produced no measurable impact on the taxing and spending policies of one city that has consolidated—Jacksonville, Florida.

Berman, B. J. C. (2006). "The Voices of the People: Missing Links in Performance Measurement and Management." *Government Finance Review* 22(3): 16-20.

> The purpose of this article is to convey to readers the importance of listening to and understanding how the public judges governmental performance so that you can develop, review, produce, and report performance measures. Failing to involve the public in performance measurement and reporting can lead to dissonance between the government and its constituents, and result in misalignment of government programs.

Bewley, J. (2003). Burlco Promotes Joint Plan for Energy; Officials Say Forming a Co-op to Buy Electricity Would Save $100,000 a Year. A Similar Plan Was Rejected 3 Years Ago. *The Philadelphia Inquirer*: B01 - B02.

> This newspaper article from Burlington County, New Jersey discusses the rationale behind the county's attempts to bulk purchase electricity for its constituent municipalities. It reports on the progress of this effort and the estimate of savings if the energy is purchased under a county bid.

Bish, R. (2001). Local Government Amalgamations: Discredited Nineteen-Century Ideas Alive in the Twenty-First. *Communiqué*, C. D. Howe Institute.

> The twenty-first century will be one of rapid change and great need for institutional adaptability. Yet, in the critical area of the relationships among citizens, the civil community, and local governance, some provincial governments are imposing an intellectual fashion of the nineteenth century in the form of an almost religious faith in monolithic organizations and central control. This Commentary undertakes a comprehensive review of 50 years of evidence on the relationship between the structure and performance of local governments in metropolitan areas.

Bish, R. L., and Vincent Ostrom (1973). *Understanding Urban Government: Metropolitan Reform Reconsidered.* Washington, D.C., American Enterprise Institute.

> This book provides an introduction to "public choice" analysis of urban problems. The authors argue that a critical rethinking of the problem of urban government is vitally needed and long overdue. As a means to this new perspective, they offer the public choice approach, which takes as its starting point the diversity of individual preferences and the diverse nature of public goods and services. Bish and Ostrom analyze a number of studies that compare the traditional alternative of metropolitan consolidation with the public choice alternative of a dynamic mix of multi-level public and private services. Another source referenced this book.

Blume, L., and Tillmann Blume (2007). "The Economic Effects of Local Authority Mergers: Empirical Evidence for German City Regions." *Annals of Regional Science*(41): 689-713.

> Cooperation of neighboring local authorities in the provision of regional public goods can be efficiency enhancing due to economies of scale, a better realization of fiscal equivalence or dynamic efficiency gains. While the need for such cooperation between local

authorities is undisputed, there are different positions concerning the form the cooperation should take. Some argue that local authority mergers are the most efficient and democratic strategy. Others argue that functional cooperation is more appropriate and that mergers reduce the welfare enhancing effects of competition between local authorities.

Bodkin, R. G., and David W. Conklin (1971). "Scale and Other Determinants of Municipal Government Expenditures in Ontario: A Quantitative Analysis." *International Economic Review* 71(3): 465-481.

This article summarizes a study of the determinants of municipal government expenditures, which was undertaken for the Government of Ontario. It examines the abilities of large and small municipalities to deliver specific types of services efficiently.

Bolton, M. M. (2008). Shared Services Getting a Fresh Look. The Boston Globe. Boston, *The New York Times* 1 - 3 pages

This news article discusses shared services in Boston, especially police services. This article uses a report that had been released recently on regionalization as a backdrop for the discussion of a new data-sharing system among five towns. The report investigated past failed attempts at regionalization and a successful consolidated 9-1-1 county dispatch system.

Bovaird, T., and Paul Davis (1999). "Learning to Manage within Limited Resources Coping Strategies and Learning Breakthroughs in UK Local Government." *The International Journal of Public Sector Management* 12(3): 293-313.

This article outlines the main conclusions of a research project into how United Kingdom local authorities are managing within limited resources (MLR). Frameworks are developed to aid authorities to plan their approaches to MLR and to situate what they have already done and what they plan to do within a wider portfolio of tactics and strategies. An evaluation is made of how well local government is learning its way through to getting "more from less" and of what local authority support agencies need to do to help authorities to accelerate their learning. Finally, the authors argue that existing learning systems like benchmarking and quality management, while developing rapidly in local government, need further significant refinement if the costs and benefits of resource management strategies are to be systematically evaluated.

Bowerman, M., Amanda Ball, and Graham Francis (2001). "Benchmarking as a Tool for the Modernisation of Local Government." *Financial Accountability and Management* 17(4): 321-329.

This paper examines benchmarking as a tool of the modernization process in local government. The contradictory tensions in the Best Value scheme are explored. Benchmarking is shown to encapsulate the dichotomous nature of a modernizing philosophy which espouses innovation and local solutions alongside the government's centralizing tendencies. One consequence is the advancement of 'compulsory' and 'defensive' modes of benchmarking with local authorities benchmarking for external accountability reasons;

issues of tangible improvement are secondary concerns. These tensions are viewed as irreconcilable, the implication is that local government will need to carefully manage and evaluate its benchmarking activities.

Boyne, G., Julian Gould–Williams, Jennifer Law, and Richard Walker (2002). "Plans, Performance Information and Accountability: The Case of Best Value." *Public Administration* 80(4): 691-710.

The current UK government emphasizes the importance of mechanisms of accountability that involve the planning and public reporting of performance. One example of this is the Best Value performance plan. However, there has been little evaluation of the quality of the information provided in this type of document. This paper draws on literature on stake holding and user needs to identify the data required for accountability. It then assesses whether the plans produced by Best Value pilot authorities in Wales provide appropriate information. The analysis shows that very few of the plans contained the relevant material. Interviews in the pilot authorities highlighted two key reasons for the poor level of data: a lack of performance indicators prior to Best Value and limited staff expertise in performance measurement. The evidence suggests that documents such as performance plans currently make little contribution to the accountability of public organizations.

Boyne, G. A. (1992). "Local Government Structure And Performance: Lessons From America?" *Public Administration* 70(Autumn): 333-357.

The debate in the UK on the reform of local government structure is poorly informed by empirical evidence. This article bridges part of the empirical gap by drawing upon analyses of structural effects in the USA. Two main dimensions of structure are outlined: fragmentation and concentration, both of which can vary vertically and horizontally. Fourteen structural hypotheses are identified and categorized as technical, competitive and political effects.

Boyne, G. A. (1996). "Scale, Performance and the New Public Management: An Empirical Analysis of Local Authority Services." *Journal of Management Studies* 33(6): 809-826.

New public management (NPM) arguments on strategy and structure suggest that performance is enhanced if large organizations are disaggregated into smaller units. The NPM perspective reflects the views of public choice theorists who claim that big organizations are unresponsive to public needs, inefficient and fail to achieve their formal goals. These arguments have underpinned many recent changes in the structure of public services at both central and local levels. This paper uses data on six local government services to test the NPM hypothesis that there is a negative relationship between scale and performance. Five dimensions of performance are analyzed: service coverage, quality, speed of provision, efficiency, and administrative effectiveness. Scale is measured through indicators of service output, caseload and needs. The impact of scale is tested in multivariate statistical models which control for other potential influences on variations in performance across local authorities.

Boyne, G. A. (2003). "Sources of Public Service Improvement: A Critical Review and Research Agenda." *Journal of Public Administration Research and Theory* 13: 357-394.

> Evidence from sixty-five empirical studies of the determinants of public service performance is critically reviewed. The statistical results are grouped on the basis of five theoretical perspectives: resources, regulation, markets, organization, and management. The analysis suggests that the most likely sources of service improvement are extra resources and better management. A research agenda for further work is identified, and recommendations are made to enhance the theoretical and methodological qualities of studies of public service improvement

Braadbaart, O. (2007). "Collaborative Benchmarking, Transparency and Performance: Evidence from The Netherlands Water Supply Industry." *Benchmarking: An International Journal* 14(6): 677-692.

> The purpose of this paper is to investigate how benchmarking affects transparency and economic performance in the public sector. The paper applies a quasi-experimental method to 1989-2000 time series data on benchmarking and non-benchmarking water utilities in the Netherlands. The main limitation of this study is its single-industry scope.

Bretschneider, S., Frederick J.Marc-Aurele, Jiannan Wu (2005). ""Best Practices" Research: A Methodological Guide for the Perplexed." *Journal of Public Administration Research and Theory* 15(2): 307-323.

> The purpose of this article is two-fold. First, it critically examines the underlying assumptions associated with "best practices research" in Public Administration in order to distill an appropriate set of rules to frame research designs for best practice studies. Second, it reviews several statistical approaches that provide a rigorous empirical basis for identification of "best practices" in public organizations - methods for modeling extreme behavior (i.e., iteratively weighted least squares and quartile regression) and measuring relative technical efficiency (data envelopment analysis, known as DEA).

British Columbia Ministry of Community Services (2006). Primer on Regional Districts in British Columbia. Retrieved July 13, 2010 from http://www.cd.gov.bc.ca/lgd/gov_structure/library/Primer_on_Regional_Districts_in_BC.pdf.

> The primer provides the history and rationale for regional districts, which were established in British Columbia in the 1960's. It discusses the underlying principles and the structure of the districts, and describes how they make decisions and maintain accountability. It emphasizes the consensual nature of the districts and how they have proceeded with flexibility to evolve for over forty years.

Brookings Institution Center on Urban and Metropolitan Policy (2002). Beyond Merger: A Competitive Vision for the Regional City of Louisville, The Brookings Institution: 1-11.

> In November 2000, voters in the City of Louisville and Jefferson County approved a referendum to unify their two governments, effective January 2003. This report investi-

gates the functions that are unaffected by the merger as well as evaluating departments whose fate has been left to the determination of the Metro Mayor and Council. Building on a superb body of local data collection and analysis, the document seeks to present the new Regional City of Louisville with its first complete look at itself as it embarks on merger, in order to help it define a new vision of competitiveness. To that end, the report endeavors to provide a new map of the critical demographic, land use and economic trends altering the new city, and then follow up with an agenda of potential policy choices that will help the region shape the trends to its benefit.

Brown, T., and Matthew Potoski (2003). "Transaction Costs and Institutional Explanations for Government Service Production Decisions." *Journal of Public Administration Research and Theory* 13: 441-468.

> Governments not only choose which services to deliver to citizens, but they also choose how to deliver those services. Governments can produce services themselves or through a variety of external production mechanisms, including contracting with other governments, private firms, and non-profit agencies. This article applies a transaction cost framework complemented with institutional and market theories to examine governments' service production decisions. A 1997 International City/County Management Association survey shows how governments choose service production mechanisms to manage the transaction costs inherent in delivering different types of services.

Brown, T. L. (2008). "The Dynamics of Government-To-Government Contracts." *Public Performance & Management Review* 31(3): 364-386.

> This paper explores the dynamics of government-to-government contracting at the local level in order to examine how governments' shared organizational characteristics, notably a governance structure based on political accountability, potentially make them more attractive vendors for services that risk contract failure. Relying on panel data from the 1992 and 1997 International City/County Management Association's (ICMA) Alternative Service Delivery surveys along with data from the U.S. Census and other sources, this paper identifies service areas in which governments most frequently turn to government vendors. In particular, a comparison of public works and transportation services - service areas with low risks of opportunism leading to contract failure - and health and human services - a service area with high risks of opportunism leading to contract failure - shows that contracting governments are more likely to utilize governments over private firms and non-profits for high-risk services. This is not the case for low-risk services, suggesting that governments view other governments as trusted contract vendors.

\Byrnes, J., and Brian Dollery (2002). "Do Economies of Scale Exist in Australian Local Government? A Review of the Research Evidence." *Urban Policy and Research* 20(4): 391-414.

> The 1990s witnessed a major era of structural reform in Australian local government. Amalgamation programmes in all six states resulted in a substantial decrease in the number of local authorities in Australia. The chief rationale underlying local govern-

ment mergers lay apparently in the belief that larger municipalities would exhibit greater economic efficiencies. Despite its widespread acceptance amongst policy elites, this argument did not derive from a solid empirical base. This article seeks to evaluate available research evidence on the controversial question of economies of scale in Australian local government.

Campbell, R., and Sally Coleman Selden (2000). Does City-County Consolidation Save Money? The Unification of Athens-Clarke County Suggest it Might. *Public Policy Research Series*: 1-2.

The article discusses a city-county merger in Georgia. Two of the four successful consolidations in the United States since 1990 have occurred in Georgia: Athens-Clarke County (1991) and Augusta-Richmond County (1998). The authors studied the finances of the Unified Government of Athens-Clarke County which began operating in FY1992. They examined expenditures between 1990 and 1997 in order to examine both the short and long-term financial impacts of consolidation.

Carey, M., Ashok Srinivasan, and Robert Strauss (1996). "Optimal Consolidation of Municipalities: An Analysis of Alternative Designs." *Socio-Economic Science* 30(2): 103-119.

The authors present a model for estimating the cost of providing local government services, and then introduce the notion of the "optimal" size of a municipality. In this paper, they present an analytic framework for the geographic aggregation of municipalities into larger and more populous municipal districts in order to reduce the costs of providing public services. The model allows the authors to determine the optimal number of districts for a fixed population size in a given geographic area, and to arrive at the extent of cost savings possible in the absence of additional considerations.

Carruthers, J. I., and Gudmundur F. Ulfarsson (2002). "Fragmentation and Sprawl: Evidence from Interregional Analysis." *Growth and Change* 33(summer): 312-340.

Recent years have witnessed widespread expansion of state and regional planning programs in the United States. A major purpose of these efforts is to reduce urban sprawl,— low density, discontinuous, suburban-style development, often characterized as the result of rapid, unplanned, and/or uncoordinated growth—by promoting jurisdictional cooperation and regulatory consistency across metropolitan areas. This paper evaluates the efficacy of this approach by examining the relationship between governmental fragmentation and several measureable outcomes of urban development: density, urbanized land area, property value, and public expenditures on infrastructure. The four dimensions are modeled in a simultaneous equations framework, providing substantive evidence on how fragmentation and other exogenous factors affect metropolitan growth patterns.

Cassese, S. (2008). Garbage Collection Savings Seen. *Newsday*: 1-1.

This newspaper article examines a report which was about to be released by Nassau County, which provided estimated cost comparisons between garbage collection services controlled by the town or controlled by the sanitation district within the county. It provides an estimate of the overall cost savings in the county if towns controlled the service and gave some comparisons for specific communities.

Cauchon, D. (2006). Big Government? N.J. Has Scads of Little Ones; State Looks at Consolidation to Cut Taxes. *USA Today*: 1-2.

This newspaper article coincided with the beginning of the New Jersey special legislative session on property taxes. The article presented the perspectives of the governor, legislators, local officials and the public, as reflected in a Gannett poll. The USA Today article analyzed New Jersey local government to be only slightly more costly than that of the average state.

Center for Government Research (2003, July). "Cooperate, Collaborate, Consolidate: Options for Local Government in Monroe County."

Local governments in Monroe County are caught in the convergence of several trends that are producing current and projected multi-million dollar budget deficits in the two largest governments—the city and the county—and have strained town, village and school district budgets as well. These trends are (1) the rising cost of government at all levels; (2) a stagnating local economy; and (3) high local taxes. The primary objective of this report was "To inform and update the public about opportunities to make government more effective and efficient through cooperation, collaboration, and/or consolidation."

Center for Government Research (2006). "CGR Experience with Consolidation & Shared Services Across New York State ". Retrieved November 1 2008, from http://www.cgr.org/ar2006/docs/SharedServices.pdf.

This government consulting firm reviews some of their experience with municipalities in New York State regarding shared services in various counties. The review includes developing a two-tiered government approach involving private contracting, consolidation of fire and police services, and other agreements brokered between counties and cities. The article discusses various service types in different size entities..

Chalos, P., and Joseph Cherian (1995). "An Application of Data Envelopment Analysis to Public Sector Performance Measurement and Accountability." *Journal of Accounting and Public Policy* 14(2): 143-160.

Public sector performance measures have been advocated by numerous regulatory bodies (FASB 1980; CCAF 1987; CICA 1988; GASB 1989). Proposed Service Effort and Accomplishment (SEA) disclosures include measures of inputs and input-output efficiency ratios (GASB 1989). Such metrics, it is argued, improve internal control and external accountability. To date, SEA disclosures are not widely disseminated. The study examined the potential utility of SEA disclosures in determining public policy in education. Specific concerns of the Illinois State Board of Education and the state legislature with respect to fiscal neutrality and tax referenda in education were examined. As proposed by the GASB (1989, x-xii), educational input and output indicators were compiled for 207 school districts. To overcome specification problems, DEA analysis was used to measure input-output efficiency. Non parametric hypothesis tests were performed on the resulting efficiency and effectiveness measures.

Chan, Y.-C. L. (2004). "Performance Measurement and Adoption of Balanced Scorecards: A Survey of Municipal Governments in the USA and Canada." *International Journal of Public Sector Management* 17(3): 204-221.

> To deal with financial constraints and increasing demand on accountability, government administrators have begun implementing modern management tools in their organizations. The balanced scorecard, a performance and strategic management system, has been adopted in for-profit organizations with success and its application in the government sector is explored in this study. Results of a survey of municipal governments in the USA and Canada show that there is limited use of the balanced scorecard. Most municipal governments, however, have developed measures to assess their organizations' financial, customer satisfaction, operating efficiency, innovation and change, and employee performance.

Cheung, R. (2008). "The Interaction between Public and Private Governments: An Empirical Analysis." *Journal of Urban Economics* 63 (3): 885-901.

> Private governments, found in planned developments and condominiums, are increasingly common methods of delivering local services to residents. This paper provides the first empirical study of their impact on local public finance. A novel data set of homeowners' associations allows construction of a panel of private governments in California. Panel methods test whether public expenditures respond to private government prevalence. The study employs a very large data set, 110 cities with 38-year time series, yielding reasonably convincing results.

Claps, M. (2008). Case Study: Business Process Analysis Underlies Launch of Local Government Shared Service in the U.K.: 1-8.

> This article is a case study set in U.K. regarding shared services and partnerships when three local U.K. councils came together to reduce cost and share services. Taxes and revenue sharing are discussed as well as the intricacies of U.K. partnerships. Different stages of the partnering are discussed as well as the success factors and lessons learned.

Coe, C. (1999). "Local Government Benchmarking: Lessons from Two Major Multigovernment Efforts." *Public Administration Review* 59(2): 110-123.

> Benchmarking and performance measurement are increasingly "hot" subjects among public administrators. Among research based efforts encouraged by the performance measurement drive are two projects that attempt to develop uniform measures so that managers can compare the performance of different city and county governments. This

article compares the methodology used in the ICMA and IOG projects. It begins with a brief overview of each benchmarking effort and then looks at the often unexpected obstacles the projects encountered and how they attempted to surmount them. It concludes with some broader lessons that these experiences suggest for local government benchmarking.

Colimore, E. (2005). South Jersey Towns Share Services, Save; Pressed to Cut Costs, More Are Exploiting Economies of Scale in Police, Fire and Development Duties. *The Philadelphia Inquirer:* 1-2.

This newspaper article reviews several efforts in Camden County, New Jersey to save money through shared services. The article projects savings for some of these efforts and discusses other plans for sharing services. It describes the statements of the Department of Community Affairs about the SHARE grant program.

Community Benchmarks Program (1999). Residential Trash Collection in Onondaga County: A Study Comparing Cost and Type of Service. Mawell School of Citizenship and Public Affairs, Syracuse University. Retrieved June 2, 2009 from http://www.state.nj.us/dca/lgs/share/joint/sharedsvcsrefguide.pdf.

This is a report from the study of residential trash and recyclables collection in 36 local governments within Onondaga County, New York. Total costs are compared for direct delivery of the service by the government, privatized delivery, and abandonment of service delivery in which the citizen is required to select the private hauler. One special district operating in a portion of a municipality was included in the comparisons. For the municipalities that abandoned the service delivery to the individual choice of their residents, the study compared the cost to the residents.

Confessore, N., and Jeremy Peters (2008). State Could Save $1 Billion a Year by Consolidating Services, Report Says. *New York Times.*

This news article describes the recommendations for sweeping changes to local government across the State of New York, which could save $1 billion a year. The report targeted special districts and other governments distinct from county, city, town, and village governments, that have appointive jobs and which Governor Paterson referred to as "patronage mills." The report recommended centralizing many services. It also recommended the State Commissioner of Education be given the power to order the consolidation of school districts. It was criticized by union leaders and school superintendents. Most recommendations will require approval by the legislature.

Conti, K. (2008). Shared Firehouse Brings Relief, and Trepidation. *The Boston Globe.* Boston: 1.

This newspaper article reviews the controversy surrounding a fire station built by a developer to provide service to its new large housing development. In particular, several groups have raised issues of how response will be affected. The Towns of Revere and Malden will share the station.

Cortés-Vázquez, L. A. (2008). Local Government Shared Services Progress Report 2005-2007. N. Y. S. State Department: 1-24.

> This NY Department of State press release speaks about a shared services report that was compiled very recently. New York created a shared services grant in 2005 for municipalities to partner with each other to share costs through difficult economic times. The highlight of the report claims that $245 million in projected savings could be realized through local government partnership and cooperation. Progress in each of the shared service areas has been analyzed and examined.

County and Municipal Government Study Commission (1970). Joint Services—A Local Response to Area Wide Problems.

> This 1970 report was referenced in the LUARCC project reports to provide evidence of the on-going nature of the interest in shared services and the effficiency of local government

Courty, P., Carolyn Heinrich, and Gerald Marschke (2005). "Setting the Standard in Performance Measurement Systems." *International Public Management Journal* 8(3): 321-347.

> A fundamental challenge in the design of performance measurement and incentive systems is the establishment of appropriate benchmark levels of performance, also known as performance standards. Drawing from the information economics, contract theory and public administration literatures, the authors derive theoretical implications for the construction of performance standards. They then assess alternative methods that are commonly used to construct performance standards and consider their application in performance measurement systems in public programs. The authors draw out important lessons for the establishment of performance benchmarks and other implications for performance standards system design in public organizations.

Curry, M. (1999). An Analysis of a Proposed Four Fire District Merger in Ada County. (An applied research project submitted to the National Fire Academy as part of the Executive Fire Officer Program): 1-44.

> This research project was an application of the first phase of the four phases Change Management Model, found in the Executive Management of Change course taught at the National Fire Academy. In Ada County, Idaho, various fire district chiefs had been discussing the possibilities of a fire district merger for some time; however the problem was that no formal analysis had taken place. The purpose of this research project was to do a formal analysis of this four fire district merger. Historical, descriptive and evaluative research methods were used to determine (a) what were the organizational conditions, including mission statements, standards, operational procedures or other values that would be impacted, (b) what were the potential destabilizing forces that may exist, (c) what would be the impact of organizational conditions or destabilizing forces, and (d) what the organizational change requirements necessary to make the merger successful would be.

Davis, P. (1998). "The Burgeoning of Benchmarking in British Local Government: The Value of "Learning by Looking" in the Public Services." *Benchmarking for Quality Management & Technology* 5(4).

> A large number of benchmarking initiatives have now been established in UK local gov-ernment and, in most cases, these activities have grown organically from a variety of local pilot schemes and from the social interaction fostered through professional networks, to the point where some classification and clarification is possible. This growth has been powered by a small number of key stimuli. The "Inter Authorities Group" (IAG), the largest voluntary benchmarking club in local government, emerged from the concern over consistent costing data. This article evaluates the current status of benchmarking in UK local government.

Davis, T. (2005). "Shared Services and the Economies of Scale They Provide Local Govern-ments." *University of Michigan, Taubman College of Architecture and Urban Planning, Urban and Regional Planning, Economic Development Handbook.* Retrieved November 12, 2008, from http://www.umich.edu/~econdev/jointservice/.

> With shrinking revenues and growing service demands, Michigan communities are join-ing forces to provide services to their constituents. Joint, or shared, services are agree-ments between local governments to combine resources to provide a service to their communities. This combination is a cost saving method for municipalities that want to maintain service levels but find that tax laws inhibit their ability to fund them individu-ally. The result is a classic example of economies of scale, providing a community with increased general fund flexibility and improvements to quality of life that contributes to the supply side of economic development. Stable general funds will allow communities to finance capital improvement projects and offer incentives to potential firms, while offering services that will attract residents that build the tax base and provide employees to those potential firms.

Deller, S. C., Carl H. Nelson, and Norman Walzer (1992). "Measuring Managerial Efficiency in Rural Government." *Public Productivity & Management Review* 15(3 (Spring)): 355-370.

> Structural limitation and narrow managerial capacity have consistently hampered both an effective and efficient decision-making process in small rural governments. Due to small size and relative isolation, rural governments are inherently limited in developing either effective policy or efficient delivery systems. These structural barriers have pre-vented many rural public officials from developing the capacity, resources, and expertise needed for managing increasingly complex problems. This article provides a brief review of the performance measurement literature and suggests an alternative approach to assessing the efficiency of producing local public services. The proposed method seeks to incorporate microeconomic theory into the measurement process. The case of produc-ing low-volume rural road services in the Midwest is examined to illustrate the method. The data used to study managerial efficiency in the production of rural road services were

gathered from a mail survey of Illinois, Minnesota and Wisconsin township road officials and the 1982 Census of government. The sample contains 435 independent observations of Midwestern townships.

Deller, S. C., and John M. Halstead (1994). "Efficiency in the Production of Rural Road Services: The Case of New England Towns." *Local Economics* 70(20): 247-59

An analysis of size and managerial efficiency of northern New England towns in the production of rural road services is reported. A stochastic cost frontier was used as the normative efficiency reference set. Empirical results provide evidence of economies of size in the production of road service in New England and evidence that size inefficiencies are present. Results also suggest that managerial inefficiencies, or input use inefficiencies, are present and costs may be 40 percent higher than necessary. At issue is the effectiveness of current institutional arrangements: small town governments may best match local demand with services, but at high cost.

Dollery, B., and Andrew Johnson (2005). "Enhancing Efficiency in Australian Local Government: An Evaluation of Alternative Models of Municipal Governance." *Urban Policy and Research* 23(13): 73-85.

Broad consensus exists in Australian policy circles on the need to enhance the efficiency of local government. However, the question of the most appropriate model for local governance remains controversial. Quite apart from larger amalgamated municipalities, a range of promising alternative options can be identified that may be able to effectively combine more efficient service delivery with vibrant local democracy.

Dollery, B., and Joel Byrnes (2005). "Alternative to Amalgamation in Australian Local Government: The Case of Walkerville." *UNE Working Paper Series in Economics* 2005-4: 1-25.

Structural reform chiefly through council amalgamation has long been the most favored means of enhancing municipal efficiency by Australian state government policy makers. However, the disappointing results of most amalgamation programs have led to a growing skepticism in the local government community and a search for alternative methods of improving council efficiency. Not only have scholars designed generic models suitable for Australian conditions, but individual councils and group of councils around the country have also developed several de facto alternatives to amalgamation. An embryonic body of research has now begun to examine the efficacy of these alternative organizational arrangements. The present paper seeks to augment this nascent literature evaluating the outcomes achieved by Walkerville; an Adelaide suburban council that escaped the South Australian merger program completed in 1998.

Dollery, B., Alexandr Akimov and Joel Byrnes (2009). *Shared Services in Australian Local Government: Rationale, Alternative Models, and Empirical Evidence.* Retrieved July 13, 2010 from http://www.solgm.co.nz/NR/rdonlyres/445ABA53-364C-4F32-88AE-A9B22B95F4CC/ 43703/ConferencePaperBackgroundBrianDollery.pdf.

> Accompanying the loss of enthusiasm for municipal amalgamations in Australian, resulting from the disappointing outcomes, has been an increasing interest in shared services. This paper attempts to fill the voids of a rationale for the effectiveness of the shared services model, a comparison to alternative models of service delivery, and empirical evidence supporting the shared services model.

Drake, L., and R. Simper (2000). "Productivity Estimation and the Size-Efficiency Relationship in English and Welsh Police Forces: An Application of DEA and Multiple Discriminant Analysis." *International Review of Law and Economics* 20(1): 53-73.

> This article utilizes data envelopment analysis (DEA) to estimate the productivity of the English and Welsh police forces and to determine whether there are categorical scale effects in policing using multiple discriminant analysis (MDA). The article demonstrates that by using DEA efficiency results it is possible to make inferences about the optimal size and structure of the English and Welsh police forces.

Drake, L., and R. Simper (2002). "X-Efficiency and Scale Economies in Policing: A Comparative Study Using the Distribution Free Approach and DEA." *Applied Economics* 34(15): 1859-1870.

> This study uses both parametric and nonparametric techniques to analyze scale economies and relative efficiency levels in policing in England and Wales. Both techniques suggest the presence of significant scale effects in policing and considerable divergence in relative efficiency levels across police forces.

Eagle, K. (2004). "Translating Strategy: Public Sector Applications of the Balanced Scorecard." *Government Finance Review*: 16-22.

> This article discusses the evolution of strategy development and performance measurement in the City of Charlotte, with an emphasis on the lessons learned from nearly 10 years of using the Balanced Scorecard model. Developed for the private sector in an effort to balance measures of organizational performance between financial results and other critical success factors, the Balanced Scorecard has been adapted for the public sector by a number of local governments. From implementing and using the Balanced Scorecard to the most recent challenge of linking strategy to resource allocation, Charlotte's story is one characterized by continuous improvement.

El-Khoury, T. (2005). Consolidating Fire Agencies A Big Cost Saver, Report Says. *St. Petersburg Times*

This newspaper article presents some cost savings estimates from a study by MGT of America evaluating the consolidation of county and city fire departments in Pinellas County, Florida. This report was presented to the County's Charter Review Commission. MGT recommended that the county form a single fire district.

Estrada, S. M. (1999a). Audit Finds Finances in Good Shape. *St. Petersburg Times.*

This newspaper article reports on the presentation of the annual audit in North Redington Beach, Florida. The audit showed $100,000 in savings for eliminating the police department, but it appeared eliminating the fire department did not represent a cost savings, since the cost of using the Indian Rocks Fire District is about the same. In the next year, this cost will be removed from the town budget and will be billed directly to the resident through the county tax bill.

Estrada, S. M. (1999b). North Redington to Get Property Tax Break. *St. Petersburg Times.*

This article discusses how the Mayor and Commission in North Redington Beach, Florida determined to set the tax rate in light of cost savings that would be realized from sharing fire services with the Indian Rocks Fire District and eliminating the police department because the Sheriff's Office is providing police services. The Mayor and Commissioners argued over whether the savings should be used to offset taxes or offset increased expenses for other purposes.

Estrada, S. M. (2007). City close to a deal with the sheriff. *St. Petersburg Times.*

This newspaper article discusses the deliberations on police services that will occur at the upcoming Belleair Beach, Florida city council meeting. The city has received proposals to provide policing from the County Sheriff's Office and from Belleair, but the Sheriff's arrangements were described as more attractive. The Sheriff has offered to waive start-up costs in exchange for some of the existing equipment owned by Belleair Beach and has agreed to hire any officer now serving and in good standing at Belleair Beach.

Feiock, R., Scott Lamothe, and Meeyoung Lamothe (2004). Vertical Integration in Municipal Service Provision. *2004 Annual Meeting of the American Political Science Association.* Chicago, IL.: 1-33.

Tremendous attention has been given to contracting or outsourcing service productions. What has gone virtually unnoticed is that many of these services have experienced "vertical integration of production" where the service is taken in-house by the providing government. Building on three typologies of service characteristics that are prominent in the literature, the authors examine whether vertical integration is systemically associated with certain types of goods and test whether the likelihood of vertical integration increases when mismatches occur between the service types and the modes of service delivery. Vertical integration can also be a response to market conditions, capacities for production and administration within government, or political, preferences of public decision makers. Vertical integration is the product of transaction problems relating to the characteristics of goods, production agents, and markets.

Fessenden, F. (2006). Two Villages, Together but Apart. *The New York Times.* New York.

This newspaper article demonstrates the difficulties of consolidation in the real experience of Pelham Manor and the Village of Pelham in New York. A village trustee cited fear of loss of services as the reason for failure to consolidate and the Mayor suggested an additional factor was the unequal property valuation in the two towns, which would lead to potential tax increases for some residents even if total costs went down.

Foltin, C. (1999). "State and Local Government Performance: It's Time to Measure Up!" *The Government Accountants Journal* 48(1): 40-46.

State and local governments must do more with less. This has been the task for nearly three decades. Resources have decreased due to slowed population growth, recessions in the 1970s and 1980s, reduced federal funding and reluctance of citizens to pass new taxes. Furthermore, unfunded mandates, inflation, worn out infrastructure and increasing wage and benefit costs have caused expenditures to skyrocket. In light of these conditions this paper encourages the use of performance measurement and provides help in understanding the basic concepts.

Foroutan, F. (1992). "Regional Integration in Sub-Saharan Africa: Experience and Prospects, Volume 1 ". Retrieved December 2, 2008, from <http://econ.worldbank.org/external/default/main?pagePK=64165259&theSitePK=469372&piPK=64165421&menuPK=64166093&entityID=000009265_3961003095633>.

The emphasis of regional integration in Sub-Saharan Africa should shift from the integration of goods markets to the regional coordination of macroeconomic and microeconomic policies, the harmonization of administrative rules and regulations, and the joint provision of public goods. Such steps are likely to make Sub-Saharan African markets more attractive to domestic and foreign investors and to improve economic growth. Still, this paper provided no concrete evidence supporting potential benefits from regional integrations.

Fox, W., and Tami Gurley (2006). Will Consolidation Improve Sub-National Governments?, World Bank.

Local government size varies dramatically around the world. In Sudan, Côte d'Ivoire and the United Kingdom municipalities average more than 125,000 people. Those in many European countries have less than 10,000 people. Countries often consider consolidation of local governments as a means to lower service delivery costs, improve service quality, enhance accountability, improve equity or expand participation in government. The paper reviews a number of theoretical arguments and empirical findings concerning the size of sub-national governments. Countries should not presume that amalgamation will solve the problems because benefits and costs are situation specific. Success depends on many factors including getting incentives right for the various players and managing the transition properly. The effects on costs must be examined in terms of all changes occurring with consolidation, including geographic size.

Fry, J. C. (2004). Performance Measurement—The Basics. *New Jersey League Of Municipalities Annual Conference.* Atlantic City, NJ.

> The PowerPoint presentation was sponsored by the New Jersey League of Municipalities and the New Jersey Municipal Managers Association. The presentation was oriented to an audience of practitioners in municipal government who had limited experience with performance measurement. It defines performance measurement, provides the basic steps to do it, describes the benefits, lists the types of indicators, provides sources of indicators, elaborates on types of targets, and discusses what should be done to achieve results.

Gabler, L. R. (1969). "Economies and Diseconomies of Scale in Urban Public Service." *Journal of Land Economics* 45(4): 425-434.

> Previous studies have yielded somewhat different conclusions as to the effect of population size on city per capita expenditures. The analysis in this article was motivated not only by the differing conclusions, but also by the increased concern expressed by policy-makers with the effects of population growth and redistribution on urban areas in general and cities in particular. This article attempts to assess the effects of three population factors—size, density, and rate of change—on the provision of certain public services.

Gabler, L. R. (1971). "Population Size as Determinant of City Expenditures and Employment—Some Further Evidence." *Land Economics* 47(2): 130-138.

> The influence of various population factors on the level of per capita expenditures has attracted increased attention in the recent past, both in the professional journals and among policy-makers at all government levels. Differences in city expenditures per capita have been linked with variations in such factors as city size, rate of population growth, and population density. Yet, earlier studies, using different units of observation and analytical approaches, have, not surprisingly, reached different conclusions. The purpose of this article is to utilize the now available 1967 Census data and to expand an earlier inquiry to encompass eight—as opposed to three—states.

Garcia-Sanchez, I. (2006). "Efficiency Measurement in Spanish Local Government: The Case of Municipal Water Services." *Review of Policy Research* 23(2): 355-371.

> In this study, the authors established a procedure for evaluating the efficiency of providing the water supply. This procedure has allowed the authors to find that the proposed indicators have a discriminating capability in the analysis of the service, and to reject criticisms traditionally assigned to the sensitivity of the data envelopment analysis (DEA) technique in relation to degrees of freedom. The article studies efficiency but is also illustrative of the use of the technique of Data Envelopment Analysis.

Gelders, D., Mirjam Galetzka, Jan Pieter Verckens, and Erwin Seydel (2008). "Showing Results? An Analysis of the Perceptions of Internal and External Stakeholders of the Public Performance Communication by the Belgian and Dutch Railways." *Government Information Quarterly* 25(2): 221–238.

> Performance measurement and communicating about it with the broader public is not self-evident if one looks at public services organizations. In Belgium and the Netherlands, one organization that has been under constant surveillance from its stakeholders is the railroad company. Originally a national public service, it has changed through a European directive to operate in a liberalized transportation market. In this paper, the authors present the results of a qualitative study into what the Belgian and Dutch railway companies measure about their performance towards travelers, how they measure it, and specifically how they communicate it to their employees and stakeholders. Although we might expect the Dutch railway company (NS) to be more transparent than the Belgian railway company (NMBS/SNCB), in reality the two organizations do not differ that much from each other.

Gonzales, S. (2004). Inverness Begins Dismantling Police. *St. Petersburg Times.*

> The news article reports the results of a city council vote in Inverness, Florida to dissolve the police department. The vote was not unanimous with some council members contending it was too emotional an issue to act on at this time. Concerns were addressed about response times, since the Inverness response had traditionally been quicker than the Sheriff's Office, which will now assume responsibility. Inverness would now enjoy the higher standards and additional capacity and expertise in the Sheriff's Office. The Sheriff's Office considered the following factors in developing the plan accepted by the Council: loss of local control and police identity, the future of Police Department employees, level of service and cost.

Gorcester, S., and Rhonda Reinke (2007). "Dashboards Simplify Performance Reporting." *Government Finance Review* 23(5): 53-56.

> Successful performance management demands effective performance reporting. Software dashboards, in particular, offer elegant simplicity to the otherwise difficult task of reporting performance for quick interpretation by both the numbers people and the ideas people. The Washington State Transportation Improvement Board (TIB) implemented its performance dashboard in 2003 and followed the government management, accountability and performance directive (GMAP) in earnest after its adoption in 2004 by the State of Washington.

Government Accounting Standards Board (1994). Concepts Statement No.2, Service Efforts and Accomplishments Reporting

> In 1994, after extensive research on SEA, the GASB issued Concepts Statement No. 2, Service Efforts and Accomplishments Reporting. That Statement provided the opportunity to elaborate on accountability in government and the importance of reporting SEA

performance information as part of general purpose external financial reporting (GPEFR). The Board stated that SEA performance information is necessary for assessing accountability and in making informed decisions: "Therefore, to be more complete, general purpose external financial reporting needs to include service efforts and accomplishments information." This report is not included in the LUARCC articles folder, although it may be purchased from GASB. GASB has continued from this point, particularly emphasizing citizen involvement in determining what should be measured and reported upon. In 2008, the Board issued an Exposure Draft of an amendment of Concepts Statement No. 2.

Grant, K. (2007). How Toronto has fared as one big city; 10 Years Old Jan. 1; Despite growing pains, there have been successes. *National Post.* Toronto: 1.

This news article looks at the successes and issues that have appeared since the consolidation of six cities into Metro Toronto ten years prior. Although the expected cost savings did not materialize, other benefits in terms of the ability to make decisions and accomplish change did occur. The author notes that much consolidation of services had already occurred prior to the final merger.

Greenblatt, A. (2006). Little Mergers on the Prairie. *Governing Magazine.*

This article examines how Iowa has addressed the concern that it has more government than it now needs. Iowa has 3,000 cities and towns, 99 counties as well as special districts. The Governor proposed to replace all local governments with 15 regional governments. With a stagnant tax base, Iowa has few options. The Governor's proposal was met with resistance, but, on a positive note, Iowa municipalities are working more together. "For local officials, saving a lot of money right away isn't as great a concern as doing things more efficiently when they can, whether that means streamlining internally or reaching out to new partners."

Grossman, P. J. (1987). "The Optimal Size of Government." *Public Choice* 53(2): 131-147.

In the economic analysis of the theory of government, two views of government are evident. The Pigovian view sees government as a benevolent actor striving to correct for the inadequacies and excesses of an unrestrained marketplace. The Public Choice' view of government portrays government as the tool of special interest groups as likely to generate distortions as to correct them. In this paper, a model of government that incorporates both views will be developed and then empirically tested. The model developed assumes that all expenditures by the government are inputs into the private sector production. Treating government expenditures as inputs into the production of private sector output, there is some optimal size of government that maximizes private sector output. The model incorporates a general production function for private sector output. Output is a function of private labor, private capital, and government expenditures. The Pigovian and Public Choice views of government are reflected in the assumed impact of G on the marginal productivities of L and K. The model is tested using United States data and a Cobb-Douglas production function.

Gunderson, M. (2008). In Tough times, officials eye shared services Regional strategy touted as efficient. *The Boston Globe.* Boston: 3.

> The news article reports on a conference in Worcester, Massachusetts on regionalizing government. The conference, sponsored by the Massachusetts Municipal Association and Northeastern University, had 200 attendees. The article presents the differing perspectives of some of the local government officials in attendance. The President of the association remarks on some legislative impediments to regionalization and cooperation.

Hanes, N. (2001). Amalgamation Impact on Local Public Expenditures in Sweden. *6th Nordic Conference on Local Public Finance.* Helsinki.

> Two extensive municipal reforms have substantially reduced the number of municipalities in Sweden. The main objective of the first municipal reform in 1952 was to form municipalities with no less than 2 000 inhabitants in order to increase administration efficiency and to exploit economies of scale in the provision of local public services. This paper studies whether the growth in local public expenditures differed between the newly formed municipalities and the ones that were not affected by the reform. The empirical analysis is based on data for the years 1951, 1953 and 1959.

Hatry, H., and Joseph J. Wholey (1999). *Performance Measurement: Getting Results.* Urban Institute Press.

> Long before "reinventing government" came into vogue, the Urban Institute pioneered methods for government and human services agencies to measure the performance of their programs. This book synthesizes more than two decades of Harry Hatry's pioneering work on performance measurement into a comprehensive guide. The author explains every component of the process, from identifying the program's mission, objectives, customers, and trackable outcomes to finding the best indicators for each outcome, the sources of data, and how to collect them. He covers the selection of indicator breakouts and benchmarks for comparisons to actual values and suggests a number of uses for performance information. Joseph Wholey contributes a chapter on maintaining the quality of the performance measurement process. It is not available in the Articles Folder for the LUARCC project.

Hildebrand, J. (2008). Plan would pool school resources; Nassau-paid report, due out today, to show county agencies can help cut school costs by sharing services. *Newsday.*

> The news article covers the contents of a report about to be released by the Nassau County (New York) Executive on cost savings that could be realized through pooling back-office functions at the county level. The report was prepared by consultants hired by the county. It emphasizes specialized administrative services, such as legal, auditing, telecommunications, information technology, and transportation would be handled more cost effectively by using county resources.

Hirsch, W. (1959). "Expenditure Implications of Metropolitan Growth and Consolidation." *The Review of Economics and Statistics* 41(3): 232-241.

> Metropolitan areas are growing fast and so are their problems. To make this growth smoother and fiscal problems less burdensome, the consolidation of metropolitan area governments is widely advocated on the premise that it will reduce per capita expenditures of local government services. It is argued that, just as there are economies of scale in manufacturing, average municipal costs and expenditures likewise decline as the size of the local government unit increases. This paper will attempt to develop a theoretical framework for analyzing the question "What are the likely expenditure effects of metropolitan growth and consolidation?" The deductive answers will then be tested by an empirical analysis of 149 government units in the St. Louis metropolitan area and some Massachusetts cities.

Hirsch, W. Z. (1968). The Supply of Urban Public Services. *Issues in Urban Economics*. H. S. Perloff, and Lowdon Wingo, Jr. Baltimore, John Hopkins University Press: 477-525.

> This book is not available in the Articles Folder of the LUARCC project. The chapter was referenced by another author as showing mixed results about economies of scale.

Ho, A. (2004). Lessons from Past Consolidation Efforts, The Center for Urban Policy and the Environment.

> This Powerpoint presentation reviews consolidation attempts since 1805 in the United States, with particular attention to those attempted since 1990. It examines the efficiency argument for consolidation and evaluates other benefits that may accrue from consolidation.

Ho, S.-J. K., and Yee-Ching Lilian Chan (2002). "Performance Measurement and the Implementation of Balanced Scorecards in Municipal Governments." *Journal of Government Financial Management* 51(4): 8-19.

> Since the Government Accounting Standards Board released Concepts Statement No. 2, Service Efforts and Accomplishments (SEA) Reporting in 1994, about one-third of local governments participate in SEA reporting, according to a recent survey. Government administrators have applied some modern, private sector management tools to solve their management problems. However, the Balanced Scorecard, a performance management system used by about 50 percent of Fortune 1000 companies, according to a recent survey by Bain & Co., has not been well received by local governments. As a follow-up to previous studies, including one by Ho and Kidwell that showed the Balanced Scorecard to be the least prevalent tool, this article examines the current performance measurement systems of municipal governments, assesses their perceived value and quality, and compares the experience of a Balanced Scorecard implementer with that of other local municipalities. This article is not available in the articles folder for the LUARCC project but is available for purchase from the AGA.

Holzer, M., John Fry, LaMont Rouse, and Lisa Mahajan (2003). Division of Local Government Services: Joint Services Assessment Report. Newark, Rutgers University-Newark Campus: 36.

> This report was commissioned by the Division of Local Government Services to conduct a study of shared service programs among New Jersey's 566 municipalities. The purpose was to find best practice models and relate experiences through the documentation of case studies. A telephone survey was conducted for 27 case studies of shared services in municipalities throughout the state of New Jersey. The survey of managers in each of the municipalities attempted to assess cost savings or other benefits that occurred because of the cooperative agreement.

Holzer, M., Leila Sadeghi, and Richard W. Schwester (2007). Exploring State Shared Services and Regional Consolidation Efforts Prepared for publication in *The Book of the States, 2007.*

> State governments are examining the prospect of inter-local shared service initiatives as a means of reducing service delivery costs and providing tax relief, as well as streamlining local services, eliminating duplicative services, and enhancing governmental responsiveness and transparency. This article provides an introduction to the possible array of shared services; highlights best practices; discusses state funding mechanisms designed to encourage shared service agreements; and provides recommendations to state and local government leaders seeking to develop, implement, or improve existing shared service programs.

Hutchins, R. (2010) Town assumes custodial duties, hires laid-off employees. *Star-Ledger.*

> This news article reports that Woodbridge Township, New Jersey has taken over the custodial services for the Woodbridge Township School District, which is a separate unit of government, at a shared services contract cost of $4.7 million, saving the district $800,000. The School District first decided it needed to lay off 100 custodians and hire a private contractor to save money to make up for decreased state aid. The Township offered to provide the service, and the Township and District considered the total costs of privatization and shared services as alternative solutions

International City/County Management Association (2008). *What Works: How Local Governments Have Made the Leap from Measurement to Management,* ICMA Press.

> This book was written by the staff of the Center for Performance Measurement at ICMA (International City/County Management Association). The book reports how performance measurement promotes positive change using over 70 case studies in fifteen different services areas, all from local government. The Center for Performance Measurements runs the comparative performance measurement data collection effort that is now over fifteen years old and has many local governments throughout the United States as its consortium members. The book is not in the articles folder for the LUARCC project, but is available for purchase from ICMA.

Jeong, M.-G. (2006). Public and Private Joint Production: Institutional Theory of Local Governance and Government Capacity. *Annual Meeting of the Midwestern Political Science Association.* Palmer House Hilton, Chicago, Illinois: 1-27.

> The question of who should provide public services has continued to gain attention among scholars and practitioners. By focusing on the 'make' or 'buy' decision, most studies are conspicuous in their lack of addressing joint production, especially at the county level. This paper fills the research lacuna by incorporating institutional theory of local governance and government capacity. Using the 2002 ICMA Survey on Local Governments' Alternative Service Delivery, this paper examines what factors determine the adoption of joint production of public services at the county level. Probit analysis is employed to estimate county choice of joint production in 2002. Overall, the preliminary analysis suggests that the reformed counties increase the likelihood of joint production adoptions. The findings also suggest that government capacity has a modest influence on joint production.

Joassart-Marcelli, P., and Juliet Musso (2005). "Municipal Service Provision Choices within a Metropolitan Area." *Urban Affairs Review* 40(4): 492-519.

> The authors investigate the decision of municipal governments to outsource the provision of public services during the 1980s and 1990s—a period of increased responsibility for municipalities. This study extends previous empirical work on outsourcing by distinguishing the type of outsourcing used (e.g., public, private, or other types of providers) and treating the outsourcing decision as a dynamic choice. Institutional characteristics and fiscal stress are found to play an important role in explaining service choices. Multinomial logistic regressions indicate that outsourcing was more common for poor cities than for wealthier ones, with the former often relying on government agencies and the latter opting for privatization. Throughout time, these choices are likely to reinforce interjurisdictional patterns of disparity in service quality and costs.

Julnes, P. d. L., and Marc Holzer, Ed. (2008). *Performance Measurement: Building Theory, Improving Practice,* M.E. Sharpe, Inc.

> This volume in the ASPA Classics series compiles the most influential contributions to the theory and practice of performance measurement that have been published in various journals affiliated with the American Society for Public Administration. The book includes major sections of original text along with the readings, and provides students and practitioners with a handy reference source for theory development and practice improvement in performance measurement. The coverage is broad, including methods and techniques for developing effective performance measurement systems, building performance-based management systems, and sustaining performance-based budgeting. The articles are all classics in the field that have endured the test of time and are considered "must reads" on performance measurement. This book is not available in the Articles Folder for the LUARCC project.

Karcher, A. (1998). *New Jersey's Multiple Municipal Madness*, Rutgers Press.

This book provides a history of how New Jersey developed into a state with 566 towns. It elaborates on the various reasons for secession over the years. The author admits that the reasons are sometimes hard to document because they happened so long ago, but the treatise of the book is that many of these justifications are no longer appropriate today. Karcher examines reasons for changing the current situation and proposes solutions based on his knowledge and experience as a state legislator. This book is not available in the Articles Folder for the LUARCC project.

Katsuyama, B. (2003). "Is Municipal Consolidation the Answer?". Retrieved November 10, 2008, from <http://www.mrsc.org/Publications/mrnews/mrnews0603.aspx>.

This article reviews the literature on size and evaluates the effectiveness of consolidations. The article begins by stating that fragmentation is usually assumed to be inefficient, but remarks that there is a growing body of evidence indicating that this conventional wisdom may not always be true. It compares the arguments for and against consolidation and reviews some of the research and case studies. The article suggests alternatives to consolidation that may provide alternative paths to efficiency.

Keehley, P., and Sue A. MacBride (1997). "Can Benchmarking for Best Practices work for Government?" *Quality Progress* 30(3): 75-80.

This article makes the case for benchmarking in the public sector. The improvements in quality and efficiency obtained by private industry through best practices and benchmarking have been so profound and widespread that public sector agencies—organizations traditionally perceived as slow to plan and implement change - are waking up to the benefits of this powerful analytical tool. The article reviews the New York City Transit Authority's adoption of best practices. It also provides ten iterative steps to take in order to benchmark.

King, R. (2004). Costs, quality core issues of fire debate. *St. Petersburg Times*

This news article discusses the debate in Spring Hill, Florida over the consolidation of the fire and rescue service into the operation of Hernando County. The costs will go up for those with less valuable properties, but down for those who own more valuable properties, because the county rate is a flat fee, not a rate based on the property valuation. The debate also centers around the differences in the operations of the the county and the Spring Hill services.

Kouzmin, A., Elke Loffler, Helmut Klages, and Nada Korac-Kakabadse (1999). "Benchmarking and Performance Measurement in Public Sectors Towards Learning for Agency Effectiveness." *International Journal of Public Sector Management* 12(2).

There are some encouraging examples of benchmarking within the public sector. This paper critically analyzes these examples in order to establish the vulnerability points of such measurement instruments. Additional research is in order to establish the specific learning dimensions of benchmarking and to illustrate the importance of such benchmarking and learning within the highly risky, information technology (IT)-driven experiences of systems development and failure. The paper also compares the public sector motivation for benchmarking to that in the private sector, where it is better established, to provide insight into differences that may be important in public sector use of benchmarking.

Koven, S. G., and Don F. Hadwiger (1992). "Consolidation of Rural Service Delivery." *Public Productivity & Management Review* 15(3 (Spring)): 315-328.

The efficiency of rural counties in Iowa varying in size is evaluated and potential structural changes are reviewed with those findings considered. In particular, the decline of both population and revenue in counties in rural Iowa is seen as pushing the need for a structural change such as consolidation. The article also discusses obstacles to consolidation that are associated with a rural environment.

Lamothe, S., and Meeyoung Lamothe (2006). "The Dynamics of Local Service Delivery Arrangements and the Role of Nonprofits." *International Journal of Public Administration* 29(10-11): 769-797.

This article examines the relationship between "contract failure" (the bringing "in-house" of previously contracted services) and service characteristics. The connection between contract failure and nonprofit and for-profit status is also explored. The analyses are performed using International City/County Management Association data and three service typologies constructed by previous scholars.

Lamothe, S., Meeyoung Lamothe, and Richard C. Feiock (2008). "Examining Local Government Service Delivery Arrangements Over Time." *Urban Affairs Review* 44(1): 27-56.

While scholars of local service delivery arrangements are fully aware the process is dynamic, research has tended to take the form of cross-sectional studies that are inherently static in nature. In this article, the authors model the determinants of production mode accounting for past delivery decisions. They find, not surprisingly, that there are strong inertia effects; previous delivery mode is a strong predictor of the current service delivery arrangement. More interestingly, the impact of the transaction cost nature of services on production choice is conditioned on past decisions, such as the extent of contracting and the type of vendors used. There is also evidence that contract management capacity and the competitiveness of the contracting environment are influential.

Leland, S., and Kurt Thurmaier, Ed. (2004). *Case Studies of City-County Consolidation.* Armonk, NY, M.E. Sharpe Inc.

The book has 14 detailed case studies about city-county consolidations in the United States from 1967-1999. Most were unsuccessful or it took several tries. The book focuses on "what factors affect the outcome of an effort to consolidate two local governments?"

LeRoux, K., and Jered B. Carr (2007). "Explaining Local Government Cooperation on Public Works: Evidence from Michigan." *Public Works Management & Policy* 12(1): 344-358.

> In recent years, analysts have begun to study cooperation on public services among local governments. These studies often have concluded that services with scale economies are likely candidates for shared service delivery. This article contributes to the emerging literature on this topic by examining inter-local service arrangements for 10 public works services in Michigan. The authors use data on the service delivery arrangements from 468 general-purpose local governments in Michigan to examine the role played by the factors in explaining inter-local cooperation on public works.

Lindberg, A. (1999). Town to consider hiring Sheriff's Office. *St. Petersburg Times*

> This news article reports that the Kenneth City council will discuss disbanding its police department at the council meeting. The city would contract with the Pinellas County Sheriff's Office for policing services. The start-up costs would be offset to some degree by equipment that would be turned over to the county and all qualified Kenneth City officers would be hired by the county. The decision not to renew the contract of the Kenneth City police chief started the discussions of other options.

Lindberg, A. (2008). County considers closing fire station in Oakhurst. *St. Petersburg Times*

> This news article reviews the deliberations of the Pinellas County Commission in Florida to close a fire station as a cost saving measure. There has been a concern for some time about the duplication caused by two similar stations that serve adjacent areas and have a low volume of calls. The boundaries of fire districts would be re-aligned. The writer interviewed fire officials from the effected fire stations, officials from neighboring districts and county officials to present different perspectives in the controversy.

Long Island Index (2007). "A Case Study Comparing Governance, Taxes and Local Services on Long Island and in Northern Virginia: Executive Summary." *Long Island Index*. Retrieved November 10, 2008, from http://www.longislandindex.org/fileadmin/pdf/pollreport/Long_Island_Index_Case_Study_Executive_Summary.pdf.

> According to the Long Island Index 84% of Long Islanders believe that high taxes are an "extremely" or "very serious" problem and a near majority (45%) cites it as the major local problem. With an eye to finding out how other regions address the issue of local taxes, the Long Island Index compared Long Island to several peer suburban regions and found one stood out in stark contrast. Northern Virginia (including Fairfax County, Loudoun County, Fairfax City and the city of Falls Church) has significantly lower per capita property taxes than Long Island. In order to explore this question, the Long Island Index commissioned two studies. First, they asked the Center for Governmental Research (CGR) in Rochester, New York to conduct an analysis that compared local taxes in each region in order to clarify the key cost drivers. Second, they asked Stony Brook University's Center for Survey Research to conduct a survey comparing how residents in the two regions felt

about the services provided by local governments. They found there was the potential for greater cost savings coupled with higher satisfaction.

Luzerne County (2005). Luzerne County's Municipal Cooperation Community Toolkit 2005 Shared Service Success Stories

This newsletter speaks about the various shared services initiatives throughout Luzerne County in Pennsylvania and speaks specifically about the police departments initiatives. Shared services success stories such as the police department and recreation parks are also explored and expanded upon. The newsletter describes the fire department's initiatives with shared services.

Mabuchi, M. (2001). "Municipal Amalgamation in Japan." Retrieved November 24, 2008, from <http://www-wds.worldbank.org/external/default/WDSContentServer/WDSP/IB/2 005/07/26/000090341_20050726131910/Rendered/PDF/330380JP0wbi37175.pdf>.

This paper describes the causes and consequences of post-war municipal amalgamations in Japan. It shows that recent amalgamations have been inspired in part by the desire to ensure that municipalities thus formed had sufficient capacity to deliver important public services in such areas as education, sanitation and welfare. It notes that there may be cost-efficiency gains associated with amalgamation in that the costs of delivering public services in Japan appear to be lower for larger municipalities (up to a point). Furthermore, case studies of some prefectures show that voter turnout in elections is not significantly affected by amalgamations.

MacMahon, P. (2008). Trade Union warns MSPs should be wary of shared services savings cash. *The Scotsman*. Scotland: 1.

This news article reports that trade unions have publicly warned the Scottish government that shared services may not deliver the cost savings that are expected. The unions also expressed concerns about the centralization of jobs, draining them from remote communities, and the use of larger suppliers for goods, reducing the need for local businesses by the Scottish government. .

Malkawi, F. K. (2003). "Amalgamation is a Solution in Jordan." Retrieved October 13, 2008, from <http://64.233.169.104/search?q=cache:2GQDv68911oJ:www.worldbank.org/wbi/mdf/mdf4/papers/malkawi.pdf+Amalgamation+is+a+Solution+in+Jordan&hl=en&ct=clnk&cd=1&gl=us>.

This paper is about the current thinking in metropolitan governance in Jordan. In 1985, a number municipalities and village councils around Amman City were amalgamated to form what is known today as the Greater Amman Municipality. Since its inception, creating a metropolitan authority in Greater Amman was presented as a solution to a technical problem, the multiplicity of administrative units. Although one cannot connect the assumed success of this new municipality to this process of amalgamation, it is often described as such. Accordingly, amalgamation is presented in Jordan as a solution to the problem of governance in metropolitan areas. Greater Amman became a model for good governance. Steps toward implementing this model around other major cities were taken recently. This paper presents the rhetoric that produced such conclusions and argues that the idea of a unified metropolitan authority is rather a "practice" that preceded the existence of the problem.

Mante, B., and Greg O'Brien (2002). "Efficiency Measurement of Australian Public Sector Organisations: The Case of State Secondary Schools in Victoria." *Journal of Educational Administration* 40(3): 274-296.

> This paper provides a review and an illustration of the Data Envelopment Analysis (DEA) methodology for measuring the relative efficiency of public sector organizations performing similar tasks. The paper focuses on measuring the relative technical efficiency of State secondary schools in a geographical region in the Australian State of Victoria. It recognizes that state secondary schools, like other non-profit making organizations, produce multiple outcomes by combining alternative discretionary and non-discretionary inputs.

Marando, V. L. (1979). "City-County Consolidation: Reform, Regionalism, Referenda and Requiem " *The Western Political Quarterly* 32(4): 409-421.

> The article does not discuss cost efficiency in consolidation. It focuses discussion and analysis upon five aspects related to consolidation: (1) the relationship between reform as a process and adoption of consolidation; (2) the regional patterns of consolidation attempts and adoption; (3) certain political and administrative characteristics of charters which are associated with reform; (4) the relationship between referenda and adoption; and (5) future reform options including the role of state government on issues of metropolitan reorganization.

Markson, S. (2005). Push to share local facilities—Councils urged to join forces. *Sunday Telegraph*

> This newspaper article from Sydney, Australia quotes the local government minister on the formation of alliances between metropolitan councils. Alliances are operating in 13 regions. Alliance boards would consist of representatives from all member councils to govern over the council groups.

Masse, M. H., and Alexander J. DiPasquale (1975). Two-Tiered Government in Monroe County, New York. Greater Rochester Intergovernmental Panel of the National Academy of Public Administration.

> The National Academy of Public Administration sponsored this report which studied every governmental unit within the irregular boundaries of Monroe County, New York, except scholl districts, and makes recommendations concerning them—how the governmental services should be delivered and who should deliver them; how the representative bodies should be structured; how the financial impact should fall upon people; and how all of that could be implemented.

Mazerolle, L., Sacha Rombouts, and James McBroom (2007). "The Impact of COMPSTAT on Reported Crime in Queensland." *International Journal of Police Strategies & Management* 30(2): 237-256.

> The purpose of this paper is to evaluate the impact of Queensland (Australia) Police Service's version of COMPSTAT, known as "Operational Performance Reviews" (OPRs), on reported crime. The paper employed interrupted time series analytic techniques to examine the impact of OPRs on various categories of reported crime in Queensland. The analyses assessed the extent to which OPRs were associated with crime reductions across the 29 police districts in Queensland. This study was the first to provide a systematic examination of the impact of OPRs on a relatively large number of offence categories.

McAdams, R., and Liam O'Neil (2002). "Evaluating Best Value through Clustered Benchmarking in UK Local Government: Building Control Services." *International Journal of Public Sector Management* 15(6): 438-457.

> The Best Value initiative has been designated as the key framework for improving service quality and effectiveness in UK local government. In support of the framework a number of measures have been introduced to measure effectiveness. However, there are problems with using comparative performance measures within the diverse grouping of local government services. This article measures the effectiveness of Best Value in a similar group of building control services by using a clustered benchmarking approach. The mainly qualitative research involves applying a strategic benchmarking approach to the 26 units or councils within the cluster and then comparing the cluster with the best practice UK measures for building control services. To facilitate the process a benchmarking measurement framework for building control was developed

McDavid, J. C. (2002). "The Impacts of Amalgamation on Police Services in the Halifax Regional Municipality." *Canadian Public Administration* 45(4): 538-565.

> The Nova Scotia government amalgamated the Town of Bedford, the cities of Dartmouth and Halifax and Halifax County to create the Halifax Regional Municipality. The Halifax amalgamation is one in a series of such mergers that have happened recently in Ontario, Quebec and the Atlantic Provinces. This study compares the costs, resources, service levels, crime rates, workloads and citizen perceptions of police services before and after amalgamation. Claims about the efficiency and cost-effectiveness of amalgamations have tended to rest on evidence that is generally inadequate to assess the actual consequences of this kind of organizational change. The current study suggests that when predictions are tested, there is a considerable gap between the rhetoric and what actually happens when police departments are amalgamated in an urban setting.

McKay, R. B. (2004). "Reforming Municipal Services after Amalgamation: The Challenge of Efficiency." *International Journal of Public Sector Management* 17(1): 24-47.

> The differing perspectives of decision makers in newly-amalgamated municipalities may hinder the reduction of costs or introduction of efficient organizational change. The author discusses the need to address and accept differences, a process that may be essential, at least initially, to achieving efficiencies. Additionally, the author discusses the amalgamation process and the nature of the change process itself. During amalgamation the pursuit of uniformity of services in combination with a weak and/or chaotic change process (lack of committee structure, poor information, vague deadlines, shifting relationships and assertion of power) may undermine efforts to obtain efficiencies.

Mera, K. (1973). "On the Urban Agglomeration and Economic Efficiency." *Economic Development and Cultural Change* 21(2): 309-24.

> This article evaluates the effects of population size on economic development but some comments are made about the impact on government expenditures from size or other factors. The article addresses wealth of the population as a determinant of government cost per capita expenditure.

Meszaros, G., and C. James Owen (1997). "Improving through Benchmarking: A Competitive Assessment of Municipal Utility Services." *Public Works Management & Policy* 2(1): 11-23.

> This article examines the use of competitive benchmarking as a means of assessing and responding to the changing market conditions sweeping the municipal water and wastewater utility industry. The authors present an overview of the benchmarking process, and illustrate the use of benchmarking through an examination of the techniques used to develop a competitive assessment of the Utility Division of the city of Fort Wayne. The authors perceive that rising public expectations for higher-quality, more cost-effective services are radically altering the way municipalities deliver utility services. In increasing numbers, many local governments are introducing competition, through private sector contract operation companies, into their water and wastewater utilities. Once foreign to public utility managers, the concepts, behavior, and work practices of a competitive market increasingly are becoming a reality for many municipal water and wastewater utility providers.

Moore, A., James Nolan, and Geoffrey F. Segal (2005). "Putting Out the Trash: Measuring Municipal Service Efficiency in U.S. Cities." *Urban Affairs Review* 41(2): 237-259.

> The authors discuss Data envelopment analysis (DEA) as a response to their view that theliterature describing the performance of municipal services often uses imperfect or partial measures of efficiency. DEA has emerged as an effective tool for measuring the relative efficiency of public service provision. This article uses DEA to measure the relative efficiency of 11 municipal services in 46 of the largest cities in the United States over a period of 6 years. In addition, this information is used to explore efficiency differences between cities and services and provide input into a statistical analysis to explore factors

that may explain differences in efficiency between cities. Finally, the authors discuss municipal governments' use of performance measures and problems with collecting municipal data for benchmarking.

Morgan, D. R., and John P. Pelissero (1980). "Urban Policy: Does Political Structure Matter?" *American Political Science Review* 74(4): 999-1006.

> An interrupted time-series quasi-experiment is employed to test the basic hypothesis that reformed cities (with city manager, at-large elections, and nonpartisan ballots) tax and spend less than unreformed communities. Eleven cities with populations of 25,000 and above which significantly changed their political structure between 1948 and 1973 are compared with 11 matched control cities that made no changes. They found that over an 11-year period, variations in fiscal behavior were virtually unaffected by changes in city government structure

Morton, L. W., Yu-Che Chen, and Ricardo S. Morse (2008). "Small Town Civic Structure and Interlocal Collaboration for Public Services." *City and Community* 7(1): 45-60.

> Local governments are responsible for financing and providing an array of public services ranging from police, fire, and emergency medical services to streets, parks, and water. Two mechanisms, namely civic structure and interlocal collaboration, have the potential to solve the problem of providing high quality public services in the face of declining resources and increasing needs. The authors find that civic structure - citizen engagement in solving public problems - is positively and strongly associated with perceived quality of small town public services. Although many rural towns show significant positive association with citizen ratings of overall service quality, citizens seem to prefer their local government directly providing police services rather than entering into interlocal agreements. This suggests that many services are better provided directly.

National Performance Management Advisory Commission (2010). A Performance Management Framework for State and Local Government: From Measurement and Reporting to Management and Improving. Retrieved July 15, 2010 from http://www.pmcommission.org/APerformanceManagementFramework.pdf.

> The National Performance Management Advisory Commission developed the performance management framework to help governments move beyond measuring and reporting those measures to managing performance toward improved results. The framework is conceptual; even though this report provides useful information for governments for learning about and implementing performance management initiatives, the framework was not intended to be a how-to guide. For governments that currently have performance measures, it offers information on how they can use them to get better results. For governments that have not yet developed performance measures, it is a starting point for creating a performance management system. The framework is intentionally flexible and high-level so it can be used by all state, provincial, and local entities – agencies, cities, counties, school districts, the judiciary, and special districts.

Neill, L. (2007). Sheriff's Office Taking over Dispatching Duties. *St. Petersburg Times.*

> This article reports on the Hernando County, Florida, Sheriff Office taking over the 9-1-1 dispatching for Brookville. Brooksville City Council instructed the City Manager to work out the details of the contract with the Sheriff's Office, but it is estimated to save over $195,000 annually. The Council favored keeping the savings in the City's reserve account rather than reducing taxes because of financial uncertainty.

Nelson, M. A. (1997). "Municipal Government Approaches to Service Delivery: An Analysis from A Transactions Cost Perspective." *Economic Inquiry* 35(1): 82-96.

> Municipal governments are less likely to contract out for service delivery if citizen preferences for the service are heterogeneous. This conclusion is based on an analysis that extends to the public sector the empirical industrial organization literature on transaction costs and the "make or buy" decision faced by private firms. Service delivery practices for sixty-three municipal services are examined. The findings are consistent with the proposition that the cost of writing and monitoring contracts may be an important consideration in municipal service delivery approach and that bureaucratic supply may not be as inefficient as some previous studies indicate.

New Jersey Public Laws (2007). P.L. 2007, Chapter 54. N. J. S. Government.

> Chapter 54 is an act establishing the "Local Unit Alignment, Reorganization, and Consolidation Commission," performance measures for municipalities, and the Municipal Efficiency Promotion Aid Program compiled at N.J.S.A. 52:27D et seq. It also pertains to the development of performance measures by the New Jersey State Local Finance Board.

New South Wales Department of Local Government (2008). Comparative Information on NSW Local Government Councils 2005/2006. Sydney, NSW, Australia, New South Wales Department of Local Government: 245p.

> This publication of the New South Wales (Australia) Department of Local Government provides detailed performance information for three years for every municipality in New South Wales. This publication uses municipal profiles to group councils into similar groups for comparison. It represents an example of public benchmarking.

New York State Commission on Local Government Efficiency & Competitiveness (2008). Developing Intermunicipal Arrangements for Highway Services: A Guide for Local Government Officials, retrieved July 13, 2010 from http://www.nyslocalgov.org/pdf/Intermunicipal_Highway_Agreements.pdf.

> The Commission developed this guide to assist local government managers and elected officials, with varying levels of expertise and resources, to identify opportunities to share highway services and to develop and implement sharing agreements. The description elaborates on alternatives in forming a joint agreement.

New York State Office of the Comptroller (2010). New York State Legislative Commission on Rural Resources (2005). Promoting Intermunicipal Cooperation for Shared Highway Services, retrieved July 13, 2010 from http://www.dos.state.ny.us/lgss/pdfs/SharedHighway1.pdf.

> This report focuses on reducing the cost of providing highway maintenance services in New York State. The publication provides a sample resolution for use by local governing bodies to authorize the sharing of machinery, maintenance and equipment, and lending or borrowing of materials and supplies. It also offers a sample memorandum, which may be used by highway officials when equipment is rented or loaned or material is exchanged or borrowed pursuant to such authorization.

New York State Office of the State Comptroller (2006). Outdated Municipal Structures: Cities, Towns, and Villages—18th Century Designations for 21st Century Communities. A Research Series. Comptroller. 2.

> This study presents an analysis of municipalities—cities, towns and villages—including a statistical regrouping that suggests what a modern classification system might look like if we started from scratch today, based on current conditions. What emerges is an intuitively satisfying reassignment of cities, towns and villages into groups far more homogenous than the current legal designations. Big cities and immense urban towns group together, as do the smaller cities, larger villages and other urban towns. Suburban and rural areas emerge naturally. This analysis provides an illustration that suggests it may be time to refocus attention on the basic structure of local government, including State laws covering service provision, governance, revenue structure, intergovernmental aid, and the provisions under which municipalities may merge, dissolve or annex territory. A number of studies have already described problems and potential improvements in these areas (many of which are cited in this report). With today's heightened focus on local government efficiency, it makes sense to take another look at some of these basic issues.

New York State Office of the State Comptroller (2010). Local Government Snapshot. Retrieved July 15, 2010 from http://www.osc.state.ny.us/localgov/pubs/research/snapshot/0310-2snapshot.pdf.

> This short report elaborates on the number of local governments in New York State as of 2010. It distinguishes authorities to tax and incur debt possessed by the different forms of local government and provides counts of the number of each form.

Ostrom, E., and Gordon Whitaker (1973). "Does Local Community Control of Police make a Difference? Some Preliminary Findings." *American Journal of Political Science* 17(1): 48-76.

> Using a comparative research design, this study examines the consequences of organizing neighborhood patrol functions on a large scale by a city-wide police force or on a small scale by local communities. The research was conducted in three small independent communities adjacent to Indianapolis, and three matched neighborhoods within the city. The findings indicate a consistent pattern of higher levels of police performance in the independent communities when compared to the Indianapolis neighborhood. The

findings strongly suggest that in the area studied, small police forces under local community control are more effective than a large, city-wide controlled police department in meeting citizen demands for neighborhood police protection. Further studies have been initiated to ascertain if the patterns found in this metropolitan area are also present in other areas.

Ostrom, E. (1976). "Size and Performance in a Federal System." *Publius* 6(2): 33-73.

The author is concerned with the call for municipal reform based on untested theories. In particular, the assertion that the number of police jurisdictions should be curtailed in favor of larger police departments has no support from the evidence. The article summarizes empirical studies on the impact of size on efficiency of government services, particularly police services

Ouellette, P., and Valérie Vierstraete (2005). "An Evaluation of the Efficiency of Québec's School Boards Using the Data Envelopment Analysis Method." *Applied Economics* 37(14): 1643-1653.

In this paper the efficiency of Quebec's school boards during a period of severe cutbacks in their finance is examined using Data Envelopment Analysis. The average efficiency is found to be relatively high. In spite of this, potential savings could be achieved if school boards were fully efficient. Results depended heavily on school boards' socio-economic conditions. They were subjected to Tobit analysis and the boards' corrected efficiencies recalculated. The inefficiencies cost $800 million of which $200 million came from unfavorable socio-economic conditions.

Pachon, H. P., and Nicholas P..Lovrich, Jr. (1977). "The Consolidation of Urban Public Services: A Focus on the Police." *Public Administration Review* 37(6): 38-47.

A set of literature in public administration has recently emerged, associated with the Public Choice perspective, which argues against metropolitan consolidation and police consolidation specifically. This article reviews the major assertions which the "anti-consolidationists" make in specific reference to the consolidation of urban police departments: (1) that larger police departments are not more efficient or economical; and (2) that citizen satisfaction with urban police services varies inversely with the size of the municipality. On the first assertion the authors find that evidence is still inconclusive regarding the economy and efficiency of larger police departments. On the second assertion, the results indicate that, contrary to the anti-consolidationist viewpoint, citizen satisfaction with police services is more a reflection of the differentiated socio-economic characteristics of central cities and suburban cities than a function of city size.

Page, S., and Chris Malinowski (2004). "Top 10 Performance Measurement Do's and Don'ts." *Government Finance Review* 20(5): 28-32.

Performance measurement continues to gain in popularity in all levels and types of governmental organizations. Robert Kaplan's Balanced Scorecard, David Osborne's Reinventing Government, the success of the NYPD's COMPSTAT process, and the ever-increasing public pressure to report performance have made the practice of performance measurement commonplace in the public sector. While most of these efforts are well intentioned, too many performance measurement programs fail to live up to expectations or get derailed altogether because of poor execution. To help governments make the most of their performance measurement efforts, the authors compiled a "top 10 list" of performance measurement do's and don'ts, using case studies to illustrate their assertions.

Palmer, A. J. (1993). "Performance Measurement in Local Government." *Public Money & Management* 13(4): 31-36.

Emphasis on improving performance in the public sector has led to the development of systems for measuring performance in local government. This article reports on the author's research into this development, presenting information on how local authorities measure performance; which dimensions of performance they attempt to measure; and how they use performance measurement information. Existing systems of measuring performance are evaluated in relation to an ideal system. The conclusion is that, although few authorities currently have a coherent system for measuring performance, pressure for continued development of such systems should yield improvements.

Pedraja-Chaparro, F., and Javier Salinas-Jiminez (1996). "An Assessment of the Efficiency of Spanish Courts Using DEA." *Applied Economics* 28: 1391-1403.

The objective of the article is to provide a measure of technical efficiency of the Administrative Litigation Division of the Spanish High Courts. The concept of efficiency to be measured and the most adequate technique for carrying out the efficiency analysis are selected by considering the specific characteristics of public production. The analysis is undertaken by using data envelopment analysis (DEA) and various homogeneity tests (returns to scale and restrictions on weights) are applied in order to ensure a correct comparison between Courts.

Peters, J. W. (2007). Lips Move, but No Mergers Result. *New York Times.*

This newspaper article reports the perspectives of New Jersey state legislators, state officials, local mayors, and municipal consultants when they were meeting at the 2007 New Jersey League of Municipalities convention. The focus of the article is on the debate about consolidation - whether it will produce the cost savings its proponents claim.

Plumridge, N., and Bohdan Wynnycky (2007). "The "Midas" Touch: New System Will Bring Powerful Analysis Tools Online for Ontario Municipalities." *Municipal World* 117(10): 27-30.

As a response to the growing desire to access more financial and performance measurement information, the Association of Municipalities of Ontario (AMO) and the Ministry of Municipal Affairs and Housing (MMAH), with funding assistance from the Ministry of Finance's (MOF) "Strengthening Our Partnerships" program, jointly developed the Municipal Information and Data Analysis System (MIDAS). MIDAS is a powerful web-based query and analysis tool that will allow any municipal staff member to access the data compiled in the Province of Ontario's Financial Information Return (FIR) system, including the Municipal Performance Measurement Program (MPMP) data. Staff members and elected officials can query and report on this statistical, financial and operational data, examine their own historical records, and browse and make comparisons with their peer municipalities using standard and established performance measures and indicators. This increased access to financial and performance measurement data allows for an improved ability to make service delivery decisions.

Poel, D. (2000). "Amalgamation Perspectives: Citizen Responses to Municipal Consolidation." *Canadian Journal of Regional Science* 23(1): 31-48.

The 1999 Halifax Regional Municipality (HRM) Citizen Survey is used here to study citizen responses to a municipal amalgamation that created the Halifax Regional Municipality. The analysis of this survey brings forward citizen-based assessments of the amalgamation decision and subsequent municipal governance. Questionnaire items are used to create measures of citizens' views concerning amalgamation, the relationship between the urban and rural spaces of the new municipality, the performance of the HRM political leadership and the impact of amalgamation on municipal services. There are two key research questions. How did HRM citizens assess amalgamation after three years of experience? What factors best explain citizens' views towards amalgamation? The political and policy context of the amalgamation decision taken unilaterally by the Nova Scotia provincial government is briefly described.

Price Waterhouse Coopers (2005). Shared Services for Even Greater Efficieny in Local Government.

The paper provides an overview of the challenges that have prevented local authorities from delivering on the shared services agenda in the past; details the benefits the shared services model is able to deliver; and provides a guide to overcoming the barriers preventing this model from being more widely adopted in local government. At present authorities are tinkering at the edges. The authors believe a bolder approach is required to tackle the real barriers preventing authorities from succeeding.

Public Performance Measurement and Reporting Network (2009). "Public Performance Measurement and Reporting Network." Retrieved February 3, 2009, from www.PPMRN.net.

This website serves as a resource for the Rutgers University School of Public Affairs and Administration's network of over 2,000 academics and practitioners. It is available to the public and contains information and other information resources on the field of performance measurement and related topics. The goal of the Public Performance Measurement and Reporting Network is to promote the use of valid, reliable data as a key element in improving the delivery of public services. In support of the Network, the National Center for Public Performance has implemented a series of initiatives: a comprehensive and continuously updated database of publications and cases; national conferences and workshops; publications of measurement-based books and articles; an Online Public Performance Measurement Certificate; and a monthly e-newsletter.

Raaum, R. B. (2007). "Applying the Finding Paradigm to Audits of Output and Outcome Performance: A Research Perspective." *Journal of Government Financial Management* 56(2): 44-50.

> The "finding paradigm," a four-element measurement tool used to analyze government service provision, is at the foundation of one method of performance auditing. The four-element finding paradigm of criteria, condition, effect and cause is widely used by auditors and cited in auditing standards, and has proven a powerful tool for analyzing the performance of all manner of government, as well as private and nonprofit operations and programs. This article provides guidance and details for applying the finding paradigm to findings for audits of output and outcome performance.

Revelli, F., and Per Tovmo (2007). "Revealed Yardstick Competition: Local Government Efficiency Patterns in Norway." *Journal of Urban Economics* 62(1): 121–134.

> This paper investigates whether the production efficiency of Norwegian local governments exhibits a spatial pattern that is compatible with the hypothesis of yardstick competition. In order to check whether yardstick competition is really responsible for the observed spatial pattern and rule out alternative theoretical explanations, the paper exploits unique information from a survey on local politicians' attitudes towards comparative evaluation of local bureaus' performances against other jurisdictions' (benchmarking).

Richter, C. A. (2004). "The Case for Performance Standards." *Public Roads* 67(5): 18-22.

> This article makes the case for performance standards, expressed from a user perspective, as opposed to specifications in the construction of highways. The author suggested customer focused issues include street smoothness, road noise, longevity of the road, and traffic congestion. The article reviews the use of performance standards in practice throughout the United States.

Ridley, C. E. (1927). *Measuring Municipal Government,* School of Citizenship and Public Affairs, Syracuse University.

> This seminal work in the field of performance measurement is referenced for the LUARCC projects to provide a sense of the long history of attempting to measure the efficiency of government. The book is out of print, but the concepts are the basis of much of what is being implemented and studied today.

Rivenbark, W. C., and K. Lee Carter (2000). "Benchmarking and Cost Accounting: The North Carolina Approach." *Journal of Public Budgeting, Accounting & Financial Management* 12(1): 125-137.

> Benchmarking is a management tool that promotes process improvement. By comparing services units across jurisdictions, best practices can be identified and used to enhance less

efficient and effective operations. However, the lack of generally accepted criteria to compare service costs for local government has hindered benchmarking initiatives. One of the key components of the North Carolina Local Government Performance Measurement Project is the full-cost accounting model developed to ensure that localities employ the same methodology to collect and report cost data associated with performance measures. This article presents an overview of the development and implementation issues associated with that model and highlights the areas of direct costs, indirect costs, and capital costs. It is argued that accuracy and comparability of performance and cost data are the fundamental ingredients of a benchmarking and performance measurement project.

Rosenfield, R., and Laura Reese (2004). Local Government Amalgamation from the Top Down. *City-County Consolidation and Its Alternatives.* J. F. Carr, Richard. Armonk, NY, M.E. Sharpe: 219-245.

This case explores the consolidation of 12 municipalities in the Ottawa-Carleton region of Ontario, Canada based on case study interviews before and immediately after consolidation and a variety of government documents. The study analyzes whether top-down, or mandated, consolidations can produce a long-term successful implementation. It addresses questions related to motivation, goals, the new structure, effects on public employees, immediate impacts on service quantity and quality, short-term cost savings, and changes in local power structure.

Rosentraub, M. (2000). "City-County Consolidation and the Rebuilding of Image: The Fiscal Lessons from Indianapolis's UniGov Program." *State and Local Government Review* 32(3): 180-191.

This article describes the successful UniGov program, uniting the city of Indianapolis and Marion County in central Indiana and outlines "lessons learned" for other communities considering such a consolidation effort. Through this consolidation, the city of Indianapolis was transformed from what was described by its chamber of commerce in the 1970s as "a cemetery with lights," into a destination for those seeking a vibrant downtown area and a major sports center, as well as the nation's 12th largest city by the 1990s. Indianapolis was one of the three major consolidation or merger experiences in the 1960s and 1970s. Indianapolis's specific contribution to the experiment in governance models was a city-county consolidation program that concentrated a limited or select group of urban services at the regional (defined as county) level while permitting most other critical urban services to be delivered by administrations and agencies serving different, often much smaller, areas within the county.

Sancton, A. (1996). "Reducing Costs by Consolidating Municipalities: New Brunswick, Nova Scotia and Ontario." *Canadian Public Administration* 39(3): 267-289.

Notwithstanding a lack of interest by cost-cutting governments in Britain and the United States, municipal consolidation has emerged in at least three Canadian provinces—New Brunswick, Nova Scotia and Ontario—as a significant government priority. There is no academic evidence to suggest that consolidation produces savings. This article examines the various studies that have accompanied the consolidation efforts in the three provinces and finds them inadequate and flawed. Government reports in New Brunswick have tended to point more to non-financial benefits from consolidation, but the creation of the single-tier Halifax Regional Municipality in Nova Scotia has been justified primarily in terms of projected cost savings. In Ontario, the "Common Sense Revolution" commits the government to reducing overlap and duplication but not necessarily to consolidation. A ministry study of one Ontario municipal amalgamation purports to demonstrate savings, but the conclusions are questionable. The report of the task force on the Greater Toronto Area is significant because it specifically rejects claims that lower-tier amalgamations will save money and because it points to the benefits of municipal competition. Reducing the number of municipal governments does not necessarily mean less government.

Sancton, A. (2000). "Amalgamations, Service Realignment, and Property Taxes: Did the Harris Government Have a Plan for Ontario's Municipalities?" *Canadian Journal of Regional Science* 23(1): 135-156.

Drastic change was contemplated by The Common Sense Revolution (CSR), the election manifesto that brought Mike Harris to power as premier of Ontario in 1995; the Harris government implemented drastic change; therefore the CSR explains what the Harris government has done. The fact that this syllogism is logically flawed should be obvious. The aim of this paper, however, is to go beyond formal logic and show that, with respect to the Harris-government's municipal policies, its substance is flawed as well.

Sancton, A. (2001a). "Municipalities, Mergers and the Outward Expansion of the City." *Journal of Eastern Townships Studies* Fall (19).

As the previous discussion has shown, it is quite possible for a single urban area to evolve in such a way that it contains many separate municipalities. Adjoining rural municipalities might have become urban over time; new urban municipalities might have been established within a former part of a rural municipality; two previously distinct urban areas might have grown into each other; or all or some of these processes might have occurred simultaneously. Ever since the mid-nineteenth century, there have been politicians, civil servants, academics, and sometimes even real-estate developers who have observed such phenomena with growing concern. They began to refer to the increasing number of municipalities within a single urban area as "fragmentation." This article discusses the need for redrawing municipal boundaries, particularly in light of different demands for service in rural and urban communities.

Sancton, A. (2001b). "Canadian Cities and the New Regionalism." *Journal of Urban Affairs* 23(5): 543-555.

The new regionalism in the United States emerged because the old regionalism proved politically impossible to implement. For Canadian cities, however, provincial legislatures frequently imposed various institutional reforms of the type favored by the old regionalists. The first section of this article points out what it is that American new regionalists and Canadian policy-makers should have learned from the results of the old regionalism as it was implemented in Canada. The second section examines the relevance of the new regionalism for Canada. For those who still accept the tenets of the old regionalism, the new variety will seem irrelevant, if not counterproductive. But, for others, the new regionalism will provide a new perspective for analyzing old Canadian problems. The article's third section shows that, in some respects, Canadian cities have already gone further in implementing new regionalist principles than most American and Canadian analysts have recognized. The relevant institutions that are examined briefly in this section are the Greater Vancouver Regional District (GVRD), the Greater Toronto Services Board (GTSB), and the Montreal Metropolitan Community (MMC).

Sancton, A. (2003). "Municipal Amalgamations: A Made-in-Canada Solution to an Undefined Problem." *Canadian Issues* (February).

> The first part of this article explores the historical background to municipal amalgamation. The second looks at what has been happening in the United States. The third briefly describes the recent Canadian amalgamations and the conclusion examines their potential impacts. Since the early 1990s, municipal amalgamations have taken place within the following major Canadian cities: Sydney and Halifax in Nova Scotia; Toronto, Ottawa, Hamilton, and Sudbury in Ontario; and Montreal, Quebec City, Hull, and Longueuil in Quebec. The temptation is to assume that, like so many other changes in public policy in this period, such amalgamations are simply part of a worldwide trend relating to neo-conservatism, globalization, and/or the apparent victory of capitalism over socialism. Nothing could be further from the truth. With the exception of controversial municipal amalgamations in Melbourne, Australia and in post-apartheid South Africa, it is only in Canada, among western developed nations, that municipal amalgamations have recently been high on the policy agenda.

Sancton, A. (2005). "The Governance of Metropolitan Areas in Canada." *Public Administration and Development* 25: 317-327.

> This article briefly examines five significant Canadian developments with respect to the governance of metropolitan areas: annexations and mergers such that there is one main municipal government for the metropolitan area, two-tier metropolitan government, the amalgamation of two-tier metropolitan systems into a single municipality, demergers in Quebec, and the creation of flexible and innovative entities for metropolitan governance. Special attention is paid to the Greater Toronto Area, a continuous built-up urban area that transcends at least three metropolitan areas as defined by Statistics Canada. In the absence of any authority covering the entire metropolitan area, it now appears that the Ontario provincial government is becoming the key policy maker. As an example of a flexible and innovative form of metropolitan governance, the Greater Vancouver Regional District merits attention elsewhere in the world. Canada's experiences with so

many different institutional arrangements in recent years means that there is much to be learnt from their obvious failures and occasional successes.

Santucci, J. (2006). "The Missing Half: Ensuring Fair Representation in Essex, Vermont." *National Civic Review* 95(3): 42-50.

> This article discusses the proposed merging of the Vermont municipalities of the Town of Essex and the Village of Essex Junction as a way to revitalize local representation in government. The two entities already share a town selectboard, but the town outnumbers the village in population, which causes taxation without representation for the villagers and voter apathy in both municipalities. Alternative voting systems are analyzed, most notably Proportional Voting. The author warns that unless an alternative voting system, as used in other U.S. municipalities, is implemented, the gains made by efficiency will be impeded by loss of equity. Rushing to consolidate two municipalities can cause loss of representation for neighborhoods and other minority groups.

Savitch, H. V., and Ronald K. Vogel (2000). "Metropolitan Consolidation versus Metropolitan Governance in Louisville." *State and Local Government Review* 32: 198–212.

> New Regionalism differs from past metropolitan reforms. Historically, local government reorganization was promoted as a way to enhance efficiency in metropolitan service delivery. Now metropolitan reform aims to reduce disparities between the cities and their suburbs and enhance the ability of the city region to compete in the global economy. There are two main routes to New Regionalism and regional governance: (1) metropolitan consolidation, which represents a government strategy, and (2) metropolitan governance, which reflects a governance approach.

Schmandt, H. J., and G. Ross Stephens (1960). "Measuring Municipal Output." *National Tax Journal* 13(4): 369-375.

> The Article describes findings of a study made of the local governments in Milwaukee county to test the assumption that population size is unrelated to per capita municipal expenditures even when service levels are considered. Comparing 19 cities, they found that the use of per capita municipal expenditures shows only that one city is spending more or less than another, it tells nothing about either the quantity or quality of service that the respective public receives.

SEMCOG (2003). "Intergovernmental Cooperation: A Background Paper." Part of the Series *Making Joint Public Services Work in the 21st Century.*

> This paper was part of a series sponsored by the Southeast Michigan Council of Governments and the Metropolitan Affairs Commission. It focuses on mechanisms to deliver public services and explores collaborative ventures as a means to reduce the economic costs of the service delivery. The paper also reviews the political and social benefits to collaboration, before addressing the obstacles.

Sewell, J. (2000). Mega-problems in Toronto: The forced amalgamation of one regional and six local municipalities in metro Toronto has brought cuts in services, higher costs and reduced public access to decision-makers. *The Gazette.*

> This Op-Ed editorial was written by a former Mayor of Toronto and is quite passionate about the negative implications of the consolidation. Because of the intimate knowledge, some of the changes are put into the perspective of what was already in place and not a result of the consolidation. In addition, the loss of managerial and analytic capacity provides a perspective that would not be easy for an outsider to attain. Although the author has reason for a biased interest in the events, the inside perspective of what is important to evaluate is illuminating and the overall results are supported by other authors without a personal interest.

Sharockman, A. (2004). Oldsmar: Numbers Right for Annexation. *St. Petersburg Times.*

> This newspaper article reports on the discussions about pursuing the annexation of West Oldsmar in Pinellas County, Florida. The article reported no debate on the value to both municipalities. The only issue was a legal requirement about the total percentage of land in the municipality that must be owned by registered voters in order to hold a valid referendum for annexation.

Shrestha, M. (2005). Inter-Local Fiscal Cooperation in the Provision of Local Public Services—The Case of Large US Cities *American Society for Public Administration Annual Conference.* Milwaukee, Wisconsin.

> This study explains inter-local fiscal cooperation among local governments in the provision of public goods and services. A panel data set from cities above 400,000 from 1990 to 1999 for sixteen services is employed to test the following hypotheses: 1) The higher the asset specificity of a public good, the greater the inter-local cooperation among cities will be found; 2) The higher the difficulty in metering of a public service, the greater the inter-local cooperation among cities will be found; 3) The higher the economies of scale benefits of a service, the more inter-local cooperation among cities will be found.; 4) The greater the local fiscal autonomy, the higher the inter-local cooperation among cities will be found.

Sinclair, T. (2005). Broome County Shared Services Summit. Broome County: 9.

> This report discusses the shared services implemented in Broome County, New York. This report utilized a survey conducted among elected officials as well as analysis of the cost savings mentioned. The report identifies the services most likely to be successfully shared, and specifically identifies courts, health insurance, parks and recreation, and highways as the best candidates. The report also speaks about the ideal methods of implementing and creating shared services agreements.

Singell, L. D. (1974). "Optimum City Size: Some Thoughts on Theory and Policy." *Journal of Land Economics* 50(3): 207-212.

> The author relates size to a number of factors, including municipal expenditures. The perspective of the article is that there may be a reason to control urban growth, but that absent a federal policy to do so, there is reason to believe the limitations may lead to inefficiencies. Government expenditures are only one of the variables investigated.

Slack, E. (2007). "Managing the Coordination of Service Delivery in Metropolitan Cities: the Role of Metropolitan Governance ". Retrieved November 24, 2008, from <http://econ.worldbank.org/external/default/main?pagePK=64165259&theSitePK=469372&piPK=641654 21&menuPK=64166093&entityID=000158349_20070814091849>.

> This paper examines different models of governing structure found in metropolitan areas around the world. It evaluates how well these models achieve the coordination of service delivery over the entire metropolitan area as well as the extent to which they result in the equitable sharing of costs of services. Based on theory and case studies from numerous cities in developed and less developed countries, the paper concludes that there is no "one size fits all" model of metropolitan governance.

Smothers, R. (1999). Regional Fire Service Succeeds in Its First Test. *New York Times.*

> This newspaper article reviews the beginning of operations of a regional fire department organized by five towns in New Jersey. The article reviews some of the obstacles in achieving the regionalization, mechanisms used to overcome or reduce the obstacles, and the expected cost savings.

Somerset County Municipal Managers Association (2006). A White Paper Report: Removing the Barriers to Shared Services—A Prescription for Creating Efficiency and Taxpayer Savings Through Local Government Shared Services.

> In Somerset County, the Somerset County Municipal Managers Association (SCMMA), a professional association of municipal administrators working with the Somerset County Business Partnership (SCBP), is focusing on identifying the "roadblocks" that are inhibiting municipalities from furthering shared services with other towns, the school districts and the county. Somerset County's towns have created a model shared services network that has experienced outstanding and unparalleled success. However, it is the belief of the SCMMA and the SCBP that the more reachable areas to facilitate sharing have been accomplished and, at this point, "all the low fruit has been picked." The obstacles that stand before municipalities are the significant legislative barriers that inhibit bringing shared services to the next level. This white paper makes an attempt to identify the "roadblocks" and to actively push for meaningful legislation that will streamline and facilitate the expansion of shared services.

Sorensen, R. J. (2006). "Local Government Consolidations: The Impact of Political Transaction Costs." *Public Choice* (127): 75-95.

> Local government in Norway comprises a large number of small municipalities. Cost efficiency can be improved by consolidating local authorities, and central government has designed a framework to stimulate voluntary mergers. Existing theories suggest that political transaction costs will impede consolidations. The author offers an explicit test of several efficiency and cost propositions based on data for Norwegian local government.

Spoehr, J., Anne Burger, and Steven Barrett (2007). The Shared Services Experience Report 2: Lessons from Australia, The Australian Institute for Social Research: 42.

> This report was commissioned by the Public Service Association of South Australia to identify some of the key lessons from shared service arrangements in Britain and Australia. The report provides an overview of the Australian experience, while an accompanying report details lessons from the British experience. Both reports are presented in the context of the South Australian Government's deliberations regarding the introduction of a shared service model for the provision of business services to the South Australian public sector.

Stein, R. M. (1993). "Arranging City Services." *Journal of Public Administration Research and Theory* 3(1): 66-92.

> Contemporary research on service delivery has been preoccupied with the issue of privatization. Specifically, the concern has been with whether a governmental or a nongovernmental entity is more effective and efficient in delivering publicly provided goods and services. This paper offers an alternative perspective on service delivery and examines the full array of institutional arrangements used by municipal governments to deliver different goods and services. These choices are related to characteristics of individual goods and services to derive a simple thesis. The way governments arrange for service delivery is a function of the scope and content of their service responsibilities.

Stephenson, P. (2008). Shared Services Backed but Few Bosses See Cost Benefits. *Communitycare*: 1.

> The delivery of shared services is seen as a significant benefit by social care managers, but is unlikely to save much money, a new survey has found. The survey of 178 public sector managers, by law firm Browne Jacobson, found those working in adult social care and children's services were most positive about the benefits of sharing services.

Stevens, P. A. (2005). "Assessing the Performance of Local Government." *National Institute Economic Review* 193(1): 90-101.

> This article considers the measurement of performance in the public sector in general, focusing on local government and the provision of library services by English local authorities in particular. The author considers two methodologies that assess the performance of local authorities in terms of the efficiency with which they provide services, and considers

methods that allow for the identification of exogenous influences on performance such as the socio-economic profile of the population served by the authority. The author finds that although both methods' results appear similar, the implications for potential cost savings vary widely. Omitting to account for background factors leads to an overstatement of the level of inefficiency and hence the scope for reducing expenditure.

Sun, S. (2002). "Measuring the Relative Efficiency of Police Precincts Using Data Envelopment Analysis." *Socio-Economic Planning Sciences* 36(1): 51–71.

Data envelopment analysis (DEA) is used to measure the relative efficiency of the 14 police precincts in Taipei city, Taiwan. The results indicate how DEA may be used to evaluate these police precincts from commonly available police statistical data for the years 1994–1996. To sharpen the efficiency estimates, the study uses window analysis, slack variable analysis, and output-oriented DEA models with both constant and variable returns to scale. The problem of the presence of non-discretionary input variables is explicitly treated in the models used. Potential improvements in technical efficiency of police precincts are examined by readjusting the particular output/input indicators. The analysis indicates that differences in operating environments, such as resident population and location factors, do not have a significant influence upon the efficiency of police precincts.

Tanguay, G. A., and David F. Wihry. (2008). "Voters Preferences Regarding Municipal Consolidation: Evidence from Quebec De-Merger Referenda" *Journal of Urban Affairs* 30(3): 325-345.

This article examines the results of the 2004 Quebec referenda on the mergers of municipalities to analyze the determinants of citizen preferences regarding municipal consolidation and fragmentation. The core hypotheses of the authors' empirical model are generated from the economic theory of optimal jurisdictional size. Holding constant the influences of language and of a unit's share of the merged population, the authors find voters are more likely to support de-merger when they expect that the merged unit will display a different public expenditure level than that of the municipality in which they reside. They also find support for de-merger is less when voters expect de-merger to increase the tax price of local public services.

Thurmaier, K., and Curtis Wood (2002). "Interlocal Agreements as Overlapping Social Networks: Picket-Fence Regionalism in Metropolitan Kansas City." *Public Administration Review* 62(5): 585-598.

Public policies addressing complex issues require trans-jurisdictional solutions, challenging hierarchical modes of public service delivery. Interlocal agreements (ILA's) are long-established service delivery instruments for local governments, and research suggests they are plentiful, with a majority of cities and counties involved in at least one ILA. Although ILA's are an established feature of local government operations, previous research is atheoretical, largely descriptive, and unsystematic. This article explores ILA's as social network phenomena, identifying the rationales and underlying values for various ILA's, central and peripheral actors, and brokering roles. In particular, the authors explore the utility of incorporating network exchange theory into public management network models to identify the relative power of actors in network exchange relationships. They find that a "norm of reciprocity" culture predominates an economizing value as the rationale for an abundance of service oriented policy networks that produce a picket-fence regionalism of ILA participation in the Kansas City metropolitan area.

Triantafillou, P. (2007). "Benchmarking in the Public Sector: A Critical Conceptual Framework." *Public Administration* 85(3): 829–846.

How can we critically address benchmarking? By conceptualizing benchmarking as a normalizing governing technology, a space is cleared for analyzing some of the power relations brought into play in benchmarking activities. As a device of power, benchmarking depends upon the production of normalizing knowledge and the freedom or self-governing capacities of those who are benchmarked. The fruitfulness of this conception is illustrated through an example from the Danish hospital system.

Tynan, N., and Bill Kingdom (2005). "Optimal Size for Utilities?" Public Policy for the Private Sector. Retrieved October 13, 2008, from <http://www-wds.worldbank.org/external/default/WDSContentServer/WDSP/IB/2005/02/28/000090341_20050228132513/Rendered/PDF/315620PAPER0VP2830tynan.pdf>.

Using data from 270 water and sanitation providers, this article investigates the relationship between a utility's size and its operating costs. The current trend toward transferring responsibility for providing services to the municipal level is driven in part by the assumption that this will make providers more responsive to customers' needs. But findings reported here suggest that smaller municipalities may face higher per customer costs and could lower costs (and prices for consumers) by merging.

United States Census (2007). New Jersey local governments. This electronic document was retrieved July 9, 2010 from http://www2.census.gov/govs/cog/2007/nj.pdf.

This webpage discusses local governments in New Jersey as determined by the 2007 Census of Governments. It describes the types of local governments,their purposes and the number of each of the types. The index page from http://www2.census.gov/govs/cog/2007/nj.pdf links to the page for every state.

United States Conference of Mayors (2000). "Project Scorecard Evaluates Cleanliness of New York Streets." Retrieved February 1, 2009, from http://usmayors.org/bestpractices/litter/NewYork.html.

This web page from the site of the United States Conference of Mayors was prepared when Mayor Rudolph Giuliani was in office. It presents the origins and purpose of Project Scorecard, a street and sidewalk litter rating system that was one of the first attempts in New York City to measure the results of the city's service delivery. The description provides information about how the measurement is accomplished and provides a table of street and sidewalk cleanliness results in the City's five boroughs in 1976 and 1998.

United States Office of Personnel Management (1974). Managers Guide for Improving Productivity: 24.

This report was originally written by Edward Koenig of the Office of Productivity Programs, but the Office of Intergovernmental Personnel Programs revised it for use by state and local governments. It attempts to get managers to look at their organization and its mission, collect and analyze information, make systemic changes, and continue to evaluate and monitor. It incorporates measurement and analysis of inputs, outputs, and efficiency in its methods for increasing productivity. This is an early report in the field of performance measurement, but it lays out the basics. This report is not available electronically and is not in the Articles Folder for the LUARCC project.

Van Ryzin, G. (2004). "Expectations, Performance, and Citizen Satisfaction with Urban Services." *Journal of Policy Analysis and Management*, 23(3).

This reference helps to explain the relationship between citizen expectation and citizen satisfaction with government performance. The expectancy disconfirmation model has dominated private-sector research on customer satisfaction for several decades, yet it has not been applied to citizen satisfaction with urban services. The model views satisfaction judgments as determined - not just by product or service performance - but by a process in which consumers compare performance with their prior expectations. The study uses data from a New York City citizen survey,. Additional implications for research and public management practice are discussed.

Van Ryzin, G. (2006). "Testing the Expectancy Disconfirmation Model of Citizen Satisfaction with Local Government." *Journal of Public Administration Research and Theory*, 16(4).

This reference helps to explain some of the conclusions in the report on optimal size and efficiency. It is important that public administration researchers and practitioners understand how citizens form satisfaction judgments regarding local government services. A prior study by Van Ryzin (2004) found strong support for an expectancy disconfirmation model of citizen satisfaction, which focuses on the gap between performance and expectations. This model has been tested for decades in studies of private sector customer satisfaction, yet it is little known and applied in the field of public administration. The present study seeks to replicate the Van Ryzin (2004) results, which were based on a telephone survey in New York City, using a nationwide sample and a much different survey methodology, namely, an online, self-administered survey of a national panel. In addition, this study tests the sensitivity of the results to two alternative measures of disconfirmation (or the gap between performance and expectations). Results using subtractive disconfirmation confirm the basic expectancy disconfirmation model, but results using perceived disconfirmation do not, calling into question the policy and management implications of the prior study.

Vojnovic, I. (1998). "Municipal Consolidation in the 1990s: An Analysis of British Columbia, New Brunswick, and Nova Scotia." *Canadian Public Administration/Administration Publique du Canada* 41(2): 239-283.

> Three municipal amalgamations in three different Canadian provinces are analyzed and compared in this article. There is little evidence to show substantial cost savings from the merging of larger government units. Smaller entities studied in this article have realized financial benefits, while some larger jurisdictions that merge experience diseconomies of scale; higher wages resulting from a more specialized, professionalized bureaucracy; and the tendency to move to higher service standards. The authors conclude that consolidation will depend on the history of inter-municipal cooperation, financial arrangements, collective agreements, political structure, spatial organization, and political will to amalgamate.

Vojnovic, I. (2001). "The Transitional Impacts of Municipal Consolidations." *Journal of Planning Literature* 15(3).

> This article examines the transition and short-term effects of municipal consolidation on five recently amalgamated municipalities in Canada. The data for this study were collected from provincial and municipal legislations, tax rate by-laws and finance reports, as well as surveys and interviews with a variety of municipal officials and mayors. The analysis shows that municipal consolidation involves a complex reorganization of intricate administrative and political structures. Many of the problems encountered, and successes achieved, were particular to the circumstances of the municipalities that amalgamated. Ultimately, the success of consolidation in achieving greater efficiency and effectiveness in governance and service delivery will depend on the distinct history, as well as the spatial and economic circumstances, of the region considering reform. The five case studies, however, provide some useful lessons on how to improve the success of consolidations.

Warner, M., and Robert Hebdon (2001). "Local Government Restructuring: Privatization and Its Alternatives." *Journal of Policy Analysis & Management* 20(2): 315-336.

> Local government restructuring should no longer be viewed as a simple dichotomy between private and public provision. A 1997 survey of chief elected township and county officials in New York shows that local governments use both private and public sector mechanisms to structure the market, create competition, and attain economies of scale. In addition to privatization and inter-municipal cooperation, two alternative forms of service delivery not previously researched—reverse privatization and governmental entrepreneurship - are analyzed here.

Warner, M., and Amir Hefetz (2002a). "Applying Market Solutions to Public Services: An Assessment of Efficiency, Equity, and Voice." *Urban Affairs Review* 38(1): 70-89.

> Political fragmentation in metropolitan regions makes equitable and efficient delivery of public services difficult. Regionalism, although promoted as more equitable and rational, has found limited political support. Public choice theory argues, against regional-

ism, that political fragmentation can promote competition and efficiency by creating markets for public services. The authors assess the efficacy of market solutions for metropolitan public service provision by comparing privatization with inter-municipal cooperation and evaluating each on efficiency, equity, and democracy grounds. Using probit regression analysis of a national survey of local government service delivery from 1992 and 1997, the authors find that both alternatives promote efficiency, but equity and voice are more associated with inter-municipal cooperation than privatization.

Warner, M. E., and A. Hefetz (2002b). "The Uneven Distribution of Market Solutions for Public Goods." *Journal of Urban Affairs* 24(4): 445-459.

Using data from the ICMA surveys of alternative service delivery arrangements of local governments from 1992 and 1997 and data on poverty and income from the U. S. Census of Population 1990, the authors explore whether local governmental use of market forms of service delivery differs by metropolitan status. The surveys measured the form of service delivery for 64 different public services in seven broad areas: public works and transportation, public utilities, public safety, health and human services, parks and recreation, culture and art, and support functions. This article assesses the distribution of privatization and inter-municipal cooperation across localities in the metropolitan region and finds them most common among suburbs.

Weitzman, H. S. (2007). Cost Disparities in Special Districts in Nassau County

This report analyzes what Nassau County residents pay for garbage collection, water and fire protection. It examined town-run and commissioner-run special districts, and the private companies that deliver water in many areas. The report shows that the cost to residents varies widely depending on where they live. Significant opportunities for saving taxpayers' money exist.

Williams, M. C. (2005). Can Local Government Comparative Benchmarking Improve Efficiency?: Leveraging Multiple Analytical Techniques to Provide Definitive Answers and Guide Practical Action. L. Douglas Wilder School of Government and Public Affairs. Richmond, VA, Virginia Commonwealth University: 246.

This thesis looks at the attempts at municipal benchmarking in order to discover what benchmarking tactics lead to efficiency improvements. The failed Innovation Group project and the North Carolina benchmarking project are both examined. The study examines the differing ability of municipalities to improve from the information provided from benchmarking and makes conclusions about the effectiveness of voluntary benchmarking.

Willoughby, K. G. (2004). "Performance Measurement and Budget Balancing: State Government Perspective." *Public Budgeting & Finance* 24(2): 21-39.

This research presents data from a survey conducted as a component of the multiyear effort by the Governmental Accounting Standards Board (GASB) regarding the Service Efforts and Accomplishments (SEA) research. (p.26) In addition to the case research, the multiyear effort involved a follow-up mail survey conducted in the summer of 2000 to state and local government budget officers and specific agency and department heads and program administrators. This research assesses state personnel perceptions of performance measurement use and effectiveness for both management and budgeting decisions.

Wood, R. C., and Vladimir V. Almendinger (1961). *1400 Governments: The Political Economy of the New York Metropolitan Region.* Cambridge, Mass., Harvard University Press.

The main aim of this book is to link the workings of the governmental system with that of the economic system. While other studies conducted of the New York Metropolitan Region have traced the directions in which popoulation and economic activities are moving, this book shows how the region's 1,467 governmental entities are influencing the process and how they may do so in the future. The book applies the statistical technique of factor analysis to the study of municipal finance. It is not available in the Articles Folder for the LUARCC project.

Woodbury, K., Brian Dollery, and Prasada Rao (2003). "Is Local Government Efficiency Measurement in Australia Adequate? An Analysis of the Evidence." *Public Performance & Management Review* 27(2): 77-91.

Attempts to enhance the efficiency and effectiveness of local government have lagged behind the higher tiers of governance in Australia, and it is only in the comparatively recent past that systematic efforts have been made to measure the performance of Australian local government. This paper reviews municipal efficiency measurement in Australia to advance the argument that the present reliance on partial measures of performance is inadequate and should be heavily augmented by data envelopment analysis (DEA). The authors summarize progress made in efficiency measurement on a state-by-state basis and then examine performance measurement in water and wastewater as a more detailed case study. On the basis of this evidence, the authors argue that DEA provides the best means of providing public policymakers with the necessary information on municipal performance.

World Bank (2008). "Inefficiency of Rural Water Supply Schemes in India " Policy Paper Retrieved October 13,2008, from <http://www-wds.worldbank.org/external/default/WDS ContentServer/WDSP/IB/2008/07/23/000333037_20080723003033/Rendered/PDF/4 47910PP0P09411741301PUBLIC10PAPER2.pdf>.

In the last one-and-a-half decades, there has been an annual average expenditure of about one billion US dollars in the rural water supply sector in India. This has led to an appreciable increase in coverage (from 75 percent in 1997 to 97 percent in 2006, according to official statistics), but the overall improvement in the provision of water supply in rural areas has not been commensurate with the level of expenditure undertaken due to inefficiencies and wastages of various kinds. The 10-state study on the Effectiveness of Rural Water Supply Schemes, undertaken by the World Bank at the request of the Government of India, has looked at various aspects of 'inefficiency' along with measures to address these issues.

Worthington, A. (1999). "Performance Indicators and Efficiency Measurement in Public Libraries." *Australian Economic Review* 32(1): 31-42.

A sample of one hundred and sixty-eight New South Wales local government libraries is used to analyze the efficiency measures derived from the non-parametric technique of data envelopment analysis. Depending upon the assumptions employed, 9.5 per cent of local governments were judged to be overall technically efficient in the provision of library services, 47.6 per cent as pure technically efficient, and 10.1 per cent as scale efficient. The study also analyses the posited linkages between comparative performance indicators, productive performance and non-discretionary environmental factors under these different model formulations.

Worthington, A. C., and Brian E. Dollery (2002). "Incorporating Contextual Information in Public Sector Efficiency Analyses: A Comparative Study of NSW Local Government." *Applied Economics* 34(4): 453-464.

Using the planning and regulatory function of 173 NSW local governments, several approaches for incorporating contextual or non-discretionary inputs in data envelopment analysis (DEA) are compared. Non-discretionary inputs (or factors beyond managerial control) in this context include the population growth rate and distribution, the level of development and non-residential building activity, and the proportion of the population from a non-English speaking background. The approaches selected to incorporate these variables include discretionary inputs only, non-discretionary and discretionary inputs treated alike and differently, categorical inputs, 'adjusted' DEA, and 'endogenous' DEA. The results indicate that the efficiency scores of the five approaches that incorporated non-discretionary factors were significantly positively correlated. However, it was also established that the distributions of the efficiency scores and the number of councils assessed as perfectly technically efficient in the six approaches also varied significantly across the sample.

Index